D0274769

BENSON and HEDGES
RACING YEAR
FIRST EDITION

EDITOR HOWARD WRIGHT
ASSOCIATE EDITOR JOHN OAKSEY

PELHAM BOOKS

● GOLDEN MOMENTS: A summer's day and out in the country the race for the Goodwood Cup takes shape.
Picture: GERRY CRANHAM

BENSON *and* HEDGES
RACING YEAR
FIRST EDITION

EDITOR HOWARD WRIGHT
ASSOCIATE EDITOR JOHN OAKSEY

PELHAM BOOKS

COMPILED BY
RACING POST

First Published in Great Britain by
Pelham Books Ltd
27 Wrights Lane
London W8 5TZ
1987

© 1987 by Howard Wright

All Rights Reserved. No part of this publication may be
reproduced, stored in a retrieval system, or transmitted,
in any form or by any means, electronic, mechanical,
photocopying, recording or otherwise, without the prior
permission of the Copyright owner.

British Library Cataloguing in Publication Data
Benson & Hedges racing book.
1. Horse-racing—Great Britain
1. Wright, Howard   II. Oaksey, John
798.4'00941   SF335.G7
ISBN 0-7207-1747-7

Designed and produced by Michael Shaw, Racing Post Ltd
Photoset in Nimrod, Calvert, and Helvetica by Racing Post Ltd, Raynes Park, London
Printed and bound by Hazell, Watson & Viney

Sponsor's Message

We are very pleased to be the sponsors of this the first *Benson and Hedges Racing Year*. Strange as it may seem, no such book recording the previous year's season, over the jumps and on the flat, has been produced in this form before. With the experience of our Editor Howard Wright, Associate Editor John Oaksey and expert contributors including Brough Scott and Peter O'Sullevan, we are confident that those interested in racing, whether professionally or for pleasure, will find *Racing Year* an invaluable and rewarding record of the previous year in the sport.

We would like to extend our thanks to *Racing Post* for their assistance with the compilation of the book and the publishers, Pelham Books.

PAUL RUTHERFORD
Director, Benson and Hedges

Horse of the Year

● **DANCING BRAVE: Winner of the Two Thousand Guineas, the Eclipse, the King George, and the Arc.**

Picture: GEORGE SELWYN

Contents

1. **The Classics** *Jeremy Early* 12
      1,000 Guineas 14
      2,000 Guineas 18
      The Derby 22
      The Oaks 26
      St Leger 30
      Classics Results & Breeding 33
2. **In My View** *John Oaksey* 40

3. **Dancing Brave** *Graham Rock* 44
4. **The King George, Ascot** *Paul Johnson* 52
5. **Sprinters** *Emily Weber* 56
      Group One Sprint Results & Breeding 62
6. **Milers** *Adrian Cook* 66
      Group One Mile Result & Breeding 71

7. **Pat Eddery** *J A McGrath* 74
8. **Middle Distance** *Graham Dench* 78
      Group One Middle Distance Results
      & Breeding 82
9. **Stayers** *Colin Russell* 90
      Group One Stayers Results & Breeding ... 95

10. **Two-Year-Olds** *Frank Carter* 98
       Group One Two-Year-Old Results
       & Breeding 104
11. **Sir Gordon Richards** *Brough Scott* 110
12. **Handicaps** *Will O'Hanlon* 114
13. **The North** *Ray Gilpin* 122
14. **Owners** *George Ennor* 130

15. **Trainers** *Lawrence Wadey* 138
16. **Jockeys** *J A McGrath* 146
17. **Breeders** *Adrian Cook* 154
18. **Sires** *Adrian Cook* 162
19. **France** *Desmond Stoneham* 170
20. **Arc de Triomphe** *Tim Richards* 178
21. **Irish Flat** *Tony O'Hehir* 182
22. **Michael Stoute** *Paul Haigh* 190
23. **Racing Abroad** *Robert Carter* 194
24. **USA** *Dan Farley* 202
25. **Breeders' Cup** *George Ennor* 210
26. **Odds and Ends** *John McCririck* 214
27. **Sales** *Tony Morris* 218
28. **Dawn Run** *John Oaksey* 226
29. **National Hunt** *Neil Morrice* 234
30. **Triumph Hurdle** *Peter O'Sullevan* 246
31. **Irish National Hunt** *Tony O'Hehir* 254
32. **20 To Follow** *Racing Post Team* 258
33. **Apprentices** *Mark Coton* 262
34. **Quiz of the Year** *John Randall* 264
35. **News Diary** *Mark Coton* 268
       Maps of British Racecourses 275

● **EPSOM THRILLER:**
Shahrastani holds off Dancing
Brave in a nail-biting finish to
the Ever Ready Derby
Picture: GERRY CRANHAM

CHAPTER 1

Classics

by JEREMY EARLY

O 1,000 GUINEAS: Midway Lady beats Maysoon and Sonic Lady.
Picture: TONY EDENDEN

O DERBY: Shahrastani beats Dancing Brave.
Picture: KICKSPORTS

O ST LEGER: Moon Madness beats Celestial Storm and Untold.
Picture: DAVID HASTINGS

SUGGESTIONS that the top-class thoroughbred is worse than half a century ago are as commonplace as they are unconvincing. It is, however, futile denying that the shape of racing, and perceptions of it, have changed.

The Classics were once the be-all and end-all of top three-year-olds' careers. Now the emphasis is much more on inter-age championships run in the second half of the season, notably the King George VI and Queen Elizabeth Diamond Stakes and the Prix de l'Arc de Triomphe, and the Classics have consequently lost some of their gloss.

Despite this, the five races are still of fundamental significance and synonymous with quality. No-one could complain about the 1986 editions, which combined entertainment with talent of the highest level and, in one instance, major controversy.

O **2,000 GUINEAS: Dancing Brave (fifth right) beats Green Desert (white V).** Picture: TONY EDENDEN

The Classics

by JEREMY EARLY

O **OAKS: Midway Lady beats Untold (right) and Maysoon.** Picture: KICKSPORTS

O DEFEAT OF STOUTE PARTY: Midway Lady is too good for the stablemates Maysoon and Sonic Lady in the General Accident 1,000 Guineas.
Picture: GERRY CRANHAM

1,000 Guineas

by JEREMY EARLY

THE CLASSIC fillies had a lot to live up to, coming a year after Triple Crown heroine Oh So Sharp. But as the season got under way it was common knowledge that Michael Stoute's stable housed some potential stars, and the Guineas trials confirmed the point.

In mid-April Sonic Lady put up a scintillating display in the Nell Gwyn Stakes at Newmarket, and three days later Maysoon made it a Stoute double in the Gainsborough Stud Fred Darling Stakes at Newbury. Both fillies lined up at Newmarket on 1 May for the Guineas. The 13 other runners included the second, third and fourth in the Nell Gwyn, Lady Sophie, Ala Mahlik and Embla. On the book, none of these had much hope of beating Sonic Lady, assuming she got the trip — her tendency to take a strong hold being a slight drawback.

There were three French challengers, Dear Margie, Grande Couture and Rose of the Sea, none anywhere near so good as the last French-trained winner of the race, Ma Biche in 1983.

The wild card in the pack was Midway Lady, trained by Ben Hanbury. Stamina was no problem with her, since she had won two Pattern events over a mile at two, the May Hill Stakes and Group One Prix Marcel Boussac. These successes had resulted in her being given nine stone in the Ladbroke European Free Handicap, 4lb below top-rated filly Baiser Vole.

The main doubts about Midway Lady concerned her speed against specialist milers — on breeding middle distances looked just the ticket — and her fitness. Hanbury, 40, seeking his first Classic win, had intended giving the filly her initial run in the Musidora Stakes over an extended ten furlongs, but after some highly encouraging gallops at Newmarket, he seized the bull by the horns and elected for the Guineas instead.

The ride on Midway Lady went to Ray Cochrane, also seeking his first Classic win. Cochrane had been called up late for the ride after a short-lived plan to bring

○ **CLASSIC STYLE: Maysoon wins the Gainsborough Stud Fred Darling Stakes.**   Picture: GERRY CRANHAM

○ **BACK VIEW: Ala Mahlik stays on into fourth place behind Midway Lady.**   Picture: PRESS ASSOCIATION

○ **WINNING COMBINATION: Ray Cochrane and Midway Lady after their Newmarket triumph.** Picture: MARK LEECH

trainer Lester Piggott back to take the mount foundered. Midway Lady started 10-1, fifth in the betting behind Sonic Lady, Embla, Maysoon and Lady Sophie.

Midway Lady needed 1min 41.54sec to dispel any doubts. Headstrong Rose of the Sea took them along until Sonic Lady and Walter Swinburn went on about two and a half furlongs out, where Yves Saint-Martin produced Maysoon for her attack.

The early pace had been a little vigorous for Midway Lady, but by the two-furlong mark she was finding her legs and throwing down a challenge on the inside. In the final furlong the race developed into a magnificent battle reminiscent of the 1985 renewal. And as the two Stoute fillies battled away in front, Midway Lady looked likely to come out a close third-best. Cochrane had other ideas.

Riding a superb, power-packed finish, which the filly answered with the utmost gameness, Cochrane got Midway Lady to the front 50

O CATCH ME: Midway Lady has the edge over, from left, Maysoon, Sonic Lady and Ala Mahlik.   Picture: ALAN JOHNSON

O STRIDING OUT: Midway Lady and Ray Cochrane going for the line.   Picture: ALAN JOHNSON

yards from home. Keeping on powerfully, she had threequarters of a length to spare at the line over Maysoon, who nosed Sonic Lady out of second. The next to finish were Ala Mahlik and Embla, neither of whom threatened to take a leading role in proceedings.

The win was sweet for Hanbury. A year before, his stable star Kala Dancer, also making his reappearance, had been completely eclipsed in the 2,000 Guineas, and failed to run again. It was not so sweet for Michael Stoute. Maysoon became his fourth 1,000 Guineas runner-up following in the footsteps of Fair Salinia, Our Home, and Royal Heroine.

In addition to that unfortunate statistic, Sonic Lady clearly did not run to the form she was to show over a mile later, when she beat not only the fillies but the colts as well. Stoute must be wondering what he has to do to win the race.□

O SWEEPING HOME: Dancing Brave has the General Accident 2,000 Guineas field at full stretch.

Picture: GEORGE SELWYN

2,000 Guineas

by JEREMY EARLY

TWO DAYS after Midway Lady's triumph the colts held centre stage in the 2,000 Guineas.

Form in the previous season always used to be the best guide to the race, but recently the principle has received a dent or two. In 1983 none of the first three in the Guineas had won a Pattern race at two years, and in 1985 none of the first three had even run in a Pattern race the year before.

The latest edition followed suit, at least as far as the winner was concerned. Khalid Abdullah's Dancing Brave, trained by Guy Harwood and unbeaten at two in a couple of average races at Sandown Park and Newmarket, had been written up as a top horse for a long time.

He won his Guineas trial over the course and distance, the Charles Heidsieck Champagne Craven Stakes, in taking style by a length from Faraway Dancer. The enthusiasm of Dancing Brave's rider Greville Starkey in claiming he was better than the 1981 2,000 Guineas winner To-Agori-Mou, also trained by Harwood, was entirely understandable, but at this stage the colt's promise still exceeded his track peformance. Equally, none of his 14 rivals at Newmarket had caught the imagination of punters and professionals to anything like the same degree.

Not that those rivals were a poor bunch by any means. Sure Blade, a top two-year-old, had trotted up in a trial at Thirsk; Green Desert had

○ TAKE THAT: Greville Starkey sizes up the situation on Dancing Brave with a look round to his 2,000 Guineas rivals.
Picture: TONY EDENDEN

gained a meritorious victory in Newmarket's Ladbroke European Free Handicap under top weight of 9st 7lb, and Faustus had won a tight Clerical, Medical Greenham Stakes at Newbury.

One of the two Irish challengers, Tate Gallery, had blotted his copybook in the Michael Smurfit Gladness Stakes at The Curragh, but the other, Toca Madera, was a recent Pattern winner in the Gallagher's New York 2,000 Guineas Trial at Phoenix Park. So there was no shortage of quality. Punters, though, had little doubt about the Guineas outcome. They made Dancing Brave a well-backed 15-8 favourite ahead of the 1985 Dewhurst Stakes winner Huntingdale (trying to do a Midway Lady since he was making his reappearance), Sure Blade and Toca Madera.

After only a steady gallop, set by Prix de Guiche runner-up Hail to Roberto, Green Desert and Dancing Brave challenged together about a quarter of a mile out. Both accelerated in great style, but with a furlong to go Dancing Brave quickened again and in a flash he left his rival for dead. Dancing Brave stormed three lengths clear of Green Desert, who held second place comfortably by a length and a half from Huntingdale. Sheikh Mohammed's pair Sharrood and Sure Blade came next but they might as well have been in a different race.

Allowing for the knowledge of hindsight, that the second, a classy sprinter, probably did not quite stay the trip, Dancing Brave's speed was still blinding and his performance exceptional. Sharrood and Sure Blade were not poor horses, but they looked poor by comparison with the winner. That is the mark of excellence in a thoroughbred, and few observers were in any doubt that a brilliant colt had arrived on the scene. □

◗ ON THE WAY: Green Desert (right) puts himself in the Guineas picture by winning the Ladbroke European Free Handicap from Sperry.

Picture: PRESS ASSOCIATION

◗ GUINEAS GLORY: Dancing Brave has the race in safe keeping as Green Desert (left) chases in vain.

Picture: TONY EDENDEN

○ **SECOND BEST: Shahrastani wins the Ever Ready Derby but the runner-up Dancing Brave got as much attention.**
Picture: SIMON BRUTY/ALLSPORT

The Derby

by JEREMY EARLY

IMMEDIATELY after the Guineas Guy Harwood said of Dancing Brave: "We have never considered the Derby as a race for him, this has always been his race. He showed a lot of speed and it looks like a mile probably is his best trip."

Breeding lent some support to the view, since Dancing Brave's sire (Lyphard) and dam were both best at around a mile. However, Harwood's opinion soon changed, encouraged no doubt by the fact that Bakharoff, his other star three-year-old colt and also owned by Khalid Abdullah, was beaten by

Mashkour in the Highland Spring Derby Trial at Lingfield Park.

The trials revealed at least one colt who could be expected to pose a serious threat to Dancing Brave at Epsom — Shahrastani, the son of Nijinsky, owned by the Aga Khan and trained by Michael Stoute. Shahrastani had lost his only race at two but looked a different horse in the spring when winning the Guardian Classic Trial at Sandown Park by four lengths from Bonhomie, and the Mecca Dante Stakes at York by a length and a half from Nomrood. Shahrastani's performance at York did

not satisfy everyone, but experts were more confident about his ability to stay a mile and a half than Dancing Brave's and he started a clear second favourite at 11-2 behind the Harwood colt at 2-1.

The 15 others in a representative field included the favourite's stablemate Allez Milord (winner of the Predominate Stakes), Kentucky Derby second Bold Arrangement, Mashkour, Nomrood, Dee Stakes winner Faraway Dancer, the improving Nisnas and the first three in the Irish 2,000 Guineas, Flash of Steel, Mr John and Sharrood. Prix Lupin runner-up

Arokar was the sole runner from France.

The Derby remains the main focus of owners' and trainers' attention, despite its timing — too early, in the view of many people — and the peculiarities of the track on which it is run. Epsom, with its pronounced gradients and bends, is not an ideal course on which to hold a championship race. Its configuration undoubtedly prevented the best horse, Prince Regent, winning in 1969 and arguably led to Rheingold's losing in 1972, when Dancing Brave's sire Lyphard gave Freddy Head a very uncomfortable ride.

Starkey, conscious of Dancing Brave's stamina doubts, probably intended holding up the colt. In the event he had no choice. Dancing Brave did not fare so badly as Lyphard, but he was never racing smoothly enough to take close order, and while Nomrood made the running from a group including Faraway Dancer and Shahrastani, the Guineas winner was at the rear.

Rounding the home turn with half a mile left, Dancing Brave, who had come down Tattenham hill almost like a drunk, had only two behind him. By contrast, Shahrastani was perfectly positioned in fourth behind Nomrood, Faraway Dancer and Nisnas. Dancing Brave continued sprawling in the straight. For over a furlong Starkey could do nothing besides desperately try to get his mount properly balanced again, on a part of the course which is far from level.

This delay proved crucial. While Starkey battled, Walter Swinburn drove Shahrastani into the lead over two furlongs out. At that point Dancing Brave, finally on something approaching an even keel, was ten to 12 lengths adrift of the leader, who was travelling powerfully. The acceleration the favourite produced was astonishing. At the furlong marker Shahrastani had a two-length lead over the one-paced Faraway Dancer; Nomrood was dropping back, and Dancing Brave, now

○ CLASS OF HIS OWN: Shahrastani slams the Guardian Classic Trial field to become a strong candidate for the Derby.
Picture: DAVID HASTINGS

O SWINGING FOR HOME: Nomrood leads the Derby field round Tattenham Corner, pursued by Faraway Dancer, Nisnas (rails) and Shahrastani.
Picture: PRESS ASSOCIATION

sixth and making up ground hand over fist, still had six lengths to catch up.

The last 150 yards must have been agonizing for backers of either Dancing Brave or Shahrastani. Moving forward relentlessly despite following the camber of the track and veering sharply left, Dancing Brave held out strong hopes of getting there. However, Shahrastani was not stopping and the post came just in time. The winning margin was half a length. Two and a half lengths away third came Mashkour, who made up an enormous amount of ground in the closing stages to catch Faraway Dancer and fifth-placed Nisnas.

Shahrastani gave the Aga Khan, Walter Swinburn and Michael Stoute their second Derby winner following Shergar in 1980, and a second for Nijinsky, sire of 1982 hero Golden Fleece. Shahrastani had shown himself a mile-and-a-

half performer of exceptional quality, and he reinforced the point in the Budweiser Irish Derby. But rightly or wrongly, the Derby was a story less of one horse's win than another's loss.

Many observers suspected the best horse had not won. Subsequent events confirmed this opinion, as Dancing Brave went on to trounce the best in Europe in a string of Group One events. Debate raged as the race became the most talked-about of the year, and Starkey, a convenient scapegoat, received some extremely hostile Press comment. Most of this was at odds with the facts.

The critics would have been better advised to look at the video before sharpening their pens. If blame has to be attached to a defeat, the main candidate in the 1986 Derby was not Starkey, but Epsom racecourse. □

O CLOSE CALL: Shahrastani holds off Dancing Brave. Picture: JOHN CROFTS

O **PROUD MOMENT:** The Aga Khan leads in Shahrastani and Walter Swinburn.
Picture: PADDOCK STUDIOS

O **NO DOUBTS:** It's there for all to see — Shahrastani is the Derby winner.
Picture: PADDOCK STUDIOS

○ ON THE LINE: Midway Lady is again too good for a pair of Michael Stoute-trained fillies, Untold and Maysoon, in the Gold Seal Oaks.

Picture: DAVID HASTINGS

The Oaks

by JEREMY EARLY

THE DOUBLE of 1,000 Guineas and Oaks is not an every-year occurrence, and Oh So Sharp in 1985 was the first since Mysterious twelve years previously.

Midway Lady appeared to have an outstanding chance of following suit, given that middle distances promised to show her to even better advantage than the Guineas mile. Nothing happened to alter confidence in her in the weeks running up to the Oaks, though Tralthee impressed when winning

the Sheraton Park Tower Lupe Stakes at Goodwood and Gesedeh and Rejuvenate gained admirers by winning respectively the Pretty Polly Stakes and Tattersalls Musidora Stakes.

In a field of 15, including also Maysoon, Musidora runner-up Ala Mahlik and two more Stoute fillies, Untold (having her first run of the season) and Colorspin, Midway Lady started 15-8 favourite, ahead of Tralthee at 9-2. There was no Irish or French contestant.

By happy contrast with the Derby, the race had no controversy, apart from the withdrawal of Mill on the Floss, who misbehaved badly at the start.

Ray Cochrane held up Midway Lady in the middle of the field as Asteroid Field made the running from outsider Davemma — giving Gay Kelleway a first ride for a woman in an English Classic — and Untold.

When Paul Eddery set sail for home on Untold over three

furlongs out the Guineas winner still had plenty to do in seventh place. She, Maysoon and Colorspin all made headway and over a furlong out Maysoon looked to be going best. However, her suspect stamina gave out and in the last 100 yards Untold, despite battling on courageously, was overtaken by Midway Lady, who stayed on powerfully to gain a workmanlike length success. Maysoon and Colorspin were third and fourth, so Ben Hanbury once again foiled a Michael Stoute Classic benefit. Davemma did not give Miss Kelleway a dream debut, trailing in last.

Completing the Classic double was part of a fine year for Cochrane, 29, who later signed up to ride for Luca Cumani in 1987. He did not ride Midway Lady

○ MOMENT OF GLORY: Gay Kelleway becomes the first girl to ride in a British Classic on Davema in the Oaks. Picture: GEORGE SELWYN

○ ON THE RAILS: Midway Lady is on top in the Oaks, chased by Maysoon. Picture: KICKSPORTS

O **WE'VE DONE IT: Midway Lady returns after the Oaks with owner Harry Ranier, trainer Ben Hanbury and jockey Ray Cochrane.**
Picture: KICKSPORTS

again, though, because the filly paid a price for her Epsom triumph. The ground, officially good, was too fast for her. She jarred her forelegs, which had always been suspect. Try as he might Hanbury could not get her right for the prestigious late-season prizes, and she was retired.

A Classic double from just two starts at three is an excellent achievement, and though Midway Lady's form did not put her in the super league, her combination of superior talent and courage unquestionably made her one of the season's stars. It also made the daughter of Alleged and Smooth Bore (who was by His Majesty) a highly desirable broodmare prospect.

Sent through the ring at Keeneland in 1984 for $42,000, she returned there in November as one of the choicest lots in the Keeneland Breeding Stock Sale. At the end of 1985 a half-share in her had been sold for a reported $1.5m. The purchasers did not make a loss, for she fetched $3.3m to the bid of Adrian Nicoll, acting on behalf of Maktoum Al-Maktoum's Shadwell Stud. □

○ WELL DONE: The Oaks is all over for Midway Lady.   Picture: KICKSPORTS

○ SIDE VIEW: Midway Lady strides out to beat Untold and Maysoon.   Picture: JOHN CROFTS

○ **EASING DOWN: Moon Madness and Pat Eddery have the Holsten Pils St Leger in safe keeping.**

Picture: GEORGE SELWYN

St Leger

by JEREMY EARLY

STAMINA IS A dirty word among breeders nowadays, and the St Leger is no longer an obvious target for the best middle-distance colts. The 1986 race lacked the first four in the Derbys of England, Ireland and France, so inevitably missed some of the prestige the sponsors and executive seek to regain for the final Classic.

Holsten have committed themselves to another three years' sponsorship increasing by stages, and the Doncaster executive is seeking to bring the first-entry stage back to February from July, while introducing a supplementary stage for later-maturing horses.

Whether either of these will help restore the race to its former glory is open to debate — cash injections are far from certain to change now-entrenched opinions among breeders. Either way, even if the St Leger has fallen a little in status, it is still vastly superior to several Group One races across Europe, including the Irish and French St Legers. And at least there are no plans to open up the race to four-year-olds and upwards, a recipe for failure judged on the Irish and French experience.

In the run-up to the 1986 St Leger possible candidates came and went, including Irish Derby second Bonhomie, ruled out by a setback, and Bakharoff. The field of eight on the day included two late-maturing colts, the former handicappers Moon Madness and Celestial Storm.

Moon Madness had started the season winning a maiden race at Salisbury before picking up handicaps at Newmarket, Haydock Park and Royal Ascot (the King George V Stakes). He had then stepped up in class, winning the Mecca Bookmakers' Scottish Derby at Ayr and running a close third to Nisnas, another St Leger runner, in a muddling race for the Great Voltigeur Stakes at York.

● **VAIN CHASE: Celestial Storm trails Moon Madness.**   Picture: JOHN CROFTS

Celestial Storm had also come a long way in a short time. Making his racecourse debut in July, he had improved at a terrific pace and cantered home in the March Stakes at Goodwood on his outing before the St Leger.

The other runners included Allez Milord (fifth in the Voltigeur), Oaks second and Yorkshire Oaks winner Untold, and Grand Prix de Paris winner Swink. On the face of it a competitive field, if not a top-class one. Moon Madness, a 9-2 shot behind favourite Untold and Allez Milord, showed the York form all wrong by running away with the prize.

The start was delayed by the antics of Swink's intended pacemaker Rosedale, who dumped Brent Thomson, galloped loose around the vicinity of Town Moor and had to be withdrawn. In his absence outsiders Family Friend and Sirk made the running; Pat Eddery, riding with all the confidence of a man who already

○ **UNTOLD PROMISE: The Yorkshire Oaks, and Untold's defeat of Park Express puts her in line for the St Leger.**   Picture: GERRY CRANHAM

⊙ **HERO AND HERIONE: Amanda Bryan and her St Leger winner Moon Madness.**   Picture: ALAN JOHNSON

had the jockeys' championship buttoned up, settled Moon Madness in the rear.

Eddery's confidence was entirely justified. While some of his rivals, notably Swink and Untold, were getting in a tangle, Moon Madness obtained a sweet run up the rails in the straight and took the lead off Celestial Storm a quarter of a mile out. It was no contest in the closing stages as Moon Madness, showing a fine turn of foot, put four lengths between himself and the toiling Celestial Storm.

The form was questioned in some quarters on the grounds of supposed doubtful stamina in the runner-up, third-placed Untold and last-placed Allez Milord. Celestial Storm certainly looked more a middle-distance colt than a stayer when second in the Dubai Champion Stakes, and over a mile and a half Allez Milord reversed Doncaster form with the winner to some tune in the Puma Europa Preis in Cologne.

But no-one could deny Moon Madness had shown unusual acceleration for a horse so well suited by a test of stamina. Moreover, the racing world was delighted that Lavinia Duchess of Norfolk, 70, had got off the mark in a Classic as owner-breeder, and that John Dunlop and Pat Eddery had also won their first St Leger.

Moon Madness was pencilled in for the Japan Cup, but a setback prevented his participating. Unlike the other 1986 British Classic winners, he stays in training and will have the opportunity to show his mettle as a four-year-old. □

Newmarket   GOOD   1m

General Accident 1,000 Guineas

1st £101,244 **2nd** £38,163 **3rd** £18,556 **4th** £8,327

1   **MIDWAY LADY (USA)** 3 9-00 .... R Cochrane
b f by Alleged-Smooth Bore (His Majesty)
headway 2f out, led well inside final furlong, all out **10/1**

2 ¾ **MAYSOON** 3 9-00 .... Y Saint-Martin
b f by Shergar-Triple First (High Top)
headway 2f out, led inside final furlong, ran on well **15/2**

3 *shd* **SONIC LADY (USA)** 3 9-00 .... W R Swinburn
b f by Nureyev-Stumped (Owen Anthony)
led over 2f out, hard ridden over 1f out, ran on well **6/4F**

4 ¾ **ALA MAHLIK** 3 9-00 .... G Starkey
ch f by Ahonoora-Negligence (Roan Rocket)
every chance 2f out, unable quicken final furlong **14/1**

5 2½ **EMBLA** 3 9-00 .... T Ives
headway 3f out, every chance 2f out, one pace **6/1**

6 ¾ **WEIGHT IN GOLD** 3 9-00 .... D Gillespie
no headway final 2f **50/1**

7 1½ **VOLIDA** 3 9-00 .... P Robinson
never near to challenge **200/1**

8 1½ **DEAR MARGIE (FR)** 3 9-00 .... E Legrix
never nearer **25/1**

9 3 **LADY SOPHIE** 3 9-00 .... S Cauthen
outpaced **9/1**

10 2 **SPUN GOLD** 3 9-00 .... T Quinn
no show **50/1**

11 2½ **BRIDESMAID** 3 9-00 .... M Hills
every chance 3f out, weakened 2f out **100/1**

12 *nk* **TENDER LOVING CARE** 3 9-00 .... B Thomson
no show **33/1**

13 5 **IMPROVISE** 3 9-00 .... R P Elliott
speed 6f **200/1**

14   **ROSE OF THE SEA (USA)** 3 9-00 .... C Asmussen
led over 5f **33/1**

15   **GRANDE COUTURE (USA)** 3 9-00 .... G Moore
tailed off **20/1**

15 ran
TIME 1m 41.54s
1st OWNER: H Ranier TRAINER: B Hanbury (Newmarket) BRED: Edward A Seltzer & Shadowlawn Farm, in United States
2nd OWNER: Maktoum Al-Maktoum TRAINER: M Stoute
3rd OWNER: Sheikh Mohammed TRAINER: J Alan Mactier, in United States
TOTE WIN£12.10 PL£2.40,£2.80,£1.10 DF£23.00 CSF£70.26

Midway Lady (USA)

Alleged	Hoist The Flag	Tom Rolfe
		Wavy Navy
	Princess Pout	Prince John
		Determined Lady
Smooth Bore	His Majesty	Ribot
		Flower Bowl
	French Leave	Damascus
		Marche Lorraine

Maysoon

Shergar	Great Nephew	Honeyway
		Sybil's Niece
	Sharmeen	Val de Loir
		Nasreen
Triple First	High Top	Derring-Do
		Camenae
	Field Mouse	Grey Sovereign
		Meadow Song

Sonic Lady (USA)

Nureyev	Northern Dancer	Nearctic
		Natalma
	Special	Forli
		Thong
Stumped	Owen Anthony	Proud Chieftain
		Oweninny
	Luckhurst	Busted
		Lucasland

Ala Mahlik

Ahonoora	Lorenzaccio	Klairon
		Phoenissa
	Helen Nichols	Martial
		Quaker Girl
Negligence	Roan Rocket	Buisson Ardent
		Farandole
	Malpractice	Pall Mall
		Miss Justice

Newmarket GOOD 1m

General Accident 2,000 Guineas

1st £107,145 **2nd** £40,379 **3rd** £19,627 **4th** £8,800

1	**DANCING BRAVE (USA)** 3 9-00 .... G Starkey	
	b c by Lyphard-Navajo Princess (Drone)	
	held up, quickened and led over 1f out,	
	comfortably	**15/8F**
2	*3* **GREEN DESERT (USA)** 3 9-00 .... W R Swinburn	
	b c by Danzig-Foreign Courier (Sir Ivor)	
	led well over 1f out, ridden over 1f out, no im-	
	pression	**2/1**
3	*1½* **HUNTINGDALE** 3 9-00 .... M Hills	
	ch c by Double Form-Abbeydale (Huntercombe)	
	headway 2f out, hard ridden final furlong, unable	
	quicken	**6/1**
4	*hd* **SHARROOD (USA)** 3 9-00 .... W Carson	
	ro c by Caro-Angel Island (Cougar II)	
	headway 2f out, ran on inside final furlong	**14/1**
5	*1½* **SURE BLADE (USA)** 3 9-00 .... B Thomson	
	every chance 2f out, one pace final furlong ·	**13/2**
6	*½* **HAIL TO ROBERTO (USA)** 3 9-00 .... C Asmussen	
	led over 6f, weakened final furlong	**66/1**
7	*shd* **VAINGLORIOUS** 3 9-00 .... R Curant	
	no headway final 2f	**66/1**
8	*2½* **FAUSTUS (USA)** 3 9-00 .... S Cauthen	
	never near to challenge	**12/1**
9	*shd* **TOCA MADERA** 3 9-00 .... S Craine	
	never nearer	**9/1**
10	*1* **JAZETAS** 3 9-00 .... R Cochrane	
	always behind	**100/1**
11	*shd* **EXOTIC RIVER** 3 9-00 .... G Mosse	
	outpaced	**66/1**
12	*shd* **HALLGATE** 3 9-00 .... K Hodgson	
	outpaced	**18/1**
13	*¾* **ALSHINFARAH** 3 9-00 .... A Murray	
	outpaced	**50/1**
14	*1* **TATE GALLERY (USA)** 3 9-00 .... T Ives	
	speed over 5f	**12/1**
15	**FARNCOMBE** 3 9-00 .... P Robinson	
	refused to race	**500/1**

15 ran

TIME 1m 40.00s

1st OWNER: K Abdullah TRAINER: G Harwood (Pulborough) BRED: Glen Oak Farm, in United States

2nd OWNER: Maktoum Al-Maktoum TRAINER: M Stoute

3rd OWNER: Mrs P Threlfall TRAINER: J Hindley

TOTE WIN£3.30 PL£1.20,£2.60,£1.90 DF£20.70 CSF£21.80

Dancing Brave (USA)

Lyphard	Northern Dancer	Nearctic
		Natalma
	Goofed	Court Martial
		Barra
Navajo Princess	Drone	Sir Gaylord
		Cap And Bells
	Olmec	Pago Pago
		Chocolate Beau

Green Desert (USA)

Danzig	Northern Dancer	Nearctic
		Natalma
	Pas de Nom	Admiral's Voyage
		Petitioner
Foreign Courier	Sir Ivor	Sir Gaylord
		Attica
	Courtly Dee	Never Bend
		Tulle

Huntingdale

Double Form	Habitat	Sir Gaylord
		Little Hut
	Fanghorn	Crocket
		Honeymoon House
Abbeydale	Huntercombe	Derring-Do
		Ergina
	Lucky Maid	Acropolis
		Mor'a Bai

Sharrood (USA)

Caro	Fortino	Grey Sovereign
		Ranavalo
	Chambord	Chamossaire
		Life Hill
Angel Island	Cougar	Tale of Two Cities
		Cindy Lou
	Who's To Know	Fleet Nasrullah
		Masked Lady

Epsom   GOOD   1m 4f

Ever Ready Derby

1st £239,260 **2nd** £90,483 **3rd** £44,242 **4th** £20,116

1   **SHAHRASTANI (USA)** 3 9-00 .... W R Swinburn
ch c by Nijinsky-Shademah (Thatch)
4th straight, led over 2f out, driven out   **11/2**

2   ½ **DANCING BRAVE (USA)** 3 9-00 .... G Starkey
b c by Lyphard-Navajo Princess (Drone)
*well behind 9f, pulled out 3f out, good headway 2f out,
strong run final furlong finished fast, too much to do* **2/1F**

3   2½ **MASHKOUR (USA)** 3 9-00............................ S Cauthen
ch c by Irish River-Sancta Rose (Karabas)
good headway final 2f, ran on   **12/1**

4   hd **FARAWAY DANCER (USA)** 3 9-00...................... W Ryan
br c by Far North-Prove Us Royal (Prove It)
2nd straight, every chance well over 1f out, ran on **33/1**

5   shd **NISNAS** 3 9-00.. P Waldron
3rd straight, no headway final 2f   **40/1**

6   ¾ **FLASH OF STEEL** 3 9-00............................. M J Kinane
headway 3f out, never near to challenge   **25/1**

7   ¾ **SIRK** 3 9-00.. P Robinson
well behind 9f, never nearer   **50/1**

8   1 **SHARROOD (USA)** 3 9-00............................... W Carson
always behind   **25/1**

9   hd **MR JOHN** 3 9-00.. T Ives
started slowly   **50/1**

10   ½ **ALLEZ MILORD (USA)** 3 9-00...................... C Asmussen
     8/1

11   hd **NOMROOD (USA)** 3 9-00................................. T Quinn
led over 9f   **20/1**

12   1 **JAREER (USA)** 3 9-00.................................... B Rouse
     16/1

13   3 **THEN AGAIN** 3 9-00................................... R Guest
prominent 9f   **33/1**

14 2½ **BOLD ARRANGEMENT** 3 9-00 .... C McCarron
     12/1

15 shd **AROKAR (FR)** 3 9-00............................. Y Saint-Martin
6th straight, weakened over 2f out   **18/1**

16 10 **FIORAVANTI (USA)** 3 9-00........................... C Roche
     33/1

17   **WISE COUNSELLOR (USA)** 3 9-00 ....Pat Eddery
5th straight, weakened 3f out   **16/1**

17 ran
TIME 2m 37.13s
1st OWNER: Aga Khan TRAINER: M Stoute (Newmarket) BRED: Aga Khan, in United
States
2nd OWNER: K Abdullah TRAINER: G Harwood
3rd OWNER: Prince Ahmed Salman TRAINER: H Cecil
TOTE WIN£6.10 PL£2.00,£2.30,£2.30 DF£7.00 CSF£15.16 TRICAST£116.38

Shahrastani (USA)

		Nearctic
	Northern Dancer	Natalma
Nijinsky		Bull Page
	Flaming Page	Flaring Top
	Thatch	Forli
		Thong
Shademah		Le Haar
	Shamim	Diamond Drop

Dancing Brave (USA)

		Nearctic
	Northern Dancer	Natalma
Lyphard		Court Martial
	Goofed	Barra
	Drone	Sir Gaylord
		Cap And Bells
Navajo Princess		Pago Pago
	Olmec	Chocolate Beau

Mashkour (USA)

		Never Bend
	Riverman	River Lady
Irish River		Klairon
	Irish Star	Botany Bay
	Karabas	Worden
		Fair Share
Sancta Rose		Roan Rocket
	Rosie Bang	Kazanlik

Faraway Dancer (USA)

		Nearctic
	Northern Dancer	Natalma
Far North		Victoria Park
	Fleur	Flaming Page
	Prove It	Endeavour
		Time To Khal
Prove Us Royal		Royal Hamlet
	She Jr.	O. Gay

Epsom GOOD 1m 4f

Gold Seal Oaks

1st £119,952 **2nd** £45,242 **3rd** £22,021 **4th** £9,906

1		**MIDWAY LADY (USA)** 3 9-00 .... R Cochrane

b f by Alleged-Smooth Bore (His Majesty)
6th straight, ridden over 1f out, led inside final furlong, ran on well   **15/8F**

2 _1_ **UNTOLD** 3 9-00 .... Paul Eddery
ch f by Final Straw-Unsuspected (Above Suspicion)
2nd straight, led over 3f out, ridden over 1f out, ran on   **20/1**

3 ¾ **MAYSOON** 3 9-00 .... W R Swinburn
b f by Shergar-Triple First (High Top)
headway 6f out, every chance over 1f out, ran on   **12/1**

4 _4_ **COLORSPIN (FR)** 3 9-00 .... B Rouse
b f by High Top-Reprocolor (Jimmy Reppin)
headway 3f out, ridden well over 1f out, unable to quicken   **25/1**

5 _7_ **GESEDEH** 3 9-00 .... T Ives
baulked and lost place 5f out, rallied 2f out, never nearer   **9/1**

6 _1½_ **REJUVENATE** 3 9-00 .... B Thomson
started slowly, 4th straight, no headway final 2f   **14/1**

7 _shd_ **ASTEROID FIELD (USA)** 3 9-00 .... Y Saint-Martin
led over 8f   **25/1**

8 _2_ **ALA MAHLIK** 3 9-00 .... G Starkey
outpaced   **18/1**

9 _3_ **LAUGHTER** 3 9-00 .... W Carson
3rd straight, weakened 2f out   **18/1**

10 _2_ **TRALTHEE (USA)** 3 9-00 .... Pat Eddery
5th straight, weakened over 2f out   **9/2**

11 _1½_ **BROKEN WAVE** 3 9-00 .... R Curant
100/1

12 _3_ **BONSHAMILE** 3 9-00 .... R Guest
prominent 4f, behind final 4f   **33/1**

13 _3_ **SANET** 3 9-00 .... C Asmussen
100/1

14 **VOLIDA** 3 9-00 .... P Robinson
started slowly, always behind   **100/1**

15 **DAVEMMA** 3 9-00 .... Gay Kelleway
chased leader 7f   **200/1**

15 ran
TIME 2m 35.60s
1st OWNER: H Ranier TRAINER: B Hanbury (Newmarket) BRED: Edward A Seltzer & Shadowlawn Farm, in United States
2nd OWNER: R Cowell TRAINER: M Stoute
3rd OWNER: Maktoum Al-Maktoum TRAINER: M Stoute
TOTE WIN£2.60 PL£1.10,£3.50,£3.00 DF£33.10 CSF£30.82

Midway Lady (USA)

		Tom Rolfe
Alleged	**Hoist The Flag**	Tom Rolfe
		Wavy Navy
	Princess Pout	Prince John
		Determined Lady
Smooth Bore	**His Majesty**	Ribot
		Flower Bowl
	French Leave	Damascus
		Marche Lorraine

Untold

		Forli
Final Straw	**Thatch**	Forli
		Thong
	Last Call	Klairon
		Stage Fright
Unsuspected	**Above Suspicion**	Court Martial
		Above Board
	Chevanstell	Le Levanstell
		Chevartic

Maysoon

		Honeyway
Shergar	**Great Nephew**	Honeyway
		Sybil's Niece
	Sharmeen	Val de Loir
		Nasreen
Triple First	**High Top**	Derring-Do
		Camenae
	Field Mouse	Grey Sovereign
		Meadow Song

Colorspin (FR)

		Darius
High Top	**Derring-Do**	Darius
		Sipsey Bridge
	Camenae	Vimy
		Madrilene
Reprocolor	**Jimmy Reppin**	Midsummer Night
		Sweet Molly
	Blue Queen	Majority Blue
		Hill Queen

Doncaster GOOD to FIRM **1m 6f 127y**

Holsten Pils St Leger

1st £110,592 **2nd** £41,284 **3rd** £19,742 **4th** £8,503

1 **MOON MADNESS** 3 9-00...............................Pat Eddery
   b c by Vitiges-Castle Moon (Kalamoun)
   held up and behind, last straight, headway on inside 4f
   out, led 2f out, ran on   **9/2**

2 *4* **CELESTIAL STORM (USA)** 3 9-00.....................S Cauthen
   b c by Roberto-Tobira Celeste (Ribot)
   held up, 7th straight, quickened to lead over 2f out,
   edged left, soon headed and ran on   **6/1**

3 *2* **UNTOLD** 3 8-11.................................W R Swinburn
   ch f by Final Straw-Unsuspected (Above Suspicion)
   6th straight, not much room 2½f out, ran on under pres-
   sure final 2f   **5/2F**

4 *2½* **SWINK (USA)** 3 9-00..............................C Asmussen
   b c by Liloy-Swiss (Vaguely Noble)
   5th straight, not much room 3f out, ran on one pace **8/1**

5 *1* **NISNAS** 3 9-00.......................................T Quinn
   chased leaders, 4th straight, every chance 3f out, not
   much room over 2f out, one pace   **11/2**

6 *3* **SIRK** 3 9-00.......................................M Roberts
   led 1f, 3rd straight, weakened 3f out   **18/1**

7 *8* **FAMILY FRIEND** 3 9-00............................W Carson
   led after 1f until headed 3f out, weakened 2f out **66/1**

8 *shd* **ALLEZ MILORD (USA)** 3 9-00.....................G Starkey
   soon chasing leaders, 2nd straight, led 3f out until over
   2f out, soon weakened   **4/1**

---

8 ran
TIME 3m 5.03s
1st OWNER: Lavinia Duchess of Norfolk TRAINER: J Dunlop (Arundel) BRED: Lavinia
Duchess of Norfolk
2nd OWNER: R Duchossois TRAINER: L Cumani
3rd OWNER: Sheikh Mohammed TRAINER: M Stoute
TOTE WIN£4.50 PL£1.60,£2.30,£1.10 DF£12.90 CSF£28.52

Moon Madness

		Sicambre
Vitiges	Phaeton	Pasquinade
	Vale	Verrieres
		Calliopsis
Castle Moon	Kalamoun	Zeddaan
		Khairunissa
	Fotheringay	Right Royal
		La Fresnes

Celestial Storm (USA)

		Turn-to
Roberto	Hail To Reason	Nothirdchance
	Bramalea	Nashua
		Rarelea
Tobira Celeste	Ribot	Tenerani
		Romanella
	Heavenly Body	Dark Star
		Dangerous Dame

Untold

		Forli
Final Straw	Thatch	Thong
	Last Call	Klairon
		Stage Fright
Unsuspected	Above Suspicion	Court Martial
		Above Board
	Chevanstell	Le Levanstell
		Chevarctic

Swink (USA)

		Bold Ruler
Liloy	Bold Bidder	High Bid
	Locust Time	Spy Song
		Snow Goose
Swiss	Vaguely Noble	Vienna
		Noble Lassie
	Gala Host	My Host
		Huspah

● FULL HOUSE: York plays host to a huge crowd at its August meeting but for how long will other tracks manage to attract the customers?
Picture: GERRY CRANHAM

38

In My View

by JOHN OAKSEY

In My View

_by_ JOHN OAKSEY

IT IS A very long time since the executives of British racecourses had any serious 'new' money to spend. But starting in 1987, the appearance of televised racing in Britain's betting shops will, barring accidents, put several million pounds a year at their disposal.

What's more, this will be money they can spend almost as they please, unlike grants or loans from the Levy Board.

The chosen Fairy Godmother had not actually signed her contract by Christmas 1986 but Satellite Racing Development, the Racecourse Association's announced choice in September, already had firm "orders" from 7,000 of the 10,000 betting shops.

There are, of course, those who consider Satellite Racing Development a sinister cross between a Trojan horse and a wolf in sheep's clothing! Forty-five per cent of the shares will belong to holding companies which control the big four bookmaking chains, Ladbrokes, Hills, Corals and Mecca — and that, the Jeremiahs say, is like putting the punter's head nearly half way into a hostile horse's mouth!

But 40 per cent is going to "other investors", presumably not bookmakers, so at least in theory, with the RCA keeping the remaining ten per cent and having a right of veto over certain key decisions, the bookies will be in an outvotable minority.

In my own uninformed but optimistic opinion, the "Big Bookmaker Domination" scare was never worth the loss of too much sleep.

Televised racing (two meetings a day plus one at the greyhounds) is obviously not calculated to swell racecourse crowds or strengthen the on-course market. I am not sure the effect will be quite as bad as some fear, but more than ever before, this must be the moment for racecourse managers to rack their brains and empty their cash boxes in an all-out effort to make each day's racing cheaper, more attractive and better all-round value for money.

The moment one starts thinking how this can best be done, admission prices on our racecourses become the first statistic to hit you in the face.

It is all very well (and perfectly true) to say that they have fallen in real terms since the second war and now compare quite favourably with cinemas and theatres. But the fact remains, sticking out like the sorest possible thumb, that it costs more than twice as much to go racing in England as anywhere else in the world.

The original underlying reason for this can be summed up in a word — bookmakers. In all countries with some version of a Tote monopoly, racecourses want as many people betting at the races as possible — and charge them correspondingly little to get in.

A few comparisons reveal the high price British racegoers pay, by choice, for their beloved bookies.

Depending on the rate of exchange, £1.90 to £3.15 gets the racegoer into all but the very poshest enclosure in France, £2.16 in Belgium, £1.40 in Norway and about £2 at Santa Anita. By contrast there are few, if any, British courses where it does not cost at least £5 to get into Tattersalls on an ordinary day. Most Members' enclosures cost around the £8 mark and except at a few enlightened (or prosperous?) courses, race cards and car parking still have to be paid for.

I am afraid these figures are rarely written down — for the excellent, if slightly discreditable reason that fortunate journalists never pay to get in. Quite often we get fed for nothing too, so the standard and price of racecourse catering tends to go similarly under-reported.

But that does not alter the fact that a man wishing to take his wife or girl-friend racing needs the best part of £30 to spend before either have a bet. These days that amounts to a serious deterrent — or, if you like backing horses, to a serious incentive for a walk to the betting shop instead.

The trouble is that 3,750,000 people went racing in Britain in 1985. To cut their admission charges by £1 a head would therefore use up an unhealthy proportion of the £5m which the RCA hopes to be distributing annually by 1989. Lord Wigg attempted a subsidy which had no visible effect, and such evidence as there is, suggests that a cut of £1 would be both inadequate and pointless.

But that gloomy calculation will not absolve racecourse managers from devoting most of the betting shop television money to improving the product they have for sale. By that I do not mean adding to the already inflated prize money offered for top Flat races, many of which add at least one nought to the winner's value the moment he passes the post.

A case can be made for increasing prize money for jumping and, just possibly, for Flat racing lower down the scale, but the overwhelming priority must be to improve the value of the product and then to tell the world what good value it represents in terms of entertainment.

Even if, for the reasons already given, a straight subsidy is not feasible, admission charges should at least be pegged for as long as possible. Race cards and car parking should invariably be free, and although the fragmentation of our fixture list makes good, reasonably cheap catering extremely difficult to achieve, strenuous efforts should be made to avoid the 50p cup of tea and the £2 drink extracted from a rugby scrum, where the racegoer feels he will be lucky to escape with all four limbs in place.

The Levy Board has promised £10m for improved amenities, and although that will not go far stretched over five years and 59 courses, it does seem reasonable to hope that from 1987 the fortunes of the long-suffering British racegoer may be on an upward curve. Of course, there is nothing wrong that a steady supply of winners would not cure, but failing that, let us hope we will not have to pay more to lose our money — and that we may even be allowed to bet in something approaching reasonable comfort. □

● NONE BUT THE BRAVE: A jewel of a performance as Dancing Brave wins the King George VI and Queen Elizabeth Diamond Stakes from Shardari.
Picture: GEORGE SELWYN

42

Dancing Brave

by GRAHAM ROCK

○ **MISSION ACCOMPLISHED: Dancing Brave whips the cream of Europe's thoroughbreds in the Prix de l'Arc de Triomphe at Longchamp.**

Picture: TONY EDENDEN

Dancing Brave

by GRAHAM ROCK

THAT DANCING BRAVE has become the latest candidate for the equine Hall of Fame is a compliment in itself, but does his name sit happily alongside the likes of Mill Reef, Nijinsky, Shergar, Alleged and other recent champions?

His reputation will rest, ultimately if unfairly, on one race, the Trusthouse Forte Prix de l'Arc de Triomphe. That success and his win in the King George VI and Queen Elizabeth Diamond Stakes were his most prestigious victories,

both at a mile and a half. However, few who saw Dancing Brave destroy his rivals in the 2,000 Guineas at Newmarket would deny he was one of the most impressive winners of that Classic, over a mile, and it would be wrong to dismiss him as a one-race horse.

One quality which Dancing Brave possessed in glorious abundance - and far in excess of his middle-distance contemporaries - was speed. His pedigree (by Lyphard out of the high-class American racemare Navajo

Princess) suggested a mile and a quarter would be his maximum effective distance. That he was able to win against the cream of Europe's thoroughbreds over a mile and a half was a tribute to his versatility, but in order to achieve those victories, he needed to be 'switched off', or relaxed, in the early stages of the race until unleashing his final run.

Most horses give their best when ridden from behind. The jockey lets his mount know soon after the start that maximum effort is not required immediately and the horse settles, racing at threequarter pace. In the later stages, the front-runners begin to tire and those at the rear, who have conserved their energy, are able to come through and finish ahead of the pacemakers. Occasionally, when the pace is very strong in the first half of the race, horses held up do not necessarily quicken, but merely maintain their gallop as those ahead weaken.

None of this should be surprising, since athletes face identical tactical problems; the pressure of pacemaking, the judgement of pace and the conservation of energy to strike at the optimum moment are essential ingredients of success. They gauge such variables for themselves, but thoroughbreds require a human in the saddle to take these critical decisions, even if those expert riders in the stands offer the opinion that sometimes the horse would be better off on his own!

Was Greville Starkey's judgement at fault when Dancing Brave just failed to catch Shahrastani in the Derby? Certainly the condemnation immediately after the race was almost universal, but his critics overlooked salient facts, not all apparent at the time. Starkey knew he was aboard a top-class horse at Epsom. The combination had won a slowly-run 2,000 Guineas, storming clear to leave Green Desert (the best six-furlong horse in the country) struggling like a giraffe in quicksand three lengths behind, a distance which would have been doubled in a few more strides.

There was doubt in some minds (if not in Starkey's) whether Dancing Brave would stay a mile and a half. In the end, the undulating course and the muddling pace brought about his defeat. Starkey might have won if he could have ridden the race again, but such gratuitous comment does little to illuminate his dilemma on Derby Day.

O PERFECT PAIRING: Pat Eddery and Dancing Brave.   Picture: KICKSPORTS

Scobie Breasley, the supreme artist at holding up a horse for a late run, said afterwards that a horse settled at the rear in a race could only be expected to use his burst of speed to any real effect once. If Starkey had used that power to improve his position after a couple of furlongs, when the field slowed, his mount may not have had enough left for a second burst to reach Shahrastani in the straight.

One statistic is worth quoting, though. Dancing Brave covered the penultimate furlong at Epsom in 10.3 seconds, of which any top-class sprinter would have been proud.

The Coral-Eclipse Stakes gave Dancing Brave the opportunity to reaffirm his mettle. Starkey had the confidence to let Triptych go past him two furlongs out before switching round her, after which he unleashed his own mount for an exhilarating and emphatic four-length success.

Dancing Brave's victory in the King George at Ascot was less impressive; his speed had, in part, been used by Pat Eddery to overcome interference in running before the straight. At the post Dancing Brave was hanging on by a diminishing threequarters of a length from Shardari. The bare form leaves Dancing Brave significantly behind other champions who have made their mark in the King George, but more, much more, was to come.

Guy Harwood chose the Scottish Equitable Select Stakes for Dancing Brave's reappearance seven weeks later. Starkey, who was back in the saddle, has the reputation for spending as much time looking behind as ahead when cruising in front, but this time he gave his mount a proper work-out, pushing him out to such effect that

the mile-and-a-quarter course record was clipped by half a second.

Once again at Longchamp, to the credit of Harwood, Dancing Brave looked in the peak of condition. Throughout the year his coat had shone like lacquered mahogany and under the leafy trees of Longchamp he drew murmurs of approval from the chauvinistic French crowd.

The Arc field lined up against Dancing Brave on that sunlit afternoon was the strongest in recent memory. The intervention of British bookmakers in the face of heavy support for the local hero Bering depressed Dancing Brave's price to 11-10, but those odds

seemed lean indeed as he turned for home at the rear of the field.

Thousands of English hearts sank in anticipation of the disappointment and ignominy to follow, but the large band of supporters which had followed Dancing Brave across the Channel had reckoned without Pat Eddery's daunting confidence.

Content to relax his mount until passing the two-furlong marker, Eddery switched to get a run and seeing daylight, Dancing Brave struck for home. The raw power of his challenge was matched by the surge of adrenalin through the stands and the crowds roared their approval as Dancing Brave strode past Bering and the remainder, a

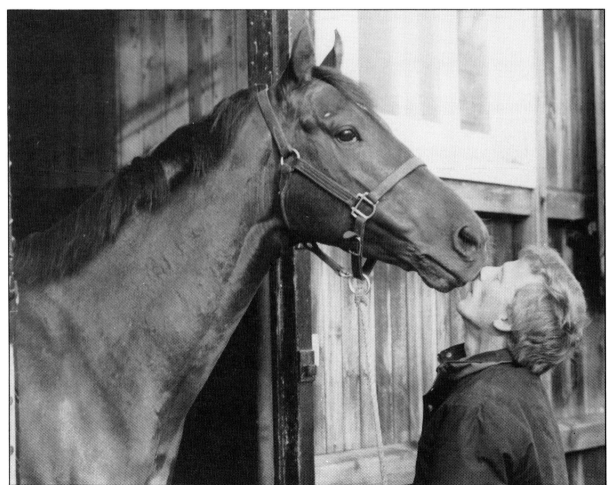

○ **LAST FAREWELL: Brian Graham, who looked after Dancing Brave at the Guy Harwood stable, says goodbye to his hero at the National Stud.**
Picture: ALAN JOHNSON

○ **BEATEN BUT UNBOWED: Dancing Brave goes down to Shahrastani in the Derby, but many considered him the moral victor.**
       Picture: GERRY CRANHAM

monarch dismissing insolent pretenders.

The raucous American hype ensured that every Californian mammal knew of Dancing Brave's 'awesome' reputation before he touched down for the Breeders' Cup Turf race at Santa Anita the following month. Matched against him were Estrapade, easy winner of the Budweiser Million at Arlington, and Manila, the best middle-distance turf horse from the East coast. Nonetheless, the European star was sent to post at lengthy odds on.

Through the unerring binoculars of hindsight, it is obvious Dancing Brave was no certainty in that alien environment. The smog, the heat, the tight left-handed course,

the long season, the rigours of the Arc and the debilitating jet lag all may have counted against him. He went, he saw, but he did not conquer, finishing a lack-lustre fourth to Manila. There was no disgrace, no permanent damage to his reputation, only the aching disappointment that sportsmen, as opposed to mere punters, can comprehend.

It was his last race. Before the Eclipse, he had been syndicated at £14m and was eventually sent to take up stallion duties at Dalham Hall Stud in Newmarket.

By any standards Dancing Brave's record was exceptional and throughout his career he was blessed with an equable temperament, vital for the

consistency he sustained from April to October. Thoroughbreds are highly-strung, born to run, but Dancing Brave had the disposition of a dormouse and would not have blinked at a firecracker jumping between his legs.

When matching him against the leviathans of the past, it is difficult to overcome the fallibilities of one's senses. His victories remain technicolor bright in the memory, while the successes of earlier champions have faded into monochrome, like dusty postcards found in a drawer, remembered affectionately but dulled by the passing of time.

Ribot, Mill Reef and Brigadier Gerard raced for three seasons and saw off the young hopefuls of

The O'Brien trio of Nijinsky, Sir Ivor and Alleged were out of the top drawer; the first two won the Derby, Alleged landed two Arcs. Dancing Brave achieved neither feat. One could sift through the evidence for hours without reaching a convincing conclusion.

Certainly Dancing Brave's racing style was spectacular; his dramatic finishing speed, seemingly more mechanical than muscular, set the spirit soaring. As much as any of our sporting champions, he will be remembered for that most exciting but elusive attribute: star quality.□

subsequent generations. Ribot took two King Georges; Mill Reef won Pattern races by distances more readily associated with three-mile chases, and Brigadier Gerard was beaten only once in 18 starts. Sea Bird's win in the 1965 Arc was, by common acclaim, the best performance by any European thoroughbred this century.

It is unlikely that Dancing Brave would have beaten Shergar in the Derby; the hero of 1986 would have been inconvenienced by the easy ground, for one thing. Shergar galloped home ten lengths clear of Glint of Gold, who went on to win six races in high-class company and was not beaten again on soft ground.

⊙ **ARC SEQUENCE: Dancing Brave's victory run.**   Picture: TONY EDENDEN

● **DIAMOND BRIGHT: Dancing Brave wins the King George VI and Queen Elizabeth Diamond Stakes at Ascot from Shardari (right) and Triptych.**
Picture: DAVID HASTINGS

CHAPTER 4

The King George, Ascot

by PAUL JOHNSON

O VICTORY MARCH: Dancing Brave lands the King George VI and Queen Elizabeth Diamond Stakes from Shardari (right) and Triptych.

Picture: PROVINCIAL PRESS

The King George, Ascot

by PAUL JOHNSON

THE RACING WORLD owes an enormous debt to Sir John Crocker Bulteel. Not only the outstanding racing official of his day, he was also the guiding hand behind the institution of the King George VI and Queen Elizabeth Stakes at Ascot in 1951.

Sir John's brainchild has become the corner-stone of the British Flat racing season and now, under the sponsorship of De Beers, it ranks second only to the Trusthouse Forte Prix de l'Arc de Triomphe in the European pecking order for three-year-olds and upwards. In one respect it can even be considered superior to the Arc, since its 1986 opening to geldings came while the French were still resisting the move in Group One races.

Followers of most sports are fascinated by comparisons between the top stars of different eras. How many sporting debates have revolved around imponderables such as whether Best was better than Matthews, how Bradman rates with Richards, could Marciano have coped with Ali? In contrast, racing fans have something to get their teeth into every July, when the top three-year-olds can put their reputations on the line against older horses over the accepted Classic distance of a mile and a half.

And, even in these days of second-season "champions" being whisked off to stud before you can say Shareef Dancer, the King George consistently attracts the calibre of older opposition to make

feasible comparisons between generations.

The impressive list of King George winners is testimony to the status of the race but it is fair to ask whether the time has come for prize money to be boosted substantially. The King George winner's purse is not matching strides with some of the other major races and, with the number of valuable counter-attractions across the globe on the increase, a dose of extra cash might pre-empt the temptation for trainers to travel further afield for mouth-watering prizes.

The 1986 Trusthouse Forte Prix de l'Arc de Triomphe netted the winner £367,985, compared to £152,468 pocketed by Dancing Brave's connections after the King

George. The disparity of £215,517 is staggering.

In 1980 Detroit's owner received £134,078 for her triumph in the Paris spectacular, less than £10,000 more than Ela-Mana-Mou earned when successful in that year's King George. In 1975 Grundy earned only £24,555 more for winning the Derby than he did for beating Bustino in that epic King George VI. But had Shahrastani managed to complete the double 11 years later, the differential would have been £86,792.

If the King George is to be sure of retaining its hard-earned and well-deserved prestige, the sponsors may be well advised to take prompt action.

The 1986 renewal had more spice than usual in its ingredients, as it featured the eagerly-awaited rematch between Epsom · Derby winner Shahrastani and runner-up Dancing Brave. Since Dancing Brave failed by half a length to catch the Aga Khan's colt at Epsom, after starting his challenge in the next parish, arguments had raged as to which was the better.

To add fuel to the debate, both protagonists went into battle at Ascot with another Group One success in the locker. Shahrastani, not given the credit he deserved after the Derby amid the welter of criticism of Starkey's handling of Dancing Brave, had made people sit up and take notice with an eight-length triumph in the Budweiser Irish Derby at The Curragh later in June. But supporters of Dancing Brave were equally cock-a-hoop after the Pulborough star routed Triptych and six others in the Coral-Eclipse Stakes at Sandown Park earlier in July.

However, in some quarters doubts still remained about Dancing Brave's ability to last out a stiff mile and a half run at a fierce pace. Not since the days of Brigadier Gerard and Mill Reef had opinion been so polarized.

The line-up also included the four-year-old Petoski, who beat Oh So Sharp in the race 12 months earlier and appeared to be returning to his best. And Shardari, also owned by the Aga Khan, had put behind him two disappointing displays at Chester and Epsom when impressively accounting for Baby Turk and Petoski in the Princess of Wales's Stakes at Newmarket earlier in the month.

Coronation Cup runner-up Triptych, tough as old boots, was dispatched from France to renew Sandown rivalry with Dancing Brave, while Clive Brittain fielded Supreme Leader, fourth in Slip Anchor's Derby and winner of two Group Three events early in 1986.

Weight of Press opinion was firmly behind Shahrastani and this was reflected in the betting, with the Derby winner favourite at 11-10, Dancing Brave at 6-4 and both Shardari and Petoski out at 14-1. Paddock inspection revealed the two principals trained to the minute, but whereas Dancing Brave looked totally relaxed, Shahrastani was beginning to sweat up by the time the jockeys arrived in the paddock.

Petoski's pacemakers Boldden and Vouchsafe went off at a rare gallop, evoking memories of the 1975 race when the same stable's Highest and Kinglet employed similar tactics in an attempt to take the sting out of Grundy on behalf of Bustino.

By Swinley Bottom the pair were ten lengths clear of Dihistan, pacemaking for his Michael Stoute stable-companions Shardari and Shahrastani and now just ahead of that pair. Dancing Brave was going well for Eddery with the Stoute trio safely in his sights. The front-runners were swallowed up half a mile from home, with Dihistan taking over the donkey work. But as Boldden went into reverse he almost stopped Eddery and Dancing Brave in their tracks. For a few strides Dancing Brave seemed in trouble, yet in a matter of yards horse and rider had combined superbly to extricate themselves from the traffic jam. Turning for home Shahrastani and Shardari were in hot pursuit of Dihistan, with Dancing Brave being manoeuvred to the outside to deliver his challenge. Two furlongs out Sharastani was clearly making heavy weather of getting to Dihistan and suddenly the Aga Khan's hopes rested on Shardari.

But no sooner had Shardari set sail for for home than Eddery asked Dancing Brave to quicken approaching the furlong pole. The response was decisive, and in no more than 50 yards the issue was settled. Although Shardari rallied in the last furlong, he could do no more than reduce the deficit to threequarters of a length. Triptych, who had found the early pace too hot, stayed on into third place, four lengths behind Shardari but five lengths ahead of Shahrastani, whom Walter Swinburn had eased.

Dancing Brave's time of 2min 29.49sec has been bettered by only four of the 20 previous winners and he became the first colt since Nijinsky to complete the double of 2,000 Guineas and King George VI in the same season.

Swinburn rightly observed that Shahrastani had failed to give his best running, and Michael Stoute added that his three-year-old colt had not changed gear when required.

There are some illustrious names on the King George roll of honour, including the mighty Ribot, Nijinsky, Mill Reef, Brigadier Gerard and Shergar. Dancing Brave's effort loses little in comparison with theirs, even allowing for Shaharastani's below-par display.

Dancing Brave had virtually reproduced his Eclipse running with Triptych and his superiority over Shardari was not emphatic enough to justify some of the more outrageous claims made on his behalf after the King George. But the speed he showed to work his way out of trouble at a crucial stage, plus the acceleration he found to go past the runner-up stamped him as something special. Later in the season we were to see how special he was. □

● **DRIVING ON:** Last Tycoon
has to pull out all the stops to
hold Double Schwartz in the
King's Stand Stakes at Royal
Ascot.
    Picture: DAVID HASTINGS

CHAPTER 5

Sprinters

by EMILY WEBER

○ **EARLY WARNING: Last Tycoon prepares for Royal Ascot by winning the Prix du Gros-Chene.**   Picture: P BERTRAND

Sprinters

by EMILY WEBER

THE LENGTH of a French loaf separated the top European sprinters in 1986. But then came the Breeders' Cup Mile. If Last Tycoon was only marginally best of the sprinters, his reputation afterwards was as golden as a newly-baked baguette.

On a day when seven other top-class horses from Europe managed only one fourth place between them, Last Tycoon's victory, in a race two and a half furlongs longer than he had won over before, was, in my view, the best performance of the season by any horse.

But it was as a sprinter that we knew him in Europe.

Before Last Tycoon, France had not produced a champion sprinter who proved himself away from home since 1975, when Flirting

Around won the King's Stand Stakes at Royal Ascot by five lengths.

In the 20 Group One sprints between that victory and Last Tycoon's in the same race in 1986, 19 French-trained horses took part for five placings.

In the William Hill July Cup, Sonoma was third to Marwell in 1981 and Sanedtki runner-up to Solinus in 1978. In the King's Stand, Realty and Hittite Glory were second and third in 1976, and Girl Friend second to Godswalk the following year.

If the French sprinters have done badly in Britain, their record in their own championship, the Prix de l'Abbaye de Longchamp, has been, if anything, even more pitiful in recent years. In the

eight runnings since Sigy won as a two-year-old in 1978, they have managed only two second places and three thirds.

Last Tycoon ran a fine fifth in the race as a two-year-old in 1985, but it was not until he came to Ascot in June for the King's Stand that he established himself at the top.

His preparation included wins in the Prix de Saint-Georges at Longchamp and Prix du Gros-Chene at Chantilly, both over five furlongs. The half-length victory in the Prix du Gros-Chene over the one-time British handicapper Premiere Cuvee did not impress the Ascot punters despite his being on 12lb worse terms than weight-for-age and he was easy to back at 9-2 especially in the face of strong support for Double Schwartz, the mount of Pat Eddery.

Double Schwartz had looked little more than a top-class handicapper at the start of the season — he had been allotted 9st 7lb in the Wokingham 12 months earlier — but he was beginning to fulfil the promise of his two-year-old days and the high opinion of his trainer Charlie Nelson.

Still, his defeat of the handicappers Clantime and Imperial Jade in Newmarket's Palace House Stakes, and Grey Desire and Petrovich in Sandown Park's Sears Temple Stakes, amounted to little, and served only to emphasize the overall lack of quality in the domestic sprinting department. The twelve other runners in the

King's Stand had won only once between them from 33 starts in 1986; they were to win eight times more in the rest of the season from 54 runs, but only twice in Pattern races.

Best of the rest in the King's Stand was Gwydion, unbeaten winner of both her races at two and now recovered from a bout of pleurisy in the spring. She, Last Tycoon, and Double Schwartz had the race to themselves in the closing stages. Gwydion had a narrow lead two furlongs out but Last Tycoon, who was held up on the wide outside, produced a terrific burst for Cash Asmussen (replacing the injured Yves Saint-Martin) to go clear a furlong out. Eddery had looked happy enough

on Double Schwartz in the middle of the field, and at the distance he started his run in earnest. But Double Schwartz had to use up his considerable finishing speed in the first 100 yards of the final furlong and after looking sure to overhaul the French colt, he failed to quicken close home, in spite of Eddery's desperate efforts. Excuses were made for him, but Last Tycoon raced on his own for most of the final furlong and was holding him once he had something to race against.

What doubts there were about whether the best horse won at Royal Ascot were multiplied after the Norcros July Cup, run over six furlongs at Newmarket less than three weeks later.

O PERFECT RUN: Green Desert wins a muddling race for the Norcros July Cup. Picture: JOHN CROFTS

Robert Collet sent Last Tycoon back to Britain convinced the son of Try My Best would stay the extra furlong, but Charlie Nelson decided to keep Double Schwartz to five furlongs, leaving Green Desert as the main challenger to the French colt.

Green Desert was a little behind the best of his generation at two years, being rated equal 28th in the European Free Handicap, a pound below Last Tycoon, but he started his second season as the first horse to win that Newmarket seven-furlong race carrying 9st 7lb.

He went on to chase home Dancing Brave at a respectable distance in the 2,000 Guineas, but failures in the Irish equivalent and to a lesser extent the St James's Palace Stakes at Royal Ascot convinced trainer Michael Stoute he would be better employed as a sprinter. Gwydion, Grey Desire and Cyrano de Bergerac, unlucky runner-up to Sperry in the Cork and Orrery Stakes, completed the July Cup field.

Green Desert had the run of the race at Newmarket. Always going sweetly just behind the reluctant pacemaker Grey Desire, Walter Swinburn allowed Green Desert to take the lead at halfway. On the heels of this pair Cyrano de Bergerac, Last Tycoon and Gwydion raced in a line. The early pace had been modest and with all five staying on as they approached the final furlong, Yves Saint-Martin, whose early positioning left something to be desired, had no place to make his challenge except by pulling back and round Gwydion.

Once faced with open space, Last Tycoon had about four lengths to make up and sensibly Saint-Martin did no more than push him out with hands and heels. Though he finished well, he was still a length and a half and a short head behind at the line. Swinburn did not have to pick up his whip on Green Desert, who gained a comfortable success, but the presence of the admirable though scarcely top-class Grey Desire threequarters of

a length behind him, and Gwydion the same distance away third, not to mention the traffic problems of the French colt, ensured only muted praise for the winner.

None of us was much the wiser about Last Tycoon's ability to stay six furlongs after the July Cup, but there was no doubting the identity of the fastest horse in Europe after the William Hill Sprint Champ-

○ ROBERT COLLET: Trainer of Last Tycoon

ionship, run at York six weeks later.

Green Desert (running for the first time since Newmarket), Double Schwartz and Gwydion came back for another try. Double Schwartz and Gwydion were fresh, if that is the right word, from a gruelling encounter in the King George Stakes at Goodwood, where Double Schwartz, fast getting a reputation for courage after a rather different one in 1985, touched off Henry Cecil's filly under a severe ride from Eddery.

Showing no ill-effects, Double Schwartz was always near the pace at York, racing on the outside, with Green Desert also close up. Last Tycoon, pulling hard and

○ FINAL BOW: Last Tycoon beats the best in the William Hill Sprint Championship.   Picture: GERRY CRANHAM

○ **HEADS DOWN: Double Schwartz (right) and Gwydion fight out the finish of the King George Stakes.** Picture: TONY EDENDEN

changing his legs, tracked Double Schwartz about three lengths behind. Steadily improving from two furlongs out, Saint-Martin asked for his effort a furlong out and Last Tycoon settled the issue in a few strides. He had to be pushed out to hold the persevering challenge of Double Schwartz by threequarters of a length, but Green Desert was outpaced in the final furlong and finished a length and a half back in third, with Gwydion a well-beaten fourth.

That was the last we saw of Last Tycoon in Europe. His contemporaries took advantage of his absence, gaining well-deserved end-of-season prizes. Green Desert was given a fright by Hallgate, who ran him to a neck in the six-furlong Vernons Sprint Cup at Haydock Park, where Double Schwartz, suited by neither the distance nor the easy ground, was fourth.

Double Schwartz made the most of a favourable draw to land the Abbaye, in which Hallgate, winner

○ **TAILS UP: Double Schwartz cheers the British contingent at Longchamp by winning the Prix de l'Abbaye.**
Picture: JOHN CROFTS

○ CROWNING GLORY: Last Tycoon ends his career by winning the Breeders' Cup Mile at Santa Anita.
Picture: ASSOCIATED PRESS

of the Diadem eight days earlier, distinguished himself a head and a neck behind the winner. Green Desert again found five furlongs too sharp and was two lengths away fourth. First and fourth ended the season with a fruitless journey to Santa Anita for the Breeders' Cup Sprint.

But it was glory all the way for Last Tycoon in the United States. Meticulously prepared for the Breeders' Cup Mile by Collet, he produced his familiar burst of speed in the short straight and held the late challenge of Palace Music by a head. The colt who had come within one-hundredth of a second of the five-furlong record at Royal Ascot had travelled 8,000 miles to defeat the best of the Americans over three furlongs farther. It is hard to think of a similar feat of versatility. His retirement to Coolmore in Ireland is very much the racegoing public's loss. □

○ SCOOPING THE POOL: Green Desert (left) hits the jackpot by beating Hallgate in the Vernons Sprint Cup.
Picture: ALEC RUSSELL

Royal Ascot FIRM 5f

King's Stand Stakes

1st £48,828 **2nd** £18,347 **3rd** £8,874 **4th** £3,931

1	**LAST TYCOON** 3 8-09................................C Asmussen	
	b c by Try My Best-Mill Princess (Mill Reef)	
	led over well over 1f out, hard ridden final furlong, ran on	
		9/2
2 *shd*	**DOUBLE SCHWARTZ** 5 9-03.....................Pat Eddery	
	b h by Double Form-Cassy's Pet (Sing Sing)	
	outpaced, good headway over 1f out, every chance inside final furlong, edged right, ran on	**9/4F**
3 *2½*	**GWYDION (USA)** 3 8-06.............................S Cauthen	
	b f by Raise A Cup-Papamiento (Blade)	
	led 2f out, ridden over 1f out, ran on	**100/30**
4 *4*	**WELSH NOTE (USA)** 3 8-06.............................T Ives	
	b f by Sharpen Up-Gaelic Logic (Bold Reason)	
	headway final 2f, never nearer	**16/1**
5 *½*	**POLYKRATIS** 4 9-03...J Reid	
	never near to challenge	**66/1**
6 *nk*	**SHARP ROMANCE (USA)** 4 9-03 ....R Cochrane	
	headway final 2f, ran on	**50/1**
7 *¾*	**FAYRUZ** 3 8-09(v)....................................P Waldron	
	every chance 2f out, weakened over 1f out	**25/1**
8 *½*	**STORM WARNING** 4 9-00....................W R Swinburn	
	good speed over 3f	**20/1**
9 *¾*	**HALLGATE** 3 8-09....................................W Carson	
	outpaced	**9/1**
10 *nk*	**ATALL ATALL** 3 8-09 ....M J Kinane	
	speed over 2f	**20/1**
11 *hd*	**NOMINATION** 3 8-09.................................T Quinn	
	outpaced	**12/1**
0	**AMIGO LOCO** 5 9-03.............................S Whitworth	
	led over 1f, weakened 2f out	**66/1**
0	**PETROVICH** 4 9-03...............................B Thomson	
		66/1
0	**STALKER** 3 8-09.................................Paul Eddery	
	led over 3f out, weakened over 1f out	**16/1**

14 ran
TIME 59.28s
1st OWNER: R Strauss TRAINER: R Collet (France) BRED: Kilfrush Stud Ltd
2nd OWNER: R Sangster TRAINER: C Nelson
3rd OWNER: S Niarchos TRAINER: H Cecil
TOTE WIN£4.30 PL£1.40,£1.30,£1.60 DF£3.80 CSF£14.13

Newmarket GOOD TO FIRM 6f

Norcros July Cup

1st £39,208 **2nd** £14,721 **3rd** £7,111 **4th** £3,140

1	**GREEN DESERT (USA)** 3 8-11..............W R Swinburn	
	b c by Danzig-Foreign Courier (Sir Ivor)	
	led 3f out, ridden over 1f out, ran on well	**7/4F**
2 *¾*	**GREY DESIRE** 6 9-06..................................K Darley	
	gr h by Habat-Noddy Time (Gratitude)	
	led 3f, ridden over 1f out, ran on	**20/1**
3 *¾*	**GWYDION (USA)** 3 8-08...........................S Cauthen	
	b f by Raise A Cup-Papamiento (Blade)	
	every chance over 1f out, ran on inside final furlong	**15/2**
4 *shd*	**LAST TYCOON** 3 8-11.........................Y Saint-Martin	
	b c by Try My Best-Mill Princess (Mill Reef)	
	headway over 1f out, ran on inside final furlong, never nearer	**9/4**
5 *¾*	**CYRANO DE BERGERAC** 3 8-11................Pat Eddery	
	held up, every chance over 1f out, one pace final furlong	**11/4**

5 ran
TIME 1m 12.25s
1st OWNER: Maktoum Al-Maktoum TRAINER: M Stoute (Newmarket) BRED: Eaton Farms Inc & Red Bull Stables, in United States
2nd OWNER: M Brittain TRAINER: M Brittain
3rd OWNER: S Niarchos TRAINER: H Cecil
TOTE WIN£2.10 PL£1.50,£4.10 DF£13.70 CSF£21.57

Grey Desire

			Sir Gaylord
Habat	**Habitat**		Sir Gaylord
			Little Hut
	Atrevida		Sunny Boy
			Palariva
Noddy Time	**Gratitude**		Golden Cloud
			Verdura
	Siesta Time		Ommeyad
			Time Call

York   GOOD TO FIRM   5f

William Hill Sprint Championship

1st £49,518 **2nd** £18,427 **3rd** £8,763 **4th** £3,722

1		**LAST TYCOON** 3 9-02 ....Y Saint-Martin

b c by Try My Best-Mill Princess (Mill Reef)
tracked leaders, steady headway to lead well inside final furlong, ran on well   **7/2**

2   ¾   **DOUBLE SCHWARTZ** 5 9-06 ....Pat Eddery
b h by Double Form-Cassy's Pet (Sing Sing)
close up, led halfway, ran on under pressure, not quicken   **5/2**

3   1½   **GREEN DESERT (USA)** 3 9-02 ....W R Swinburn
b c by Danzig-Foreign Courier (Sir Ivor)
with leaders, challenged 2f out, not quicken inside final furlong   **9/4F**

4   4   **GWYDION (USA)** 3 8-13 ....S Cauthen
b f by Raise A Cup-Papamiento (Blade)
always chasing leaders, ridden 2f out, ran on one pace   **9/2**

5   3   **MAROUBLE** 3 9-02 ....J Reid
close up 2f, soon outpaced   **33/1**

6   hd   **BRIDESMAID** 3 8-13(v)............................B Thomson
slowly into stride, behind until ran on well final furlong   **40/1**

7   hd   **GREY DESIRE** 6 9-06 ....K Darley
never went pace   **20/1**

8   **ORIENT** 3 8-13...D McKeown
led to halfway, soon weakened   **33/1**

8 ran
TIME 57.47s
1st OWNER: R Strauss TRAINER: R Collet (France) BRED: Kilfrush Stud Ltd
2nd OWNER: R Sangster TRAINER: C Nelson
3rd OWNER: Maktoum Al-Maktoum TRAINER: M Stoute
TOTE WIN£3.50 PL£1.40,£1.20,£1.40 DF£4.30 CSF£11.83

Last Tycoon

		Nearctic
	Northern Dancer	
Try My Best		Natalma
		Buckpasser
	Sex Appeal	
		Best In Show
		Never Bend
	Mill Reef	
Mill Princess		Lalun
		Sayajirao
	Irish Lass	
		Scollata

Green Desert (USA)

		Nearctic
	Northern Dancer	
Danzig		Natalma
		Admiral's Voyage
	Pas de Nom	
		Petitioner
		Sir Gaylord
	Sir Ivor	
Foreign Courier		Attica
		Never Bend
	Courtly Dee	
		Tulle

Double Schwartz

		Sir Gaylord
	Habitat	
		Little Hut
Double Form		
		Crocket
	Fanghorn	
		Honeymoon House
		Tudor Minstrel
	Sing Sing	
		Agin The Law
Cassy's Pet		
		Nasrullah
	Cassydora	
		Glen Line

Welsh Note (USA)

		Native Dancer
	Atan	
		Mixed Marriage
Sharpen Up		
		Rockefella
	Rocchetta	
		Chambiges
		Hail To Reason
	Bold Reason	
		Lalun
Gaelic Logic		
		Irish Lancer
	Irish Party	
		Party Favor

Gwydion (USA)

		Native Dancer
	Raise A Native	
		Raise You
Raise A Cup		
		Nashua
	Spring Sunshine	
		Real Delight
		Bold Ruler
	Blade	
		Monarchy
Papiamento		
		Vandale
	Commemoration	
		Anne Comnene

CHAPTER 6

Milers

by ADRIAN COOK

● **LOOK OF A CHAMPION: Sonic Lady, Europe's top specialist miler.** Picture: DAVID HASTINGS

SUPER SONIC: The Swettenham Stud Sussex Stakes falls to Sonic Lady.   Picture: TONY EDENDEN

Milers

by ADRIAN COOK

STRENGTH IN DEPTH was not one of the features among foremost milers in 1986 and there was no denying Sonic Lady's position as Europe's supreme specialist in this category.

Six Pattern-race successes in three countries established her as a top-quality performer and her failure in the Breeders' Cup Mile at Santa Anita November, behind the French-trained sprinter Last Tycoon, should not deprive her of championship status. The title should not rest on the result of one race but be earned by a series of performances throughout the season, and Sonic Lady turned in a succession of high-class efforts.

Unusually none of the winners of the 2,000 Guineas races in England, France or Ireland — Dancing Brave, Fast Topaze and Flash of Steel — ran over less than a mile and a quarter after their Classic successes. Midway Lady and Maysoon, first and second in the 1,000 Guineas at Newmarket, were also confined to middle distances subsequently, while Green Desert, the 2,000 Guineas runner-up, and Baiser Vole, the French 1,000 winner, both spent much of the year sprinting.

Britain's only Group One race over a mile open to three-year-olds and upwards is the Swettenham Stud Sussex Stakes, run at Goodwood at the end of July with a role of honour befitting its status. Classic winners Humble Duty, Brigadier Gerard, Bolkonski, Wollow, Jaazeiro, Kings Lake and On The House, plus top-notchers such as Sallust, Thatch, Artaius, Kris, Chief Singer and Rousillon won the race in the 70s and 80s.

Sonic Lady went off at 5-6 favourite to add her name to this impressive list, her rival in the betting being Pennine Walk, subsequent Arlington Million third.

Sonic Lady had lost on only one of her previous six appearances, when a close third in the 1,000 Guineas after getting worked up before the start and spoiling her chance by pulling very hard in the race. She started favourite for that event, following an impressive three-length success in the Nell Gwyn Stakes over Lady Sophie, Ala Mahlik and Embla on her reappearance.

Following Sonic Lady's defeat in the Guineas, trainer Michael

Stoute equipped her with a special Northern Perfection bridle in her races in order to prevent her pulling so hard. It did the trick, though occasionally only just.

In the Irish 1,000 Guineas she re-established herself as a top-flight miler by comfortably accounting for a 19-runner field which included Lake Champlain, Asteroid Field and Baiser Vole. Easy successes over Embla and Some-one Special in Royal Ascot's Coronation Stakes, and over Dusty Dollar and Argon Laser in the Child Stakes at Newmarket, conf-irmed her superiority among her sex, but taking on colts is always a stiffer task.

Pennine Walk, the 1985 Jersey Stakes winner, had begun the year by putting up one of the best handicap performances of the season to win the British Car Auctions Jubilee Handicap at Kempton Park under 9st 11lb, before returning to Pattern-race company. In the Diomed Stakes at Epsom he had been confidently ridden by Pat Eddery, swooping close home to beat Hadeer by half a length, with Cliveden two lengths back in third, ahead of such as Lucky Ring, Nino Bibbia, English Spring and Ever Genial.

Pennine Walk's excellent turn of foot had again been seen to advantage in the Queen Anne Stakes at Royal Ascot, where he came late to beat Teleprompter and Efisio, although he was receiving 6lb from both.

Efisio, who had earlier won the Group One Premio Emilio Turati at Milan, was again in opposition in the Sussex Stakes, this time at level weights, and started third favourite. It was thought the fast ground would be against Scottish Reel, a late withdrawal at Royal Ascot, and this stable-companion of Sonic Lady drifted from 7-1 to 20-1.

Scottish Reel had earlier shown very smart form when going down by a neck to the ill-fated Field Hand (rec 3lb) in the Trusthouse Forte Mile at Sandown in April and when beating Teleprompter (gave 5lb) and Earl of Sefton and

Westbury Stakes winner Supreme Leader in the Juddmonte Lockinge Stakes at Newbury.

The Sussex Stakes field was completed by the Kentucky Derby second Bold Arrangement, who had been out of the money in the Derby and Eclipse Stakes following his return from America, and was tried in blinkers for the first time.

Scottish Reel set out to make the running, with Sonic Lady held up in last place. In the straight he battled on bravely but had no answer when Walter Swinburn swept past on the favourite, although he held on for second money.

On her next outing Sonic Lady beat the best that Europe could offer when winning the Prix du Moulin de Longchamp Ecurie Fustok. However, she pulled so hard she had to struggle to hold off Thrill Show, the pair finishing clear of Group One winners Lirung and Magical Wonder.

Sonic Lady's owner Sheikh Mohammed also had one of the best three-year-old miling colts in Sure Blade, who has been retired

to the Kildangan Stud in Ireland. Sure Blade, who had lost his unbeaten record on his final start as a juvenile when third in the Dewhurst, went off 13-2 third favourite for the 2,000 Guineas, following a bloodless success at Thirsk on his reappearance, but finished only fifth behind Dancing Brave.

The St James's Palace Stakes at Royal Ascot gave Sure Blade the chance to turn the tables on the Newmarket second, third and fourth — namely Green Desert, Huntingdale and Sharrood — and he took the opportunity in style.

After Green Desert had surprisingly set out to try and make all, the always-prominent Sure Blade cut him down in the last furlong for a two-length success. Green Desert narrowly held off Sharrood for second place, with the other runners, Nino Bibbia, Luqman, Greenham winner Faustus and Huntingdale, finishing in Indian file.

As trainer Barry Hills was convinced Sure Blade was not moving correctly behind, the colt

○ HERE COMES THE BRIDLE: Sonic Lady poses in the equipment which helped her to settle. Picture: R H WRIGHT

○ **TOP OF THE SHOP: Sonic Lady beats the best in Europe in Longchamp's Prix du Moulin.**   Picture: JOHN CROFTS

was turned out at his owner's Rutland Stud at Newmarket and did not race again for over three months until reappearing in the Queen Elizabeth II Stakes, also at Ascot.

Sure Blade looked anything but a short-priced favourite approaching the home turn, as the gallant gelding Teleprompter bowled along in front and Sure Blade was being pushed along in fifth. But pulled to the outside in the straight Sure Blade came with a long, steady run

which enabled him to catch the 1985 Arlington Million winner Teleprompter close home and he beat him by half a length. Efisio was two and a half lengths back in third place, ahead of the improving handicapper Mtoto, the sadly disappointing Truely Nureyev, Hadeer and Moonlight Lady.

The runner-up, who was conceding 3lb more than weight-for-age, emerged with just as much credit yet amazingly has not won in Britain since the corresponding

event in 1984. Teleprompter went on to gain compensation for some sterling efforts by winning a valuable race at Phoenix Park but Sure Blade finished only eighth of 11 in the Dubai Champion Stakes, for which he started second favourite.

Britain's other main prize for milers, the Waterford Crystal Mile at Goodwood, was reckoned by many to be a good thing for the Sussex Stakes second Scottish Reel, but he finished only fifth of eight and was subsequently retired to the Cheveley Park Stud, Newmarket. The prize was won by Then Again, who had run well for a long way in the Derby but here confirmed that he is best at around a mile by beating the luckless Sharrood, with the improved handicapper Siyah Kalem pipping Supreme Leader for third.

Then Again was subsequently an unlucky loser of the seven-furlong Ricard Challenge Stakes at Newmarket. Although only a Group Three race, it has no penalties and can be considered the most important race for three-year-olds and upwards over the distance in the country.

Held up, as he is a difficult ride, Then Again made impressive progress when asked to quicken but failed by a neck to overhaul Lucky Ring after hanging left andhampering several of his rivals up the hill. He was subsequently disqualified and placed last, with his rider Greville Starkey being disqualified seven days for careless riding.

This victory marked a return to form for Lucky Ring, who had developed into a very smart

O CUTTING EDGE: Sure Blade is too good for Green Desert in the St James's Palace Stakes.   Picture: GERRY CRANHAM

performer at three but had disappointed earlier in 1986. He subsequently added a Pattern race win in Italy to this success.

Sarab, who had the distinction of winning four Pattern races in 1986 but none at home, was awarded second place. He gained his most important win in the Group One Prix de la Foret at Longchamp ten days after the Challenge Stakes, after which he was retired to the

Cleaboy Stud in Ireland.

Only seventh in the Challenge Stakes was Hadeer, who had previously picked up three Pattern races over the seven-furlong trip — the Federation Brewery Beeswing Stakes at Newcastle, Trusthouse Forte Hungerford Stakes at Newbury and Kiveton Park Stakes at Doncaster.

Hadeer's only other defeat at seven furlongs during the year

O FINDING HIS FEET: Then Again shows his quality to land the Waterford Crystal Mile from Sharrood.
Picture: GERRY CRANHAM

came when he finished fourth of 14 behind the subsequently-exported Mister Wonderful in the newly-upgraded Group Three Van Geest Criterion Stakes at Newmarket in June. In the Beeswing Stakes he had his rivals well strung out when coming home three lengths clear of Hard Round, with Tremblant two lengths back in third and the favourite Lucky Ring last of the nine runners. In the Hungerford Stakes Hadeer again accounted for Tremblant and Hard Round but had to put his best foot

forward to beat the enigmatic Truely Nureyev (rec 3lb more than weight-for-age) by a neck.

Despite a 2lb pull in the weights, Truely Nureyev finished a well-beaten seventh in the Kiveton Park Stakes, where Hadeer got up close home to pip Moonlight Lady and the sprinter Gwydion, with Sarab and the Jersey Stakes winner Cliveden further back.

Hadeer proved a bargain buy for Stetchworth Park Stud owner Bill Gredley, who purchased the colt for 13,000gns out of Michael

Stoute's stable at the 1985 Tattersalls Autumn sales, after a light and disappointing three-year-old campaign.

A $190,000 yearling purchase by Maktoum Al-Maktoum, Hadeer had looked very promising as a juvenile and finished fourth in the Gimcrack Stakes, but he became very difficult to train. A timely combination of swimming and physiotherapy and the patience of his new trainer Clive Brittain helped Hadeer to finally fulfil his potential.□

◯ BARGAIN BUY: Hadeer proves his worth by beating Truely Nureyev (right) in the Trusthouse Forte Hungerford Stakes.

Picture: ALAN JOHNSON

Goodwood GOOD TO FIRM 1m

Swettenham Stud Sussex Stakes

1st £155,225 **2nd** £57,961 **3rd** £27,731 **4th** £11,958

1		**SONIC LADY (USA)** 3 8-07 .... W R Swinburn

b f by Nureyev-Stumped (Owen Anthony)
5th straight, led over 1f out, quickened, comfortably **5/6F**

2 *1½* **SCOTTISH REEL** 4 9-07................................G Starkey
ch c by Northfields-Dance All Night (Double-U-Jay)
led over 6f, ran on well **20/1**

3 *½* **PENNINE WALK** 4 9-07................................Pat Eddery
b c by Persian Bold-Tifrums (Thatch)
4th straight, pulled out over 1f out, ridden, ran on inside final furlong **15/8**

4 *nk* **BOLD ARRANGEMENT** 3 8-10(b)................................S Cauthen
ch c by Persian Bold-Arrangement (Floribunda)
2nd straight, every chance over 1f out, unable quicken final furlong **16/1**

5 *1* **EFISIO** 4 9-07................................W Carson
3rd straight, every chance over 1f out, weakened inside final furlong **15/2**

5 ran
TIME 1m 39.65s
1st OWNER: Sheikh Mohammed TRAINER: M Stoute (Newmarket) BRED: J Mactier, in United States
2nd OWNER: Cheveley Park Stud TRAINER: M Stoute
3rd OWNER: Mrs M Niarchos TRAINER: J Tree
TOTE WIN£1.80 PL£1.30,£2.20 DF£7.00 CSF£12.56

Sonic Lady (USA)

		Nearctic
Nureyev	Northern Dancer	Nearctic
		Natalma
	Special	Forli
		Thong
Stumped	Owen Anthony	Proud Chieftain
		Oweninny
	Luckhurst	Busted
		Lucasland

Scottish Reel

		Nearctic
Northfields	Northern Dancer	Nearctic
		Natalma
	Little Hut	Occupy
		Savage Beauty
Dance All Night	Double-U-Jay	Major Portion
		Renounce
	Pretty Show	Ossian
		After The Show

Pennine Walk

		Bold Ruler
Persian Bold	Bold Lad (Ire)	Bold Ruler
		Barn Pride
	Relkarunner	Relko
		Running Blue
Tifrums	Thatch	Forli
		Thong
	Persian Apple	No Robbery
		Persian Garden

Bold Arrangement

		Bold Ruler
Persian Bold	Bold Lad (Ire)	Bold Ruler
		Barn Pride
	Relkarunner	Relko
		Running Blue
Arrangement	Floribunda	Princely Gift
		Astrentia
	Colombelle	Colombo
		Path of Peace

CHAPTER 7

Pat Eddery

by J A McGRATH

● **WITHOUT EQUAL: Pat Eddery proved himself Britain's top jockey in 1986.**   Picture: DAVID
HASTINGS

Pat Eddery

by J. A. McGRATH

PAT EDDERY (1986) was a valuable vintage. Excitement and promise gave way to style, maturity and glorious triumph as the season progressed, with the Irish-born champion gaining his fifth jockeys' title.

But the sparkle in Eddery's champagne riding career almost fizzled out, permanently, in late-1974. It was the winter following a glorious season in Britain.

Eddery, then 22, had won his first championship with 148 winners. He had also won his first Classic, the Oaks, on Polygamy for Peter Walwyn. Clearly, he was a young man with the racing world at his feet. But how dangerously close that came to disintegrating on a warm winter afternoon at tiny Happy Valley racecourse, in the heart of high-rise Hong Kong.

It was 30 November; Eddery was riding Kentucky Lad, a Hong Kong Derby winner considered one of the best horses to have raced in the British Colony. The field was strong but Kentucky Lad was backed to clear-cut favouritism in the nine-runner St Andrew's Challenge Quaich, over about nine furlongs.

When the field passed the winning post with a circuit to travel, Kentucky Lad was in the middle, racing between horses. Already Eddery was unhappy and started tugging at the reins. A matter of strides later, he faced a split-second crisis.

Eddery stood high in the stirrups as blood spurted fiercely, alarmingly, from Kentucky Lad's nostrils. The horse was literally dying beneath him.

Still going a racing gallop, Eddery aimed to the outside, hoping to get clear of other runners. But instead of leaving trouble behind, he found himself heading towards a 12ft-high brick wall on the outside of the course. It was time for another instant decision.

What followed rates as an exhibition of escapology that would have done credit to the great Houdini.

Eddery threw away the reins, kicked his feet out of the irons, somehow got one foot on the saddle and managed a backward flip of his body, out of danger. As he made a safe touchdown, the ill-fated Kentucky Lad slammed into the wall and died instantly.

The simple entry in the Stewards' report to the Royal Hong Kong Jockey Club told a chilling story: "Eddery, when interviewed, stated that he felt something was wrong with the horse's action on the stable bend and that soon after it had bled profusely from its nostrils. Although he had made every effort to pull the horse up, he had been unable to do so. The Veterinary Surgeon stated that Kentucky Lad died immediately as a result of the accident and that it had apparently suffered an internal haemorrhage and also its skull had been fractured when it hit the wall...The jockey escaped injury."

Eddery walked away from that horrific episode to finish the season in Hong Kong with 12 winners. He returned to Britain to win another three championships on the trot, with 164, 162 and 176 winners.

Throughout his career, Eddery has possessed an uncanny, sixth-sense when it comes to horses. The Hong Kong escape will come as no great surprise to those who have seen him ride over the years. He has achieved the near-impossible, in far less dramatic circumstances, to win hundreds of races since, even though at times the odds were clearly not in his favour.

He is a naturally-gifted jockey. He has the most wonderful ability to settle almost any type of horse wherever he wants in a field. But above all, his talent for "lifting" horses to win when they appear beaten puts the seal on his riding repertoire.

In 1986, he rode more winners than any other rider. He was top jockey at Royal Ascot, and gained a string of major successes, achieved with efforts in the saddle worthy of the highest praise.

His ride on Moon Madness in the Holsten Pils St Leger at Doncaster was a gem. His performances on Dancing Brave in both the King George VI and Queen Elizabeth Diamond Stakes and Prix de l'Arc de Triomphe were exciting and called for nerves of steel.

Then to crown everything, he lifted the Japan Cup on Jupiter Island, in a typically vigorous finish which left his long-standing rival Greville Starkey again in second spot, this time on Allez Milord.

On Moon Madness, Eddery came from last place at the turn into the long Doncaster straight, edging up the inside to make headway about half a mile out before he struck the front with two furlongs to run. He saved valuable ground by taking the inside passage and was rewarded with a Classic win which compensated to some extent for missing the first two such races through suspension, and then finishing last on Wise Counsellor in the Derby and 10th of 15 on Tralthee in the Oaks.

If there was one horse which turned Eddery's season from good to glorious it was Dancing Brave. And if there was one owner who seems set to consolidate Eddery's present position at the top of the tree it is Khalid Abdulla, owner of the wonder colt.

Eddery is not a man given to showing emotion on a racecourse. He is a cool customer in whichever circle he moves. But the association with Dancing Brave left him visibly overjoyed, particularly after the spectacular Arc win in October.

Coming up against such as the brilliant French colt Bering, dual Derby winner Shahrastani, and top older horses such as Shardari, Triptych, Darara and Acatenango, produced a pressure-cooker atmosphere. After Dancing Brave had come down the outside with his paralysing, late burst, Eddery was bubbling. "He's absolutely incredible," he enthused. "I gave him two cracks with the whip at the top of the straight and he nearly jumped. He took off. What a win!"

Later, when he had had time to take in the occasion, he said: "I think he's outstanding over any distance. Some people were saying after the Eclipse that he takes time to hit top gear, but that's nonsense.

"Greville Starkey rode Dancing Brave in the Eclipse and I really don't think he wanted to hit the front too early, so he steadied and allowed another horse to go around his outside. The colt is inclined to stop if he is left in front too early."

That is what happened in the King George, where Eddery came from well back with a devastating burst of speed. Dancing Brave hit the front, but Shardari was able to counter and ran him to threequarters of a length.

Eddery came in for the Dancing Brave ride in the King George when Starkey was ruled out by injury but Abdullah installed him ahead of Starkey when it came to the Arc. At that time, Eddery had already announced he was splitting with O'Brien and partners and would ride for Abdullah in 1987.

It was a dramatic parting, reminiscent of 1980 when Eddery left Peter Walwyn to join O'Brien. But it guarantees him the opportunity to stay at the top of the jockeys' list in Britain. Not

○ PAT EDDERY: No cooler customer. Picture: ALAN JOHNSON

only will the Saudi prince supply Eddery with some of the choicest racehorses in the world, he also enables him to take up further chances on a Saturday.

During his time with O'Brien, Eddery missed many Saturdays in Britain, when a host of major races are run, due to commitments in Ireland. There is little doubt Eddery would have won more than five jockeys' titles had he been permanently in this country. The elusive 200-winner mark may well be within his reach, if all goes well, this year.

Pat Eddery, champion rider, is well-known, but Pat Eddery the man is more of a mystery.

He adopts a low profile when not riding and keeps very much to his family and a few very close friends, most of whom have known him since his early days in racing.

He is intensely loyal to his friends and likes nothing better than to relax with them over a few quiet drinks.

Married to Carolyn, the late Manny Mercer's daughter, he is the father of two daughters. After a meeting, he will dash to his car and make for home, to relax in front of the television with a glass of wine and a cigar.

He watches his weight, prefers poached eggs on toast or a bacon and egg sandwich to any exotic cuisine one may associate with his buying-power, and spends most mornings in a sauna adjacent to his house. His brother-in-law Terry Ellis, married to Olive Eddery, is his manager and books his rides, takes care of much of the administration and drives him to meetings. It is a close-knit, family operation, which has proved overwhelmingly successful.

Eddery is a fierce competitor in everything he tackles. Whether it be a game of cards, darts, snooker or whatever, he loves to win, much the same as on the racecourse. He is down-to-earth, pulls no punches, but can still take a joke with his fellow jockeys and friends.

Professionally, there is no better rider in Britain today. Like Lester Piggott, he comes from a family of jockeys, on both sides of his pedigree, and has been working at his profession since a very early age.

He was eight years old when he was first legged up on a horse at Seamus McGrath's stable in Ireland, and at 11 he was riding out with such as the brilliant Australian Bill Williamson, a time he looks back on with pleasure. "I learned a lot, riding with Bill," he says.

After being with McGrath for a short period, Eddery was off across the Irish Sea to join Frenchie Nicholson, the master trainer of apprentices, who guided him to a brilliant start in racing and to such a successful career. In 1987, Pat Eddery will again be the name on everybody's lips when the big races, or the small, come around. □

CHAPTER 8

Middle Distance
by GRAHAM DENCH

● **BACK ON TOP: Dancing Brave puts Derby defeat behind him in the Coral-Eclipse Stakes at Sandown Park.**
Picture: JOHN CROFTS

○ FULL POWER: Shardari surges through to beat Baby Turk and Petoski (left) in the Princess of Wales's Stakes.
Picture: DAVID HASTINGS

Middle Distance

by GRAHAM DENCH

THE HIGH HOPES held out for an exceptional season's racing over middle distances were fully justified by a series of superb performances, though few came from the individuals touted loudest at the start of the season.

Although the up-and-coming Classic generation looked no better than average, it was widely anticipated that competition would be strong, thanks to an outstanding group of older horses which remained in training. Slip Anchor, seven-length winner of the 1985 Derby, was still around, and so too were Petoski, winner of the King George VI and Queen Elizabeth Diamond Stakes, and Pebbles, heroine of the Coral-Eclipse and Champion Stakes.

That expectations were realised is remarkable, considering the contribution of Slip Anchor (retired after an early defeat at Newmarket) and Petoski was minimal, and that Pebbles failed to race at all, being retired to stud because of recurring lameness.

Fortunately their shortcomings were more than compensated by such as Shardari and Triptych among the older generation and, more importantly, by a handful of less exposed three-year-olds who exceeded all expectations. Dancing Brave developed into one of the most outstanding middle-distance performers of modern times, and Shahrastani and Midway Lady were no ordinary supporting act.

One of the features of Dancing Brave's defeat of Green Desert in the General Accident 2,000 Guineas was his brilliant finishing speed at the end of a slowly-run race, and on breeding he was no certainty to be suited by middle distances. There can be no doubt he would have made an equally outstanding miler had trainer Guy Harwood chosen, and the decision to campaign him over middle distances enriched that scene to an extent it would be difficult to overstate.

Dancing Brave became the star of the show in a magnificent campaign. He went on from the Guineas to success in the Coral-Eclipse, King George VI and Queen Elizabeth Diamond Stakes and Prix de l'Arc de Triomphe, with a narrow and unlucky defeat in the Ever Ready Derby in between.

He was hot favourite on Derby Day, despite the stamina doubt, in front of Michael Stoute's Shahrastani, who had beaten Bonhomie readily in the Guardian Classic Trial at Sandown Park and had defeated Nomrood in rather more workmanlike fashion in the Mecca-Dante at York, and his stablemate Allez Milord, easy winner of the Schroder Predominate Stakes at Goodwood.

Dancing Brave's controversial half-length defeat by Shahrastani, ahead of the Henry Cecil-trained pair Mashkour and Faraway Dancer, was one of the talking points of the season, and criticism of Greville Starkey's riding of Dancing Brave, who many felt was given far too much to do, tended to overshadow the superb ride Walter Swinburn gave the winner.

While Shahrastani was targeted for the Budweiser Irish Derby, Dancing Brave waited for the Eclipse at Sandown, the first significant clash between the three-year-olds and their elders over middle distances.

Dancing Brave started 4-9 in a field of eight, which included pacemakers for Bill Watts' Arlington Million winner Teleprompter and for Clive Brittain's Bold Arrangement, a good second to Ferdinand in the Kentucky Derby and bidding to repeat the stable's success with Pebbles a year earlier. Opposition was anticipated principally from Dick Hern's popular gelding Bedtime and the French filly Triptych, recently second to her compatriot Saint Estephe (ahead of Petoski and Shardari) in the Coronation Cup at Epsom. But nothing could live with Dancing Brave once

Starkey made his move, and he quickened away impressively for a four-length win over Triptych, with Teleprompter a further length and a half away third.

Shahrastani trounced the opposition in the Irish Derby, storming home eight lengths clear of Bonhomie, winner of the King Edward VII Stakes at Royal Ascot, with Bakharoff third, as he had been behind Bering in the French equivalent, the Prix du Jockey-Club Lancia. Interestingly, Bakharoff, who had topped the International Classification as a two-year-old but then became disappointing, was beaten five lengths farther by Shahrastani than by Bering, and fourth-placed Mashkour was beaten six lengths more than he had been in the Derby at Epsom. There was therefore more than a suggestion that Shahrastani had improved.

Shahrastani's stable-companion Shardari beat Baby Turk in the Princess of Wales's Stakes at

○ FRENCH COLLECTION: Saint Estephe (left) and Triptych trounce their English rivals in the Coronation Cup. Picture: PRESS ASSOCIATION

○ **GOING AWAY: Shardari (rails) gallops on too well for Triptych in the Matchmaker International at York.**

Picture: GERRY CRANHAM

Newmarket's July Meeting, to redeem a reputation tarnished by a shock defeat at the hands of 33-1 chance Brunico in the Ormonde Stakes and another disappointing effort in the Coronation Cup. He also ensured that the King George was going to be more than a two-horse race.

Dancing Brave took his revenge over Shahrastani at Ascot, but few would claim the Derby winner was anywhere near his best. With the aid of three pacemakers, including the Hardwicke Stakes winner Dihistan, subsequently also successful in the September Stakes, the King George was a true test of his stamina. Dancing Brave held Shardari by only three-quarters of a length, with Triptych four lengths back in third, after looking as though he would come clear away when quickening into the lead over a furlong out. Shahrastani was beaten nearly ten lengths into fourth place, but there was no joy for the 1985 winner Petoski, who trailed in only sixth,

his last race before retirement to the National Stud.

Unfortunately, save for a prep race in modest company at Goodwood before his magnificent Arc win, Dancing Brave was not raced again in Britain, and nor was Shahrastani. But the domestic scene was hardly dull in their absence. Shardari was improving with every race and he and the remarkable French filly Triptych had a share of the limelight at last.

Shardari, who had looked an Arc prospect when decisively slamming the opposition in both the Cumberland Lodge and St Simon Stakes late on in his season as a three-year-old, was switched back to ten and a half furlongs for the Matchmaker International, formerly the Benson and Hedges Gold Cup, at York.

This was a bold move with so powerful a galloper, who in the King George at Ascot had run as though a mile and a half were his minimum requirement. However, with Dihistan helping to force the

pace again and with Swinburn committing him early in the straight, it paid off handsomely.

Shardari and Triptych had the finish to themselves, with the colt staying on in determined fashion to prevail by threequarters of a length, after Triptych had looked to be going much the better when beginning her challenge. That was the end of Shardari's British, campaign, although he went on to be a fine fifth in the Arc and finally second in the Rothman's International at Woodbine.

The best had still to be seen of Triptych. The very embodiment of modern racing's international flavour, she gained a richly deserved and hugely popular success in the Dubai Champion Stakes at Newmarket, the last major race of the domestic scene.

A runner in no fewer than five classics in 1985, winning the Irish 2,000 Guineas and finishing second to Oh So Sharp in the Oaks, she had made the most of her only opportunity outside Group One company in 1986, winning La Coupe at Longchamp. And since the Matchmaker she had been third to the Irish filly Park Express in the Phoenix Champion Stakes and to Dancing Brave and Bering in the Arc.

Astonishingly, trainer Patrick Biancone was able to produce Triptych as fresh as paint for the Champion and she proceeded to give the former Hong Kong-based rider Tony Cruz a dream start to his new association with the French stable. When Cruz dashed her into a clear lead well over a furlong out, she looked for a moment as though she would come home alone, but she is not one to be in front too long and held on by only threequarters of a length from Celestial Storm, who found a mile and a quarter on the sharp side after finishing second to Moon Madness in the half-mile longer St Leger at Doncaster. Triptych was the seventh filly to win the Champion in the last ten runnings and her victory provided a superb climax to her European campaign,

from which subsequent defeats in the United States and Japan detract little.

It was disappointing not to see more of Midway Lady, the best of the home-trained fillies, but she was jarred up after completing the double of General Accident 1,000 Guineas and Gold Seal Oaks and her next public appearance was in November, when she went through the sale ring for $3.3m.

Trainer Ben Hanbury had her fit enough to beat the Michael Stoute pair Maysoon and Sonic Lady on her reappearance in the Guineas and then sent her straight for the Oaks. At Epsom rider Ray Cochrane again produced her inside the last furlong, scoring by a length from Untold, who this time headed a trio of Stoute-trained fillies. Although the fourth-placed Colorspin went on to score impressively in the Gilltown Stud Irish Oaks and Untold beat Park Express in the Yorkshire Oaks, the middle-distance fillies trained in England made little impact during the season.

No discussion of the middle-distance scene would be complete without mention of the sterling late-season achievements of Clive Brittain's veteran Jupiter Island who, after being sidelined with a hoof injury in California in April, returned to win the St Simon Stakes and the Japan Cup. His narrow Tokyo win over Allez Milord in a British one-two did much to restore international prestige after the bitter disappointments experienced in the Breeders' Cup.

Few of the established British middle-distance stars will be around in 1987, for Dancing Brave, Shahrastani and Shardari have been retired. But Triptych will be attempting to plunder some of the best British prizes again and the four-year-olds in training will include Bonhomie, Celestial Storm, El Cuite and Moon Madness. There are some exciting middle-distance prospects among last year's juveniles too, so who is to say 1987 will not be a repeat of 1986? Time will tell. □

O CRUISING ALONG: Triptych and Tony Cruz have the call over Celestial Storm in the Dubai Champion Stakes.　　　　　　　　　　　　　　　　　　　Picture: GERRY CRANHAM

Epsom GOOD 1m 4f

Coronation Cup

1st £49,086 **2nd** £18,261 **3rd** £8,681 **4th** £3,682

1 **SAINT ESTEPHE (FR)** 4 9-00 .... Pat Eddery
b c by Top Ville-Une Tornade (Traffic)
*headway 3f out, edged left over 1f out, led inside final
furlong, ridden out* **20/1**

2 *shd* **TRIPTYCH (USA)** 4 8-11 .... E Legrix
b f by Riverman-Trillion (Hail To Reason)
*3rd straight, led 2f out, hard ridden inside final furlong,
ran on well* **12/1**

3 *3* **PETOSKI** 4 9-00 .... W Carson
b c by Niniski-Sushila (Petingo)
*4th straight, every chance when bumped over 1f out, un-
able quicken* **5/2**

4 *½* **SHARDARI** 4 9-00 .... W R Swinburn
b c by Top Ville-Sharmada (Zeddaan)
*led over 5f out, edged right over 1f out, one
pace* **EvensF**

5 *10* **NEMAIN (USA)** 4 9-00 .... C Roche
*6th straight, hard ridden 2f out, weakened final fur-
long* **20/1**

6 *3* **PHARDANTE (FR)** 4 9-00 .... G Starkey
*5th straight, not clear run over 2f out, weakened over 1f
out* **7/1**

7 *2* **GOLD AND IVORY (USA)** 5 9-00 .... S Cauthen
never nearer **25/1**

8 **ST HILARION (USA)** 4 9-00 .... A Clark
*dwelt, 2nd straight, not clear run over 2f out, weakened
well over 1f out* **33/1**

9 **SUPER MOVE (USA)** 4 9-00 .... M T Browne
tailed off final 6f **66/1**

10 **BOLDDEN** 4 9-00 .... B Procter
led over 6f, tailed off **100/1**

---

10 ran
TIME 2m 34.87s
1st OWNER: Y Houyvet TRAINER: A Fabre (in France) BRED: M Darix, Mme Anne-
Marie Balbus & Pierre Dubois, in France
2nd OWNER: A Clore TRAINER: P-L Biancone
3rd OWNER: The Dowager, Lady Beaverbrook TRAINER: W Hern
TOTE WIN£10.50 PL£2.60,£2.30,£1.40 DF£71.50 CSF£205.39

Saint Estephe (FR)

		Derring-Do
	High Top	Derring-Do
Top Ville		Camenae
	Sega Ville	Charlottesville
		La Sega
	Traffic	Traffic Judge
Une Tornade		Capelet
	Rough Sea	Herbager
		Sea Nymph

Triptych (USA)

		Nasrullah
	Never Bend	Nasrullah
Riverman		Lalun
	River Lady	Prince John
		Nile Lily
	Hail To Reason	Turn-to
Trillion		Nothirdchance
	Margarethen	Tulyar
		Russ-Marie

Petoski

		Northern Dancer
	Nijinsky	Northern Dancer
Niniski		Flaming Page
	Virginia Hills	Tom Rolfe
		Ridin' Easy
	Petingo	Petition
Sushila		Alcazar
	Shenandoah	Vieux Manoir
		Vali

Shardari

		Derring-Do
	High Top	Derring-Do
Top Ville		Camenae
	Sega Ville	Charlottesville
		La Sega
	Zeddaan	Grey Sovereign
Sharmada		Vareta
	Shireen	Prince Taj
		Clair Obscur

Sandown   GOOD   1m 2f

Coral-Eclipse Stakes

1st £134,460 **2nd** £50,618 **3rd** £24,559 **4th** £10,963

1	**DANCING BRAVE (USA)** 3 8-08 ....G Starkey

b c by Lyphard-Navajo Princess (Drone)
*5th straight, ridden 2f out, quickened and led well over
1f out, ran on well*   **4/9F**

2 *4* **TRIPTYCH (USA)** 4 9-04 ....E Legrix
b f by Riverman-Trillion (Hail To Reason)
*4th straight, led over 2f out, ridden and no im-
pression*   **9/1**

3 *1½* **TELEPROMPTER** 6 9-07(v) ....T Ives
b g by Welsh Pageant-Ouija (Silly Season)
6th straight, ridden 3f out, one pace final 2f   **9/1**

4 *nk* **IADES (FR)** 4 9-07(b) ....F Head
b c by Shirley Heights-Isabella Moretti (Sir Gaylord)
*outpaced, headway over 1f out, ran on well inside final
furlong*   **28/1**

5 *shd* **BOLD ARRANGEMENT** 3 8-08 ....M Roberts
no headway final 2f   **14/1**

6 *4* **BEDTIME** 6 9-07 ....W Carson
3rd straight, led over 3f out, weakened 2f out   **7/1**

7 **COME ON THE BLUES** 7 9-07 ....C Rutter
2nd straight, weakened over 2f out   **500/1**

8 **GRAND HARBOUR** 6 9-07 ....N Connorton
led over 6f   **500/1**

8 ran
TIME 2m 6.18s
1st OWNER: K Abdullah TRAINER: G Harwood (Pulborough) BRED: Glen Oak Farm, in
United States
2nd OWNER: A Clore TRAINER: P-L Biancone
3rd OWNER: Lord Derby TRAINER: J Watts
TOTE WIN£1.40 PL£1.10,£1.30,£1.60 DF£3.60 CSF£5.04

Dancing Brave (USA)

		Nearctic
Lyphard	Northern Dancer	Natalma
	Goofed	Court Martial
		Barra
Navajo Princess	Drone	Sir Gaylord
		Cap And Bells
	Olmec	Pago Pago
		Chocolate Beau

Triptych (USA)

		Nasrullah
Riverman	Never Bend	Lalun
	River Lady	Prince John
		Nile Lily
Trillion	Hail To Reason	Turn-to
		Nothirdchance
	Margarethen	Tulyar
		Russ-Marie

Teleprompter

		Tudor Minstrel
Welsh Pageant	Tudor Melody	Matelda
	Picture Light	Court Martial
		Queen Of Light
Ouija	Silly Season	Tom Fool
		Double Deal
	Samanda	Alycidon
		Gradisca

Iades (FR)

		Never Bend
Shirley Heights	Mill Reef	Milan Mill
	Hardiemma	Hardicanute
		Grand Cross
Isabella Moretti	Sir Gaylord	Turn-to
		Somethingroyal
	Imprimitura	Sing Sing
		Isabella Piccini

Ascot GOOD — 1m 4f

King George VI & Queen Elizabeth Diamond Stakes

1st £152,468 **2nd** £57,367 **3rd** £27,808 **4th** £12,387

1 DANCING BRAVE (USA) 3 8-08 .... Pat Eddery
b c by Lyphard-Navajo Princess (Drone)
headway on inside over 3f out, 5th straight, quickened and led over 1f out, ran on well **6/4**

2 ¾ SHARDARI 4 9-07... S Cauthen
b c by Top Ville-Sharmada (Zeddaan)
3rd straight, led well over 1f out, ran on well inside final furlong **14/1**

3 4 TRIPTYCH (USA) 4 9-04 .... Y Saint-Martin
b f by Riverman-Trillion (Hail To Reason)
in rear 8f, good headway final 3f, never nearer **25/1**

4 5 SHAHRASTANI (USA) 3 8-08 .... W R Swinburn
ch c by Nijinsky-Shademah (Thatch)
2nd straight, every chance 2f out, one pace, eased when beaten inside final furlong **11/10F**

5 2 DIHISTAN 4 9-07... A Kimberley
led over 4f out, weakened well over 1f out **100/1**

6 1½ PETOSKI 4 9-07... W Carson
6th straight, no headway final 2f **14/1**

7 SUPREME LEADER 4 9-07.................................. A Murray
headway 5f out, 4th straight, weakened 2f out **150/1**

8 VOUCHSAFE 4 9-07.. B Procter
chased leader over 7f **1000/1**

9 BOLDDEN 4 9-07... P Cook
led over 7f **1000/1**

9 ran
TIME 2m 29.49s
1st OWNER: K Abdullah TRAINER: G Harwood (Pulborough) BRED: Glen Oak Farm, in United States
2nd OWNER: Aga Khan TRAINER: M Stoute
3rd OWNER: A Clore TRAINER: P-L Biancone
TOTE WIN£2.20 PL£1.20,£1.70,£1.60 DF£10.90 CSF£18.48

Dancing Brave (USA)

Lyphard	Northern Dancer	Nearctic
		Natalma
	Goofed	Court Martial
		Barra
Navajo Princess	Drone	Sir Gaylord
		Cap And Bells
	Olmec	Pago Pago
		Chocolate Beau

Shardari

Top Ville	High Top	Derring-Do
		Camenae
	Sega Ville	Charlottesville
		La Sega
Sharmada	Zeddaan	Grey Sovereign
		Vareta
	Shireen	Prince Taj
		Clair Obscur

Triptych (USA)

Riverman	Never Bend	Nasrullah
		Lalun
	River Lady	Prince John
		Nile Lily
Trillion	Hail To Reason	Turn-to
		Nothirdchance
	Margarethen	Tulyar
		Russ-Marie

Shahrastani (USA)

Nijinsky	Northern Dancer	Nearctic
		Natalma
	Flaming Page	Bull Page
		Flaring Top
Shademah	Thatch	Forli
		Thong
	Shamim	Le Haar
		Diamond Drop

York GOOD 1m 2f 110y

Matchmaker International

1st £117,288 **2nd** £43,850 **3rd** £21,025 **4th** £9,116

1 **SHARDARI 4 9-06**.................................W R Swinburn
b c by Top Ville-Sharmada (Zeddaan)
*prominent, 5th straight, led well over 2f out, ridden and
ran on very well* **13/8F**

2 ¾ **TRIPTYCH (USA) 4 9-03**........................J Reid
b f by Riverman-Trillion (Hail To Reason)
*held up, 6th straight, headway on bit 3f out, effort 2f
out, ran on* **5/1**

3 6 **DAMISTER (USA) 4 9-06**....................Pat Eddery
b c by Mr Prospector-Batucada (Roman Line)
*led 1f, 8th straight, stayed on under pressure final 2f,
never able to challenge* **9/1**

4 ½ **MR JOHN 3 8-10**...................................G Starkey
ch c by Northfields-Ashton Amber (On Your Mark)
*chased leaders, 2nd straight, outpaced 3f out, kept
on* **33/1**

5 hd **BOLD ARRANGEMENT 3 8-10(b)**.....................T Ives
effort 4f out, never troubled leaders **12/1**

6 3 **WYLFA 5 9-06**..B Rouse
*prominent, 4th straight, brought wide, every chance until
weakened 2f out* **50/1**

7 **DIHISTAN 4 9-06**................................A Kimberley
*led after 1f until well over 2f out, gradually lost
place* **33/1**

8 **ASTEROID FIELD (USA) 3 8-07**............B Thomson
never near leaders **25/1**

9 **BEDTIME 6 9-06**....................................W Carson
snatched up after 2f, never dangerous after **12/1**

10 **FITNAH 4 9-03**.......................................G Moore
7th straight, soon outpaced **7/1**

11 **FIORAVANTI (USA) 3 8-10**........................C Roche
pulled hard, never dangerous **16/1**

12 **KADIAL 3 8-10**....................................S Cauthen
chased leaders, 3rd straight, soon weakened **20/1**

12 ran
TIME 2m 8.28s
1st OWNER: Aga Khan TRAINER: M Stoute (Newmarket) BRED: Aga Khan
2nd OWNER: A Clore TRAINER: P-L Biancone
3rd OWNER: K Abdullah TRAINER: J Tree
TOTE WIN£2.40 PL£1.50,£1.60,£2.60 DF£3.80 CSF£9.40

Shardari

			Derring-Do
		High Top	Camenae
Top Ville			Charlottesville
		Sega Ville	La Sega
			Grey Sovereign
		Zeddaan	Vareta
Sharmada			Prince Taj
		Shireen	Clair Obscur

Triptych (USA)

			Nasrullah
		Never Bend	Lalun
Riverman			Prince John
		River Lady	Nile Lily
			Turn-to
		Hail To Reason	Nothirdchance
Trillion			Tulyar
		Margarethen	Russ-Marie

Damister (USA)

			Native Dancer
		Raise A Native	Raise You
Mr Prospector			Nashua
		Gold Digger	Sequence
			Roman
		Roman Line	Lurline B.
Batucada			Double Jay
		Whistle A Tune	Siama

Mr John

			Nearctic
		Northern Dancer	Natalma
Northfields			Occupy
		Little Hut	Savage Beauty
			Restless Wind
		On Your Mark	Super Scope
Ashton Ambler			Gratitude
		Ashton Jane	Rye Girl

York   GOOD   1m 4f

Yorkshire Oaks

1st £42,672 **2nd** £15,895 **3rd** £7,573 **4th** £3,230

1   **UNTOLD** 3 9-00...G Starkey
ch f by Final Straw-Unsuspected (Above Suspicion)
*7th straight, stayed on well to lead inside final
furlong*   **5/1**

2 ¾ **PARK EXPRESS** 3 9-00...............................J Reid
br f by Ahonoora-Matcher (Match III)
*always prominent, 3rd straight, led well over 2f out until
inside final furlong, ran on*   **9/2**

3 ½ **IVOR'S IMAGE (USA)** 3 9-00 ....S Cauthen
b f by Sir Ivor-Embryo (Busted)
*behind, 9th straight, ran on under pressure final 3f,
nearest finish*   **16/1**

4 4 **COLORSPIN (FR)** 3 9-00 ....W R Swinburn
b f by High Top-Reprocolor (Jimmy Reppin)
*held up, 8th straight, steady headway on outside 3f out,
every chance over 1f out*   **9/4F**

5 1½ **FLEUR ROYALE** 3 9-00 ....C Roche
*chased leaders, 4th straight, every chance 2f out, soon
ridden and one pace*   **9/1**

6 8 **QUEEN HELEN** 3 9-00...........................W Carson
chased leaders, 5th straight, no impression   **12/1**

7   **REJUVENATE** 3 9-00 ....B Thomson
*chased leader until led entering straight, headed well over
2f out, soon weakened*   **16/1**

8   **GESEDEH** 3 9-00 ....T Ives
*pulled hard, led, unbalanced, headed and 2nd straight,
soon beaten*   **14/1**

9   **GULL NOOK** 3 9-00 ....Pat Eddery
11th straight, never dangerous   **100/30**

10   **THREE TIMES A LADY** 3 9-00....................B Rouse
held up and 10th straight, never dangerous   **100/1**

11   **SPUN GOLD** 3 9-00...............................T Quinn
some headway and 6th straight, beaten 3f out   **25/1**

11 ran
TIME 2m 30.37s
1st OWNER: Sheikh Mohammed TRAINER: M Stoute (Newmarket) BRED: R Cowell
2nd OWNER: P Burns TRAINER: J Bolger
3rd OWNER: S Fraser TRAINER: M Stoute
TOTE WIN£5.50 PL£1.80,£1.60,£5.90 DF£9.20 CSF£28.66

Untold

Final Straw	Thatch	Forli
		Thong
	Last Call	Klairon
		Stage Fright
Unsuspected	Above Suspicion	Court Martial
		Above Board
	Chevanstell	Le Levanstell
		Chevartic

Park Express

Ahonoora	Lorenzaccio	Klairon
		Phoenissa
	Helen Nichols	Martial
		Quaker Girl
Matcher	Match	Tantieme
		Relance
	Lachine	Grey Sovereign
		Loved One

Ivor's Image (USA)

Sir Ivor	Sir Gaylord	Turn-to
		Somethingroyal
	Attica	Mr Trouble
		Athenia
Embryo	Busted	Crepello
		Sans Le Sou
	Royal Danseuse	Prince Chevalier
		Star Dancer

Colorspin (FR)

High Top	Derring-Do	Darius
		Sipsey Bridge
	Camenae	Vimy
		Madrilene
Reprocolor	Jimmy Reppin	Midsummer Night
		Sweet Molly
	Blue Queen	Majority Blue
		Hill Queen

Newmarket GOOD   1m 2f

Dubai Champion Stakes

1st £86,750 **2nd** £32,638 **3rd** £15,819 **4th** £7,044

1   **TRIPTYCH (USA)** 4 9-00 ....A Cruz
b f by Riverman-Trillion (Hail To Reason)
held up, quickened and led well over 1f out, edged left,
pushed out   **4/1**

2 ¾ **CELESTIAL STORM (USA)** 3 8-10 ....R Cochrane
b c by Roberto-Tobira Celeste (Ribot)
good headway 2f out, ran on well inside final furlong **9/1**

3 *4* **PARK EXPRESS** 3 8-07 ....J Reid
br f by Ahonoora-Matcher (Match III)
led over 8f, unable quicken final furlong   **3/1F**

4 ¾ **BAILLAMONT (USA)** 4 9-03 ....F Head
b c by Blushing Groom-Lodeve (Shoemaker)
every chance 2f out, hard ridden over 1f out, one
pace   **25/1**

5 *shd* **DAMISTER (USA)** 4 9-03 ....Pat Eddery
every chance 2f out, weakened inside final furlong **9/1**

6 *4* **UNTOLD** 3 8-07 ....W R Swinburn
chased leader 8f   **15/2**

7   **DOUBLE BED (FR)** 3 8-10 ....Paul Eddery
pulled out 3f out, every chance 2f out, weakened over 1f
out   **14/1**

8   **SURE BLADE (USA)** 3 8-10 ....B Thomson
every chance over 2f out, weakened well over 1f
out   **100/30**

9   **TREMBLANT** 5 9-03 ....S Cauthen
outpaced   **50/1**

10 **SIYAH KALEM (USA)** 4 9-03 ....W Carson
outpaced, tailed off   **66/1**

11 **MONA LISA** 3 8-07 ....M Hills
always behind, tailed off   **300/1**

11 ran
TIME 2m 9.49s
1st OWNER: A Clore TRAINER: P-L Biancone (France) BRED: N B Hunt & Edward L
Stephenson, in United States
2nd OWNER: R Duchossois TRAINER: L Cumani
3rd OWNER: P Burns TRAINER: J Bolger
TOTE WIN£3.60 PL£1.20,£2.10,£1.90 DF£19.20 CSF£35.04

Triptych (USA)

Riverman	Never Bend	Nasrullah
		Lalun
	River Lady	Prince John
		Nile Lily
Trillion	Hail To Reason	Turn-to
		Nothirdchance
	Margarethen	Tulyar
		Russ-Marie

Celestial Storm (USA)

Roberto	Hail To Reason	Turn-to
		Nothirdchance
	Bramalea	Nashua
		Rarelea
Tobira Celeste	Ribot	Tenerani
		Romanella
	Heavenly Body	Dark Star
		Dangerous Dame

Park Express

Ahonoora	Lorenzaccio	Klairon
		Phoenissa
	Helen Nichols	Martial
		Quaker Girl
Matcher	Match	Tantieme
		Relance
	Lachine	Grey Sovereign
		Loved One

Baillamont (USA)

Blushing Groom	Red God	Nasrullah
		Spring Run
	Runaway Bride	Wild Risk
		Aimee
Lodeve	Shoemaker	Saint Crespin
		Whipcord
	Locust Time	Spy Song
		Snow Goose

● GOLDEN BOY: Longboat, narrowly beaten in the 1985 Gold Cup at Royal Ascot, comes home alone.
Picture: DAVID HASTINGS

CHAPTER 9

Stayers

by COLIN RUSSELL

○ GOLD STANDARD: Longboat and Willie Carson start a treble of Cup wins, at Royal Ascot.

Picture: PADDOCK STUDIOS

Stayers

by COLIN RUSSELL

MAJOR STAYING races in 1986 were dominated by Longboat and Valuable Witness, though at five and six years old respectively they were veterans in Flat racing terms. Unfortunately their paths never crossed, although that was not deliberate policy.

It was perhaps inevitable, for they show their best form on differing types of going. Whereas Longboat is a confirmed top-of-the-ground horse, Valuable Witness, prone to leg problems, is rarely risked on anything firmer than good. With wins in the Gold Cup at Royal Ascot, and Goodwood and Doncaster Cups, Longboat took the accolade as champion stayer of 1986.

His early campaign was geared to the Gold Cup, in which only Gildoran had beaten him in 1985. With Gildoran retired for stallion duties in Australia, Longboat began the season as heir apparent to his crown. His claims were in no way dented when he was soundly beaten in the Aston Park Stakes at Newbury first time out.

Nothing was in his favour. He had not run since the previous Royal Ascot; the distance of a mile and five furlongs was too short, and most important, the going was soft. Not surprisingly, he finished only sixth, six lengths behind his former stable-companion Kaytu.

It was a different story nine days later when Longboat was among ten runners for the Mappin and Webb Henry II Stakes at Sandown Park. The going had dried out, and the distance of two miles was far more suitable. Although only second favourite behind the Yorkshire Cup runner-up Seismic Wave, Longboat laid claims to the Gold Cup with a decisive victory. Willie Carson tracked the leader Eastern Mystic until the straight, but once he joined battle, the outcome was never in doubt. Longboat went clear in the final quarter-mile, beating the favourite by two and a half lengths.

The race did produce one horse who looked as though he could stand between Longboat and the Gold Cup. That was Eastern Mystic.

The former handicapper, bought cheaply at Newmarket during his three-year-old career, came out of the Sandown race with distinction. He was no match for the winner, and was beaten just over three lengths into third place, but he was conceding 3lb. Although tapped for speed early in the straight, it was significant that he was closing on Longboat in the last furlong. In another half mile the verdict might have been less clear cut.

The Gold Cup, open to geldings for the first time, attracted a field of 11, numerically well up to standard but disappointing in terms of quality. There was no

Valuable Witness, and not one challenger from the French.

International competition was provided by the Irish four-year-old Rising, and the Swedish-trained Erydan, who originated from Poland. Neither looked to have the credentials to prove a serious threat, and were virtually ignored in the betting, which was dominated by Longboat and Eastern Mystic.

Although none of the leading contenders had a pacemaker, this great stayers' test was, for once, run at a true gallop. Petrizzo led for the first mile, after which Pat Eddery took over the role on Eastern Mystic. Unfortunately the match that many pundits had forecast never materialized. Longboat was always going too well.

Carson moved him up before the straight, and, just as he had done at Sandown, went for home over two furlongs out. There was no counter attack, because though

Eastern Mystic, who seemed likely to drop right out, fought back courageously, it was only for second place. Longboat had gone, the Gold Cup was his.

The form book shows a winning margin of five lengths, with a head between the runner-up and third-placed Spicy Story and a further three lengths back to the enigmatic Petrizzo, who ran on to take fourth.

The courage of Eastern Mystic, who broke down before the straight but refused to throw in the towel, cannot be underestimated. With four sound legs, he might have been a Gold Cup winner. That we will never know, for he never raced again, and has been sold to Brazil as a stallion.

The day belonged to Longboat, who gave trainer Dick Hern his second Gold Cup in four years. Surprisingly, it was the first success in the race for owner-breeder Dick Hollingsworth, whose Arches Hall Stud has produced

○ OPENING SHOT: Valuable Witness begins the season with a short-head success over Ramich John (left) in the Sagaro Stakes.

Picture: GEORGE SELWYN

numerous good stayers, notably Band, winner of the Yorkshire Cup and runner-up in the French and Irish St Legers.

Longboat is by the miler Welsh Pageant. His stamina appears to emanate from his dam Pirogue, winner of the Ribblesdale Stakes and from a family noted for producing high-class stayers.

With his crown in place, Longboat raced only twice more in 1986, completing the treble of Ascot, Goodwood and Doncaster Cups, a feat last achieved by Le Moss in 1979. The Goodwood race enhanced his reputation, for he was barely out of a strong canter to beat his Ascot victims Spicy Story and Petrizzo by ten lengths and eight lengths.

It was a different story at Doncaster six weeks later. The anticipated showdown between Longboat and Valuable Witness failed to materialise for the ground rode fast; the rain stayed away, and so did Valuable Witness. So it looked a formality for the Gold Cup winner, who started at 1-5. Anyone brave enough to lay the odds drew their winnings, but only with the help of the Stewards.

Longboat failed to show his true colours. Driven along from early in the straight, he mastered the handicapper The Prudent Prince over two furlongs out, but having won that duel, he had to contend with a new threat from Petrizzo, who was given an inspired ride by Cash Asmussen. The pair passed the post locked together, but the photo revealed that Petrizzo had got there by a short head.

A Stewards' inquiry was announced immediately. Petrizzo had been hanging left, defying Asmussen's efforts to keep him straight. Interference took place; the question was whether or not it had affected the result.

Longboat, racing against the rails, was squeezed and Carson did have to stop riding for a couple of strides, but close home Petrizzo, who had also hung fire, quickened again to beat him. It was not considered a controversial decision when the Stewards came down on the side of Longboat. He deserved to win, but on the day there were grounds for thinking that in spite of his antics, Petrizzo was the best horse in the race, but for the second time in three years he lost the Doncaster Cup in the Stewards' room.

Even though he was conceding 11lb to his rival, Longboat did not run up to form. The reason was diagnosed to be a pulled muscle and with time running out, Longboat did not race again. He finished the season with four

O FULL STEAM AHEAD: Longboat carries off the Goodwood Cup

Picture: DAVID HASTINGS

Group successes from five starts.

He galloped over 12 miles to earn £105,120 in prize money, scant reward considering Shahrastani's prize for winning the Every Ready Derby was more than twice that amount, and his stroll at The Curragh for the Budweiser Irish version netted him Ir£299,800. These successes also guaranteed Shahrastani a life in the stud paddocks of America. Not so for Longboat, not in the immediate future at least, for he stays in training as a six-year-old.

With a little luck he will come across Valuable Witness, and a clash between them at Royal Ascot would be both informative and entertaining.

Risked only three times on home soil in 1986, Valuable Witness stretched his unbeaten run to seven races. His most important win came at Newmarket in October, when he took the Jockey Club Cup. Although the ground was hardly soft enough, and the distance of two miles barely far enough, he won by a short head in a race which will best be remembered for the fine riding of Pat Eddery.

Taking over in front a furlong out, Valuable Witness was unable to shake off the attentions of Phardante, who stayed on to such purpose that he forced the issue to a photo. Eddery was the epitome of coolness. Apparently confident he had the measure of Phardante, he never resorted to the whip. Riding with hands and heels, he kept the old horse going. The margin between them diminished to a short head.

As Phardante, who had won only two of his previous eight races, was conceding 2lb, it did not appear to be a vintage performance by the winner. However, 12 lengths behind the first two came the luckless Spicy Story, running his seventh and final race of an unrewarding season.

Eddery had not received the same accolade when successful on Valuable Witness in the Lonsdale Stakes at York six weeks earlier.

O COOL HAND: Pat Eddery at his finest as he keeps Valuable Witness ahead of Phardante (left) in the Jockey Club Cup.   Picture: JOHN CROFTS

Faced with what appeared to be a simple task, Valuable Witness, who had been off the course since winning the Insulpak Sagaro Stakes in April, cruised home by two and a half lengths from the handicapper Majestician and Lemhill.

Although the win was facile, it was not confirmed until after lengthy deliberation by the Stewards. After hitting the front a furlong and a half out, Valuable Witness edged to his left. Eddery appeared to do little to correct him, and in consequence caused interference to third-placed Lemhill, who had a wretched run.

The winner's deviation from a straight line almost certainly cost Lemhill second place. So under Rule 153 the Stewards were entitled to disqualify Valuable Witness, even though he was undoubtedly the best horse in the race. Their findings, that interference was accidental and had no effect on the result, was a triumph for common sense, but not as an interpretation of the Rules of Racing.

The only defeat suffered by Valuable Witness came in the Prix Royal-Oak at Longchamp at the end of October. Over a distance 100 yards short of two miles, he was beaten less than a length into third place behind El Cuite and Alesso.

It was not a satisfactory race. Nobody was keen to go on, so Eddery was forced into making the running, alien tactics to the horse but necessary to ensure a true test of stamina. Valuable Witness battled back after looking likely to be swallowed up when passed by Faburola a furlong and a half out.

By winning the Prix Royal-Oak, El Cuite, trained by Henry Cecil, stamped himself as a high-class stayer. His only win in Britain in 1986 was in a handicap at Newbury in August after which he took the mile-and-a-half Gran Premio d'Italia at Milan, beating the much-travelled Tommy Way by a neck.

Unfortunately the plans are for El Cuite to tread the modern, more profitable path in middle-distances races this season, leaving few youngsters with apparent claims to ousting Longboat from his throne.

His trainer Henry Cecil has one likely candidate in Paean. After winning his maiden at Newbury, the Bustino colt spent most of his racing days at far-flung points in the North picking up small money in small races. He did, however, capture one good prize, the newly instituted George Stubbs Stakes at the final Newmarket meeting.

Although unimpressive when he beat Rosedale (gave 9lb) by half a length, Paean may yet venture into Group-race company in 1987. A dry summer would hinder his progress though, for he is at his best on soft ground.

Such conditions rarely prevailed in the latter part of 1986, though the rain came in time for the filly Orange Hill, who gained a hard-fought win in the Tote-Cesarewitch. The other major staying handicaps went to proven campaigners, as Sneak Preview maintained his improvement to win the Newcastle "Brown Ale"

O ONE TO NOTE: Paean shows promise for the future with a Newbury success over Rosedale. Picture: GEORGE SELWYN

Northumberland Plate, Rikki Tavi beat Otabari (who went on to win the Queen Alexandra Stakes) in the Ascot Stakes and the well-handicapped Primary turned the Tote-Ebor into a one-horse affair.

The outlook for stayers remains bleak. Success in a major long-distance race usually ensures a colt has no attraction to breeders of Flat horses, and his future lies less profitably as a sire of jumpers, or he is sold abroad for a fraction of the price commanded by a successful performer over middle distances.

Perhaps Ardross will reverse the trend, but until and unless he does, the immediate future for stayers remains on the racecourse and not in the paddocks. Inevitably this commercial rule means that these days few top performers over a mile and a half make their way into Cup races. Even St Leger winner Moon Madness is likely to be restricted to middle distances.

Each year the top staying events are dominated by two or possibly three outstanding horses. It looks that way for 1987. The six-year-old Longboat and the gelding Valuable Witness seem set to lord it over their rivals again. But given good ground at Royal Ascot in June, a clash between the pair would, for some enthusiasts at least, be one of the highlights of the year.□

O IT'S A PIPPIN: Orange Hill has the soft ground in her favour as she beats Marlion in the Tote-Cesarewitch. Picture: KICKSPORTS

Royal Ascot   FIRM   2m 4f

Gold Cup

1st £44,688 **2nd** £16,760 **3rd** £8,080 **4th** £3,551

1	**LONGBOAT** 5 9-00..W Carson	
	b h by Welsh Pageant-Piroque (Reliance II)	
	2nd straight, led over 2f out, ran on well **EvensF**	
2	*5* **EASTERN MYSTIC** 4 9-00.........................Pat Eddery	
	b c by Elocutionist-Belle Pensee (Ribot)	
	led over 12f out, hard ridden well over 1f out, no impression final quarter mile, fin lame **7/2**	
3	*hd* **SPICY STORY (USA)** 5 9-00...............S Cauthen	
	b h by Blushing Groom-Javamine (Nijinsky)	
	headway 5f out, 3rd straight, one pace final 2f **11/1**	
4	*3* **PETRIZZO** 5 9-00.....................................C Asmussen	
	b h by Radetzky-Perianth (Petingo)	
	led over 7f, 4th straight, weakened well over 1f out **100/1**	
5	*1½* **TALE QUALE** 4 9-00.................................T Ives	
	6th straight, hard ridden well over 1f out, no response **9/1**	
6	*4* **SEISMIC WAVE (USA)** 5 9-00.............B Thomson	
	5th straight, headway 5f out, weakened over 1f out **10/1**	
7	**KUBLAI (USA)** 4 9-00.................................P Waldron	
	never nearer **50/1**	
8	**BOURBON BOY** 4 9-00............................W R Swinburn	
	always behind **20/1**	
9	**RISING** 4 9-00...G Curran	
	always behind **33/1**	
10	**I WANT TO BE (USA)** 4 8-11................G Starkey	
	well behind final 7f **20/1**	
11	**ERYDAN (POL)** 5 9-00..............................D Persson	
	headway 7f out, every chance 5f out, weakened 4f out, tailed off **66/1**	

11 ran
TIME 4m 22.11s
1st OWNER: R Hollingsworth TRAINER: W Hern (West Ilsley) BRED: R Hollingsworth
2nd OWNER: R Harden TRAINER: L Cumani
3rd OWNER: P Mellon TRAINER: I Balding
TOTE WIN£2.00 PL£1.30,£1.40,£2.10 DF£2.90 CSF£4.78

Longboat

		Tudor Minstrel
Welsh Pageant	Tudor Melody	Tudor Minstrel
		Matelda
	Picture Light	Court Martial
		Queen Of Light
Pirogue	Reliance	Tantieme
		Relance
	Cutter	Donatello
		Felucca

Eastern Mystic

		Gallant Man
Elocutionist	Gallant Romeo	Gallant Man
		Juliet's Nurse
	Strictly Speaking	Fleet Nasrullah
		Believe Me
Belle Pensee	Ribot	Tenerani
		Romanella
	Solid Thought	Solidarity
		Unforgettable

Spicy Story (USA)

		Nasrullah
Blushing Groom	Red God	Nasrullah
		Spring Run
	Runaway Bride	Wild Risk
		Aimee
Javamine	Nijinsky	Northern Dancer
		Flaming Page
	Dusky Evening	Tim Tam
		Home By Dark

Petrizzo

		Derring-Do
Radetzky	Huntercombe	Derring-Do
		Ergina
	Selina Fair	Hugh Lupus
		Raggoty Ann
Perianth	Petingo	Petition
		Alcazar
	Armandia	Alcide
		Success

● **FIRST TO LAST:** Forest Flower beats Minstrella in the Tattersalls Cheveley Park Stakes, only to be disqualified a fortnight later.
Picture: JOHN CROFTS

CHAPTER 10

Two-Year-Olds

by FRANK CARTER

○ RECORD BREAKER: Minstrella beats the clock with an impressive win from Chime Time (left) in Royal Ascot's Chesham Stakes.
Picture: ALAN JOHNSON

Two-Year-Olds

by FRANK CARTER

RARELY has the two-year-old scene been dominated by two individuals for so long as the 1986 generation was by Forest Flower and Minstrella. Their marvellous combined achievements might have been surpassed by others in terms of merit, but their three thrilling but also controversial encounters were among the most lasting memories of the season.

These fillies gave the answer to those critics of Flat racing who harp on about here-today-gone-tomorrow equine heroes (or heroines). It was a battle rejoined the like of which we have not seen since Kings Lake and To-Agori-Mou vied for mile supremacy in 1981. For once, potential stud value was not allowed to interfere with bold racing policy.

Nobody could have guessed that their first meeting, in the Pritchard Services Cherry Hinton Stakes at the Newmarket July Meeting, would be only the prologue to the main play.

Forest Flower was 4-5 against Minstrella (rec 2lb) on the strength of her smooth win in the Queen Mary Stakes at Royal Ascot, where she had looked exceptional. However, Charlie Nelson's grey also had an impressive victory, in record time for a two-year-old in the Chesham Stakes at the Royal meeting, to her credit.

When Minstrella went to the front on the bridle over a furlong out at Newmarket, Forest Flower had a fight on her hands. It was then that the little Green Forest filly, roused by Tony Ives, revealed

her high trump card – courage. Thrusting her head forward, she responded well and forged threequarters of a length clear in the last 100 yards. The class of the principals was emphasised by the seven lengths back to the third.

Despite this setback, Nelson did not lose faith in his daughter of The Minstrel. He looked forward to a rematch at level weights in Europe's richest two-year-old race, the Heinz "57" Phoenix Stakes at Phoenix Park the following month, maintaining that Minstrella had "improved".

His bullish confidence was fully justified. The powerful grey, always in the front line, quickened to gain a decisive lead entering the final furlong and galloped on strongly as Forest Flower, brought under maximum pressure by Pat Eddery (who was widely criticised for his free use of the whip), made a desperate attempt to recover ground lost when she had to be switched left to find room below the distance.

Forest Flower, who had appeared to be crowded by Polonia, did not enjoy the run of the race and many thought her an unlucky loser. Polonia, a length away third, completed a clean sweep for the fillies and the merit of the form was underlined by subsequent events. Polonia won the Lowther at York, where Wiganthorpe (fourth at Phoenix Park) captured the Scottish Equitable Gimcrack Stakes, and Sizzling Melody (fifth) went on to land the Brian Swift Flying Childers Stakes at Doncaster.

Widespread fears that a mite like Forest Flower would not get over such a gruelling test in yielding ground gravely underestimated her toughness and durability. She returned to action six weeks later and her comfortably-gained half-length victory over Shady Heights and seven other colts in the Rokeby Farms Mill Reef Stakes at Newbury went a long way to dispelling those ideas.

Meanwhile, Minstrella had added further to her reputation on a return visit to Ireland for the Moyglare Stud Stakes at The Curragh. With Polonia setting a strong pace, this was run to suit the odds-on Minstrella, who having enjoyed a tow until inside the final furlong, quickened clear.

Thus the scene was set for the decider in the Tattersalls Cheveley Park Stakes at Newmarket. Unfortunately, as is so often the case in events which are built up in this way, the race raised more questions than it answered.

The local stewards, with comparatively little time to reach their verdict on race-day, the first of October, overruled an objection to Forest Flower on behalf of Minstrella, who was beaten two and a half lengths into second place. When the Jockey Club

○ TROUBLE LOOMS: The smiles after Forest Flower's Tattersalls Cheveley Park success disappeared on her disqualification. Picture: TONY EDENDEN

Disciplinary Committee heard an appeal lodged by Minstrella's connections in London on 14 October, with boundless time to review the race at length, they overturned the original decision, and deeming that Tony Ives had been "reckless" in switching to his right over two furlongs out, disqualified Forest Flower and suspended Ives for 12 days.

The idea that David could intimidate Goliath is fairly preposterous, but this seems the key to a controversial contest.

The crucial manoeuvre ended with Minstrella receiving a bump which momentarily knocked her out of her stride. Minstrella appeared to regain her balance quickly, but her rhythm had gone. She does a great deal on the bridle

and, once off it, as she was then, she looks in trouble. John Reid was soon niggling at her but she kept on only at one pace as Forest Flower sprinted clear for a two-and-a-half-length victory.

While the Rules were ultimately adhered to, it is debatable whether justice was done when Forest Flower was disqualified; it cannot have been easy to deprive a trier of

⊙ FUTURE CHAMPION?: Reference Point romps away with the William Hill Futurity at Doncaster. The official distance was five lengths.   Picture: JOHN CROFTS

what appeared her thoroughly deserved reward.

It is to be hoped Forest Flower will have a chance to prove the point in the 1,000 Guineas at Newmarket on 30 April.

Periodically, Ian Balding has trained an exceptionally fast two-year-old to become a top-class three-year-old. He did the trick with Mill Reef and Mrs Penny; now Forest Flower (both of whose parents did well in their second seasons) looks to come from the same mould.

For the record, Minstrella amassed a European record prize-money haul for a two-year-old with £218,076. Her victory at Phoenix Park alone was enough to take her past Horage's previous best by a British-trained youngster.

Of course, it would be absurd to think of the year as a private party. There were a number of lesser lights, who perhaps have not been given the credit they deserve, but two late arrivals, Ajdal and Reference Point, behaved very much like gate-crashers as they demanded, and received, attention.

Reference Point put up an outstanding performance to make all the running in the William Hill Futurity Stakes at Doncaster. It was a display which, with Slip Anchor's pillar-to-post victory at Epsom still fresh in mind, had the word Derby written all over it.

Henry Cecil, who trained Slip Anchor, had his eyes firmly set on the Blue Riband after the Doncaster triumph, which was gained by the widest margin

○ STUDY IN STYLE: Ajdal strides out to beat Shady Heights in the William Hill Dewhurst Stakes.   Picture: MARK CRANHAM

(officially five lengths, but actually at least six and a half) for the race since Vaguely Noble lorded over his contemporaries in 1967.

Reference Point, who had been touted for the Derby before being well beaten at Sandown Park on his debut, first revealed his quality by leading all the way in juvenile record time for a mile on the same course. Mulhollande, eight lengths second, went on to be beaten a head in a Group Three race at Leopardstown.

Stable jockey Steve Cauthen preferred to ride the unbeaten Suhailie rather than Reference Point at Doncaster, because it was thought he would act better in the yielding going. But this previously

unbeaten colt was struggling over two furlongs out as Reference Point, on whom Pat Eddery had dictated an ordinary pace to halfway, stepped up the gallop. The farther he went the better he looked, pulling steadily clear.

His rivals were made to look second-rate but as they were headed by the Royal Lodge Stakes winner Bengal Fire they were hardly nonentities. Indeed, Love the Groom, who was disputing last place with only three furlongs remaining, is probably better than the bare result indicates.

Ajdal finished his first season unbeaten in three races and a warm favourite for the 2,000 Guineas. But this bare summary hides an enigmatic performance in the William Hill Dewhurst Stakes, which casts a slight shadow over his future.

On the evidence of effortless successes at Doncaster and Ascot, here was the class colt we had searched for in vain in the prestige events for the greater part of the season. He looked sure to confirm his potential as he coasted to the

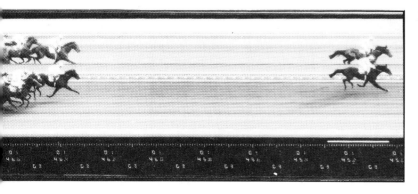

○ PHOTO FINISH: The Futurity margin seems to be 6½ lengths.
RACECOURSE TECHNICAL SERVICES

front a furlong out at Newmarket; he quickly established a lead of two lengths, but when it appeared to be all over, he began to hang fire and shortened his stride. Shady Heights, who had been outpaced in the Dip, ran on powerfully and might have created an upset with a little farther to go.

Ajdal is the sixth son of Northern Dancer to win the Dewhurst. Nijinsky, The Minstrel and El Gran Senor went on to greater things in their second seasons, but Try My Best and Storm Bird failed to train on. This historical footnote may give Michael Stoute cause for concern.

Ajdal, Reference Point, Forest Flower and Minstrella are the leading representatives of what is probably a slightly above-average crop of two-year-olds. If this is not the case, the Irish and French have a poor lot.

British-trained horses made a clean sweep of the Irish Group One two-year-old races (Minstrella two, Lockton one); Gulf King won the Panasonic Beresford Stakes (Group

O **UNFORGETTABLE: Richard Hannon is back in the big time with Don't Forget Me, winner of the Laurent Perrier Champagne Stakes.**
Picture: DAVID MUSCROFT

O **STAR FILLY: Milligram makes a winning debut at Newbury.**
Picture: DAVID HASTINGS

Two), and Sanam and Sea Dara landed Group Three prizes.

Lockton seemed an unlucky loser of France's premier contest, the Grand Criterium, in which he had difficulty obtaining a clear run and was bumped but still failed by only a length to catch Danishkada. Lockton, whose best effort on home soil was probably his third (after a poor run) to Shining Water and Sanam in the Glen International Solario Stakes at Sandown, would certainly be considered inferior to the best here. Noble Minstrel, having been beaten in a Newmarket nursery, won the Criterium de Maisons-Laffitte (Group Two) only to be disqualified following a positive dope test.

Milligram found one too good in the Prix Marcel Boussac, the principal cross-Channel staying event confined to fillies, dividing the Prix de la Salamandre one-two Miesque and Sakura Reiko. The

○ **WHIPS FLY: Invited Guest gets the better of Mountain Memory in the Hoover Fillies' Mile.** Picture: TONY EDENDEN

reverse side of the coin showed that French-trained colt Cedrico (seventh to Don't Forget Me in the Laurent Perrier Champagne Stakes at Doncaster) and Indian Forest (below par when fourth in the Cornwallis Stakes) failed badly in attempts to redress the balance.

Polonia, in winning the Lowther in a pulsating finish with Interval, gave the Irish their solitary success in this country.

Milligram's main rival for the title of leading staying filly was Invited Guest. She had built an unblemished record over four outings, and gained her major successes in the Waterford Candelabra Stakes and the Hoover Fillies' Mile. Her reputation was such that she started 8-11 for the Ascot race but, having been settled behind as usual, she took a surprisingly long time to reach Mountain Memory and Shining

Water and did not appear to have much to spare.

Another who staked a realistic, but less obvious, claim for next year's fillies' Classics is unbeaten Percy's Lass, who worked up to a five-length victory in an Ascot nursery, showing surprising speed for a daughter of Blakeney.

Hiaam looked very smart when she readily outpaced Mountain Memory at Ascot on King George day and may not have been right when disappointing behind Polonia at York.

Michael Stoute suffered an even more serious reverse at the York meeting when Classic Tale, who jumped a path after a furlong, finished a long way behind Bellotto in the Acomb Stakes. The Blushing Groom colt's running was too bad to be true for he had been most impressive at Ascot in July. Bellotto was hailed as a future star

at York, but subsequent events devalued the form. He missed his Dewhurst engagement because he disappointed in a gallop the week before.

Another unexpected absentee from the Newmarket race (he had gone in his coat) was Don't Forget Me, who had displayed notable courage when he fought off all challengers in Group races at Goodwood and Doncaster. Richard Hannon was most enthusiastic after the latter event, drawing favourable comparisons with his 1973 2,000 Guineas winner Mon Fils.

One obvious gap in the ranks was a sprinting star. Game and consistent Sizzling Melody, whose season started at lowly Leicester in March and included Group-race successes at Royal Ascot and Doncaster, was the pick at five furlongs.

Wiganthorpe, best at six furlongs, seems roughly on a par with Sizzling Melody. His Gimcrack victory confirmed him the best two-year-old trained in the North, ahead of On Tap and Chime Time.

Noticeable by their absence from the important autumn juvenile tests were Guy Harwood's horses. In fact, only New Attitude, beaten favourite in the Solario Stakes, represented him.

Henry Cecil also had fewer runners in the prestige races than usual, but he had warned early in the year that he had many more backward types than in previous seasons. However, he has a powerful-looking team for 1987. Besides Reference Point, he has Legal Bid, Scarlet Blade and Suhailie among the colts, and smart filly prospects like At Risk, Gayane, Laluche and Scimitarra.

The message is clear that some of the big stables have plenty of talent in reserve, which is not surprising as it was a late spring last year. Dancing Brave and Shahrastani did not compete at the highest level as two-year-olds and their successors are likely to be similarly unexposed.□

Newmarket GOOD TO FIRM 6f

Tattersalls Cheveley Park Stakes

1st £38,710 **2nd** £14,549 **3rd** £7,040 **4th** £3,122

1	MINSTRELLA (USA) 2 8-11 ....J Reid

ro f by The Minstrel-Flight Dancer (Misty Flight)
held up, bumped 2f out, led over 1f out, hard ridden final furlong, unable quicken, fin 2nd, 2½l, awarded race **11/10F**

2	CANADIAN MILL (USA) 2 8-11 ....W Carson

br f by Mill Reef-Par Excellence (L'Enjoleur)
chased leader, led 2f out, one pace final furlong, fin 3rd, 2½l, placed 2nd **7/1**

3	SHAIKIYA 2 8-11...S Cauthen

b f by Bold Lad (Ire)-Shaiyra (Relko)
every chance 2f out, weakened final furlong, fin 4th, 2½l, placed 3rd **14/1**

4	INDIAN LILY 2 8-11 ....Pat Eddery

led 4f, fin 5th, 3l, placed 4th **40/1**

0	FOREST FLOWER (USA) 2 8-11 ....T Ives

ch f by Green Forest-Leap Lively (Nijinsky)
held up, bumped 2f out, led inside final furlong, ridden, ran on well, fin 1st, disqualified **13/8**

Original result stands for betting purposes. Forest Flower later disqualified at Jockey Club Disciplinary Committee inquiry for 'intentional interference at about the 2f marker'.

5 ran

TIME 1m 12.5s (slow by 0.5s)

1st OWNER: E Evans TRAINER: C Nelson (Lambourn) Bred: E Evans, in United States

2nd OWNER: Maktoum Al-Maktoum TRAINER: W Hern

3rd OWNER: Aga Khan TRAINER: R Houghton

TOTE WIN£2.80 PL£1.10,£1.20 DF£1.40 CSF£3.51

Forest Flower (USA)

		Shecky Greene	Noholme
Green Forest			Lester's Pride
		Tell Meno Lies	The Axe
			Filatonga
Leap Lively		Nijinsky	Northern Dancer
			Flaming Page
		Quilloquick	Graustark
			Quillobelle

Minstrella (USA)

		Northern Dancer	Nearctic
The Minstrel			Natalma
		Fleur	Victoria Park
			Flaming Page
Flight Dancer		Misty Flight	Princequillo
			Grey Flight
		Courbette	Native Dancer
			Gallorette

Canadian Mill (USA)

		Never Bend	Nasrullah
Mill Reef			Lalun
		Milan Mill	Princequillo
			Virginia Water
Par Excellence		L'Enjoleur	Buckpasser
			Fanfreluche
		Cam Shaft	Fleet Path
			Cambalee

Shaikiya

		Bold Ruler	Nasrullah
Bold Lad (Ire)			Miss Disco
		Barn Pride	Democratic
			Fair Alycia
Shaiyra		Relko	Tanerko
			Relance
		Asharaz	Sicambre
			Vareta

Newmarket GOOD TO FIRM 6f

Tattersalls Middle Park Stakes

1st £33,184 **2nd** £12,431 **3rd** £5,980 **4th** £2,615

1   **MISTER MAJESTIC** 2 9-00 .... R Cochrane
   b c by Tumble Wind-Our Village (Ballymore)
   made all, ridden final furlong, ran on well   **33/1**

2   *nk* **RISK ME (FR)** 2 9-00 .... S Cauthen
   ch c by Sharpo-Run The Risk (Run The Gantlet)
   chased winner, every chance final furlong, ran on   **10/1**

3   *hd* **GENGHIZ (USA)** 2 9-00 .... T Ives
   ch c by Sir Ivor-Royal Caprice (Swaps)
   headway 2f out, every chance inside final furlong, ran
   on   **9/1**

4   *1½* **MANSOOJ** 2 9-00 .... Pat Eddery
   ch c by Thatching-Senta's Girl (Averof)
   every chance over 1f out, unable to quicken inside final
   furlong   **7/4**

5   *¾* **MOST WELCOME** 2 9-00 .... Paul Eddery
   never near to challenge   **11/8F**

6   *4* **WHIPPET** 2 9-00 .... P Robinson
   outpaced   **33/1**

7   **CROFTER'S CLINE** 2 9-00 .... J Reid
   good speed over 3f   **16/1**

7 ran
TIME 1m 13.75s
1st OWNER: D Johnson TRAINER: R Williams (Newmarket) BRED: Miss E Haughey
2nd OWNER: L Norris TRAINER: P Kelleway
3rd OWNER: P Wetzel TRAINER: L Piggott
TOTE WIN£29.20 PL£6.20,£2.70 DF£92.50 CSF£253.44

Mister Majestic

		Windy City
	Restless Wind	Lump Sugar
Tumble Wind		Endeavour
	Easy Stages	Saturday Off
		Ragusa
	Ballymore	Paddy's Sister
Our Village		Le Levanstell
	Epona	Astridama

Risk Me (FR)

		Atan
	Sharpen Up	Rocchetta
Sharpo		Falcon
	Moiety Bird	Gaska
		Tom Rolfe
	Run The Gantlet	First Feather
Run The Risk		Silly Season
	Siliciana	Anippe

Genghiz (USA)

		Turn-to
	Sir Gaylord	Somethingroyal
Sir Ivor		Mr Trouble
	Attica	Athenia
		Khaled
	Swaps	Iron Reward
Royal Caprice		Royal Charger
	Miss Royalea	Leading Home

Mansooj

		Forli
	Thatch	Thong
Thatching		Abernant
	Abella	Darrica
		Sing Sing
	Averof	Argentina
Senta's Girl		Chanteur
	Senta	Naval Patrol

Newmarket GOOD 7f

William Hill Dewhurst Stakes

1st £39,165 **2nd** £14,690 **3rd** £7,082 **4th** £3,113

1 **AJDAL (USA)** 2 9-00 .... W R Swinburn
b c by Northern Dancer-Native Partner(Raise A Native)
pulled out over 2f out, quickened and led 1f out, pushed out **4/9F**

2 ¾ **SHADY HEIGHTS** 2 9-00 .... S Cauthen
b c by Shirley Heights-Vaguely (Bold Lad, Ire)
shaken up 2f out, every chance over 1f out, ran on **5/2**

3 1½ **GENGHIZ (USA)** 2 9-00 .... W Carson
ch c by Sir Ivor-Royal Caprice (Swaps)
held up, ridden final furlong, ran on well **18/1**

4 1½ **MISTER MAJESTIC** 2 9-00 .... R Cochrane
b c by Tumble Wind-Our Village (Ballymore)
led 6f, one pace **20/1**

5 4 **RUMBOOGIE** 2 9-00 .... Pat Eddery
chased leader 5f, weakened over 1f out **50/1**

5 ran
TIME 1m 28.99s
1st OWNER: Sheikh Mohammed TRAINER: M Stoute (Newmarket) BRED: Ralph C Wilson Jr, in United States
2nd OWNER: G Tong TRAINER: R Armstrong
3rd OWNER: P Wetzel TRAINER: L Piggott
TOTE WIN£1.40 PL£1.10,£1.50 DF£1.20 CSF£1.89

Ajdal (USA)

		Nearco
	Nearctic	Lady Angela
Northern Dancer		Native Dancer
	Natalma	Almahmoud
		Native Dancer
	Raise A Native	Raise You
Native Partner		Tom Fool
	Dinner Partner	Bluehaze

Shady Heights

		Never Bend
	Mill Reef	Milan Mill
Shirley Heights		Hardicanute
	Hardiemma	Grand Cross
		Bold Ruler
	Bold Lad (Ire)	Barn Pride
Vaguely		Silly Season
	Vaguely Mine	Tantalizer

Genghiz (USA)

		Turn-to
	Sir Gaylord	Somethingroyal
Sir Ivor		Mr Trouble
	Attica	Athenia
		Khaled
	Swaps	Iron Reward
Royal Caprice		Royal Charger
	Miss Royalea	Leading Home

Mister Majestic

		Windy City
	Restless Wind	Lump Sugar
Tumble Wind		Endeavour
	Easy Stages	Saturday Off
		Ragusa
	Ballymore	Paddy's Sister
Our Village		Le Levanstell
	Epona	Astridama

Doncaster   Straight: GOOD   1m

William Hill Futurity Stakes

1st £44,120 **2nd** £16,611 **3rd** £8,060 **4th** £3,599

1   **REFERENCE POINT** 2 9-00.............................Pat Eddery
b c by Mill Reef-Home On The Range (Habitat)
made all, stayed on well final 2f, gradually drew clear **4/1**

2   5   **BENGAL FIRE** 2 9-00.............................M Roberts
br c by Nishapour-Gerardmer (Brigadier Gerard)
always prominent, 3rd straight, effort 3f out, ran on one pace   **6/1**

3   ¾   **LOVE THE GROOM (USA)** 2 9-00.............................P Robinson
b c by Blushing Groom-Nell's Briquette (Lanyon)
behind, switched outside 2f out, edged left, ran on, nearest finish   **14/1**

4 *shd* **MR EATS** 2 9-00.............................G Baxter
gr c by Nishapour-Breathalyser (Alcide)
behind until stayed on well final 3f   **50/1**

5   ½   **ARABIAN SHEIK (USA)** 2 9-00.............................C Asmussen
held up, 5th straight, smooth headway 3f out, ridden 2f out, one pace, hampered close home   **3/1**

6   3   **TOLUCA LAKE** 2 9-00.............................R Cochrane
headway 3f out, never able to reach leaders   **8/1**

7   3   **SUHAILIE (USA)** 2 9-00.............................S Cauthen
in touch, 6th straight, effort 3f out, beaten 2f out   **2/1F**

8 1½ **SANTELLA SAM (USA)** 2 9-00.............................N Day
prominent, 4th straight, outpaced final 3f   **50/1**

9   **STILLMAN** 2 9-00.............................M Birch
held up, effort halfway, soon ridden and beaten   **50/1**

10   **SHINING WATER** 2 8-11.............................J Reid
close up, 2nd straight, weakened quickly 3f out   **12/1**

10 ran
TIME 1m 45.03s
1st OWNER: L Freedman TRAINER: H Cecil (Newmarket) BRED: Cliveden Stud
2nd OWNER: N Phillips TRAINER: C Brittain
3rd OWNER: Mrs V Gaucci del Bono TRAINER: J Dunlop
TOTE WIN£4.20 PL£1.70,£1.70,£4.00 DF£24.00 CSF£27.81

Reference Point

Mill Reef	Never Bend	Nasrullah
		Lalun
	Milan Mill	Princequillo
		Virginia Water
Home On The Range	Habitat	Sir Gaylord
		Little Hut
	Great Guns	Busted
		Byblis

Bengal Fire

Nishapour	Zeddaan	Grey Sovereign
		Vareta
	Alama	Aureole
		Nucciolina
Gerardmer	Brigadier Gerard	Queen's Hussar
		La Paiva
	Hants	Exbury
		Intaglio

Love The Groom (USA)

Blushing Groom	Red God	Nasrullah
		Spring Run
	Runaway Bride	Wild Risk
		Aimee
Nell's Briquette	Lanyon	Cornish Prince
		Lemon Souffle
	Double's Nell	Nodouble
		Tota Nell

Mr Eats

Nishapour	Zeddaan	Grey Sovereign
		Vareta
	Alama	Aureole
		Nucciolina
Breathalyser	Alcide	Alycidon
		Chenille
	Dinant	Abernant
		Dairymaid

● **SIR GORDON RICHARDS: A great jockey and a great man.**
Picture: GERRY CRANHAM

CHAPTER 11

Sir Gordon Richards

by BROUGH SCOTT

O FIRST AT LAST: Pinza gives Gordon Richards his first Derby success, beating the Queen's colt Aureole in 1953.
                                                                    Picture: SPORT & GENERAL

Sir Gordon Richards

by BROUGH SCOTT

It was appropriate that Sir Gordon Richards, as well as being a great jockey, was also famous for his sense of humour. He would have needed it for his own memorial service.

It's not that St Margaret's in Westminster, Parliament's own parish church beside the Abbey, was not a suitable place to honour racing's man of the century. It was simply that the service immediately became embroiled in more natural disasters than a flag start at the old Lincoln meeting.

You can bet they didn't have scaffolding across the nave and heavy boots overhead when Winston married Clemmie here in 1908. You can guarantee that the whole of London's Flying Squad were not hurtling round the square, sirens howling, when poor old headless Sir Walter Raleigh was buried here in 1618.

But that was what Sir Gordon's memorial had to be put up with — and quite a bit more.

Whatever central heating has been installed in the 300 years

since Samuel Pepys' wedding never looked like beating the bitter chill of a mid-December Tuesday. And if man-made inventions have circled the heavens and earth since William Caxton was laid beneath these Westminster flagstones, they had not stretched to providing a working microphone for the memory of the jockey whose deeds were acclaimed around the world.

So racing's homage was always going to be an event where a bad draw would give less chance than a wide box at Chester. One poignant sight was the dark-suited chief usher craning forward to catch Scobie Breasley's warm but quietly spoken address. Lester Piggott's hearing was never equipped for this.

Yet, as a real loss can never be ridiculed and a true star will not be dimmed by its setting, so good came out of adversity. As we could not hear what Scobie had said, it became necessary to ask him about it; and he wanted to talk.

"Ah, but he was a wonderful man," said Breasley. "He was a great jockey and a fine trainer. But he was also one hell of a guy. He was so good to so many people." Scobie is into his seventies now but he has not lost the sunshine from that famous Australian voice, nor the relish of one champion looking back at another.

"Its funny, really," he added, repeating a story told to the Racing Post. "When I first came to ride here in 1950, I had heard so much about Gordon Richards but when I saw him, all loose and upright, I wasn't very impressed. Then one day I was on the stand at Newmarket, looking straight down the Rowley Mile. And suddenly I could see that through all the pushing and the waving, Gordon's balance was true as steel."

The metaphor is apt for much more than Gordon's balance. Listening to Scobie, you had to marvel again at the incredible engine that must have driven a frame which some wag was later to dub affectionately "the shortest knight". What a force there must have been inside the little miner's son from Oaken Gates in Shropshire.

His 26 jockeys' championships and 4,870 winners are only outline statistics and they omit three central themes — that Richards took three seasons to ride more than ten winners and took six years to become champion; that after being struck down by then killer disease of tuberculosis at only 21, he was always nervous about his health; and above all else that while Gordon played hard, he

played fair.

In these days of "grudge matches" and foul-mouthed "superbrat megastars", it is worth remembering that Gordon Richards' success was one of the greatest of all denials to the credo that "nice guys finish last".

"Out on the track you have no friends," said Breasley, "and Gordon could tighten you up all right. But whatever happened he never brought it back with him. I never remember him losing his temper and yet he hated, just hated, to be beaten."

Other contemporaries and old newsreel footage have given full accounts of Richards' typical relentless style of race riding. "The old foot would seem to have gone for everything two furlongs out," recalls long-time Cock of the North Billy Nevett, "but he would still stay on and beat you a neck."

Scobie Breasley, the greatest artist of the late, late finish, had one delightful sideways tribute.

○ TOGGED UP: Off to Buckingham Palace. Picture: SPORT & GENERAL

"People claimed Sir Gordon couldn't wait," he said. "But I have seen him hold up horses right to the death. He could wait ... almost as long as I could!"

Breasley had many other lovely tales: of the starter asking Gordon if he was all right and Harry Wragg chiming in with "yes sir" while Richards was facing the wrong way; of his prowess as a trainer, his qualities as a host and not least, as an after-dinner singer. "I would like to canoe you down the river" was one of his favourites, Breasley recalled. He bashfully failed to mention the other standard in Richards' repertoire, which he always used to ask for permission to render in mixed company, "I hit her on the titty with a hard-boiled egg."

Breasley had done what the memorial service was intended for. But in truth, the earlier hour at St Margaret's did have at least two moments. The first came quite soon. There was something familiar but rather eerily wrong about the straight grey suit on the sixth pew. Then one saw the walking frame and realized that most of us had not seen Dick Hern upright since his terrible accident two years ago. He was paying his tribute.

The other came when Peter O'Sullevan read the second lesson. "The Voice of Racing" likes to get the worst of things almost as little as Gordon himself did, but with no microphone, the scaffolding and another set of Z Car sirens' doing their worst, Peter and St Matthew 5 were making precious little progress. Then he came to the last verses. The famous tones racked up a notch and the words came through with the real ring of truth — "Let your light so shine before men, that they may see your good works, and glorify your Father that is in Heaven."

Jimmy Cannon, the great American sportswriter, used to say of our profession, "We work in the toy department." When you talk of Gordon Richards, it's rather more than that. □

● **HANDICAPPER'S DREAM:** All in a line as Green Ruby strikes the front in the William Hill Stewards' Cup at Goodwood.
Picture: DAVID HASTINGS

CHAPTER 12

Handicaps

by WILL O'HANLON

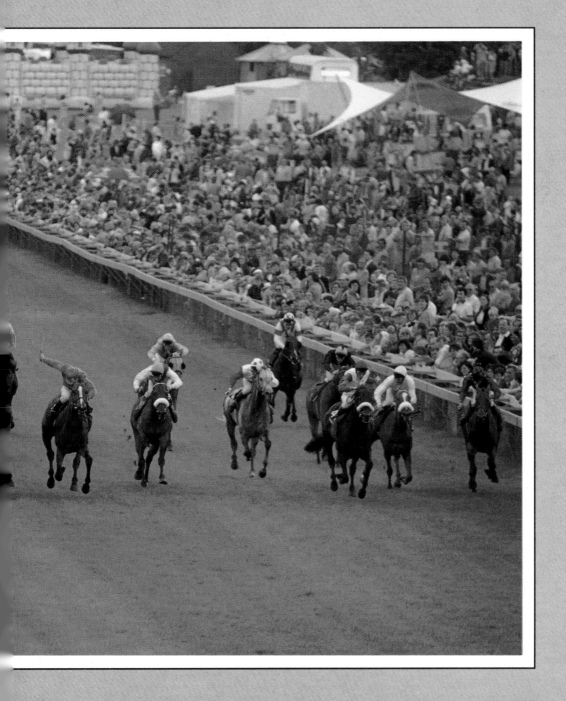

⊙ FIRST CHOICE: Primary lands the season's richest handicap, the Tote-Ebor, from Chauve Souris and Daarkom.

Picture: SPORT AND GENERAL

Handicaps

by WILL O'HANLON

HANDICAPS TELL US nothing about the intrinsic merit of the winners since their success is essentially the result of the Jockey Club Handicapper's handiwork.

Those horses on a lenient mark win races, those on too harsh a mark do not. Give or take a little training skill, it is as simple as that. And that is why a serious review of the 1986 handicap scene should include an examination of the handicapping system and how some horses become heroes at the cost of others.

Set against the prolific success of such as Dallas, Aventino, Felipe Toro and Catherine's Well, the exploits of K-Battery in 1986 make dull reading. Yet the path followed by Bill Elsey's five-year-old following his victory in the William Hill Lincoln Handicap (a first Northern-trained success in 13 years) poses an interesting question. Did K-Battery, veteran of 30 races before last season and with a solid Jockey Club rating in the 40s since September 1984, really improve by 40 per cent through 1986?

That is what the official ratings will show, with K-Battery leaping from 44 to 62 (or 18lb). The latter mark was awarded on three separate occasions: for a fifth place in the Group Three Westbury Stakes at Sandown Park; a second in the Group Three Grosser Preis von Dortmund, and a second in the Land of Burns Stakes at Ayr.

Yet on the two occasions K-Battery tried to justify such a mark in handicaps, at York in the Magnet Cup and at Newmarket in the Cambridgeshire, he was never seen with a chance.

It has been proved time and again that form shown in conditions races is the worst guide to weighing up a handicap. And so

K-Battery becomes the latest in the long line of such flops. Hadeer, Vainglorious and Glikiaa Mou were other notable examples last season.

But why is it so? Why does form gained against consistent, high-class horses in top conditions events so often fail to work out in handicap company?

One possibility is that the gap between Group-class horses and the rest has become artificially wide, so that what appears to be a much-improved performance by a horse stepping up in class is often nothing of the sort. We become dazzled by the figures, and are then surprised that come the acid racecourse test, the sums simply do not add up.

O BILL ELSEY: Bothered about lack of incentive.
Picture: PROVINCIAL PRESS

Bill Elsey's views are illuminating. "The Handicapper seems to put your horse up for having the cheek to go for a Group race in the first place," he says. "Lots of people have horses that just might be Group material, but they wouldn't dream of running them for the very reason that they are going to go up a stone without it really being justified. It's a disincentive to take a chance, but then if you don't, people go on about the bad bunch of horses north of Newmarket."

O BACK TO FORM: Clantime lands a blow for the North in the Nightrider Handicap at Epsom.
Picture: ALAN JOHNSON

O **DUNLOP DELIGHT: Stablemates Patriach (right) and Siyah Kalem dominate the Royal Hunt Cup.**

Picture: DAVID HASTINGS

Elsey's North Yorkshire neighbour Richard Whitaker was willing to take a chance with Clantime, a thoroughly game and consistent sprinter, but one who has never justified a rating of more than 50 in his long career in handicaps.

On 3 May last year, taking advantage of a decided fitness-edge, Clantime ran Double Schwartz to a length in the Group Three Palace House Stakes at Newmarket. Are we asked to believe that suddenly, on his 34th racecourse appearance, Clantime has improved by a stone? Clantime was the proverbial 'good thing' while still racing off his old mark in the David Dixon Handicap at York 10 days later, but he

offered his own interpretation of the Newmarket form - by finishing third.

To his credit, the Handicapper was quick to re-assess Clantime's worth, dropping him 12lb after the York run to the mark at which he won his only race, the Nightrider Handicap at Epsom on Derby Day.

No such wild fluctuations attended the progress of five-year-old Green Ruby, who gets my vote as the handicap star of the year for his stout defence against the marauding hordes of three-year-olds.

This was a classic case of an out-and-out handicapper showing verifiable improvement in his own

class. Rated 45 at the end of 1984 and 2lb less a year later, he had jumped to 55 by the autumn of 1986, a modest enough rise but sufficent for him to become the first horse since Greenore in 1935 to land the double of Stewards' Cup and Ayr Gold Cup.

Green Ruby's success sparked a dramatic revival in the fortunes of trainer Toby Balding, having been switched from Alan Jarvis's yard in midsummer. This does not necessarily make Balding a better trainer than Jarvis, any more than the progress of Hadeer through 1986 puts Clive Brittain on a higher plane than his previous trainer Michael Stoute.

⦿ ALL OUT: Green Ruby gets the better of Careless Whisper and Roper Row in the Harewood Handicap at York.
Picture: ALAN JOHNSON

But Green Ruby certainly found the Hampshire air to his liking. Even so, he can be counted a lucky neck winner of the big Ayr sprint. Peter Easterby's Felipe Toro (the 5-1 favourite) missed the break, then had to be switched to find a run and was closing with every stride as the pair went past the post. But few tears need be shed for Felipe Toro, who went to Ayr with five straight wins to his name, having started the season on a rating of 20 as the result of an earlier sequence - five straight zeros as a juvenile.

I can summon up even less enthusiasm for the exploits of Aventino (five wins in six weeks) and Catherine's Well (four wins in 17 days). Certainly, their success reflects credit on trainers John Sutcliffe and Mick Easterby, who long ago learned there is no better way to get a horse handicapped than through the medium of the selling race. But it also shows up an embarrassing flaw in a system whereby under-assessed horses (almost invariably three-year-olds) run up quick sequences through a penalty system which seems powerless to protect other runners. The proposed new five-day entry system may go some way towards restoring the balance, but will not in itself provide a full answer.

Newmarket trainer Tom Jones would like to see a greater number of conditions races for early three-year-olds, in the hope this would result in more accurate and fair mid-season handicapping. It is an idea which has much to commend it, if only because it must be in the long-term interest of British racing that horses in the old 55-65 rating band are not constantly forced abroad to earn their keep.

At present horses seem to be either 'ahead of the handicapper' and running riot, or 'caught by the handicapper' and unlikely to win again for the foreseeable future. So, for example, John Sutcliffe sets out with the clear intent of plundering all he can while the odds are stacked in his favour,

○ **THE BEST THINGS: Green Desert and Walter Swinburn mop up the Ladbroke European Free Handicap from Sperry.** Picture: TONY EDENDEN

then dispatches Aventino to the United States as soon as the horse's assessment rises. It never seems to enter calculations that Aventino should have a 'true' handicap mark, from which he would compete on an equal footing with other horses.

Sutcliffe's approach makes sense under the present set-up. It is the system, encouraging the quick hit-and-run attitude, which needs a sharp revision.

In defence of the Handicappers, it is difficult to see how they could have done more to get the measure of Dallas, Luca Cumani's latest handicap special. And as Dallas won his two major handicaps, the Britannia Stakes at Royal Ascot and the Cambridgeshire at Newmarket, by margins of a length and half a length, the officials need not, in any event, feel unhappy with their work. Dallas, in typical Cumani style, had won his maiden

in the lowly provinces, Brighton on this occasion.

Two other horses who won maidens at that meeting, Aldino and Landski, were given ratings of 37 and 39 respectively, about par for the course. But the Handicapper, mindful no doubt of Cumani's daunting record with such as Fish 'N' Chips and Free Guest, placed Dallas on the 53 mark, yet at the same time he rated Rue St Jacques (four and a half lengths third to him) 18lb lower.

As events were to prove, Dallas made light of his rating to win the Britannia Stakes from the luckless Navarzato, whose reward for his gallant second was an 8lb rise and a subsequently barren season. Dallas went on to win the Cambridgeshire from two penalised horses, Power Bender and Kabiyla, both still 'ahead of the handicapper' at that point. In fact,

○ **MICHAEL STOUTE: Single big handicap win.** Picture: ALEC RUSSELL

Power Bender (with Sneak Preview, the only horse older than three to run up a straight four-win sequence) went up a further 9lb after his Cambridgeshire second, with Dallas rising 11lb to 77, thus ending his handicap career.

Celestial Storm's session in handicaps was equally brief. Cumani had been happy to show his hand with this son of Roberto by finding a Newmarket maiden for his introductory win. Even off the resulting 60 mark, Celestial Storm would have won the Extel Handicap at Goodwood but for running green. In the event,

Cumani's second string, Chinoiserie, stepped into the breach to deliver the stable's third successive Extel. Celestial Storm went on to be second to Moon Madness in the St Leger!

Is it coincidence that Cumani and Michael Stoute, the two trainers who have enjoyed unparalleled success in three-year-old handicaps in recent years, are foreign imports? Cumani learned his trade in Italy; Stoute had his early grounding in the West Indies.

They, more than any others among the training elite, seem to have grasped the essential nature of how our handicapping system operates. The Handicappers, for their part, have now had plenty of time to reflect on the Cumani-Stoute modus operandi, and it was significant that Stoute, despite his magnificent year at the top level, struggled to make an impact on the 1986 handicap scene, with the singular exception of Green Desert's Free Handicap win.

O RULE BRITANNIA: Dallas goes for home in the Britannia Handicap at Royal Ascot.   Picture: ALAN JOHNSON

O LUCA CUMANI: Hard man to beat on the big occasion.
Picture: TONY EDENDEN

It will be interesting to see how Cumani fares in 1987. "Don't keep saying I'm a handicap specialist," he pleaded after Dallas's Royal Ascot triumph last June. It would take a rather large bushel to hide that particular light. Cumani is very much more than a handicap king, but it was his talent in this field which again shone out in 1986. □

O STAYING AHEAD: Another big handicap scalp as Dallas lands the William Hill Cambridgeshire.   Picture: BESPIX

● **LOOK NORTH: Away to a level break at Pontefract.**
Picture: GEORGE SELWYN

CHAPTER 13

The North

by RAY GILPIN

○ LONE STAR: Hallgate, trained by Sally Hall, was one of the few Northern-trained horses to make their mark down south in 1986.
Picture: ALEC RUSSELL

The North

by RAY GILPIN

THE GREAT DIVIDE, between North and South, showed no signs of being bridged in 1986, and more than one trainer expressed himself tempted to head off for greener pastures, their plight leaving no doubt that making the game pay north of the Trent is far from easy.

But it is not all doom and gloom, and determined efforts to re-establish popularity by such as David McHarg in Scotland and Go Racing in Yorkshire's team are reaping success.

Attendances increased last year and McHarg is one who has no great fear that satellite television in betting shops, due in 1987, will keep people away from going to the races.

He says: "Attendances hit an all-time low about three years ago, but by providing the racegoer with what he wants we have reversed the trend, and racing in Scotland has been a success this year.

"The man who goes in the betting shop is generally a different 'breed' to the regular racegoer and I don't think satellite racing will do us much harm."

However, the struggle for Northern trainers to win races with moderate horses gets no easier and the level of prize money still leaves much to be desired.

There was no sight of a Northern-based trainer in the top dozen at the end of the Flat season. And a glance at the top ten owners' list provides one of the reasons why the balance is tipped well away from the North.

Few horses stabled in the North carry the colours of Sheikh Mohammed, the Aga Khan, Khalid Abdullah and so on, but their horses are seen regularly on the Northern circuit, even as far as Edinburgh. The top Southern trainers have such strength in depth that they need to grab even the most modest opportunities to run their horses.

David McHarg is introducing more claiming races on his courses, which will help the cause of Northern trainers, and his general policy in framing races at Hamilton Park and Edinburgh is to favour moderate horses.

In contrast to the regular sorties north there were not too many raiding parties heading down the A1. Nor were Northern trainers able to keep much of a hold on the prize money offered at the major meetings on their own patch.

Chester in May brought one Northern-trained winner; the following week they took only three large bites out of the 18-race cake at York. Things got worse at York's August meeting, with a score of two out of 21 for the North, and one of those was a seller. At Doncaster in September five wins were picked up, including two sellers, from 25 races at the St Leger meeting.

But the job can be done, given the right tackle, as they say. Sally Hall proved the point with her smart sprinter Hallgate. She sent him south to win good races at Lingfield Park, Newmarket and Ascot, and then came close to setting Longchamp alight when he was narrowly beaten into third place in the Prix de l'Abbaye, Europe's top sprint. Yet Miss Hall ended the season with just a dozen winners.

Peter Easterby had a rather bigger and stronger brigade with which to go to war, and he ended top of the Northern trainers with 49 winners for a total of £156,681. Yet averaging that out, any owner who did not have a couple of winners would have finished well out of pocket, showing that much does not always equal a lot.

At one stage of the season Northern trainers were entitled to be optimistic, as several promising two-year-olds began to show their paces. Admittedly some of the shine was rubbed off Chime Time (later well sold to race in the USA), Crofter's Cline and Wiganthorpe, who gained a memorable Scottish Equitable Gimcrack Stakes victory, but they barely cost 6,000gns

○ ONE TO REMEMBER: Wiganthorpe and Willie Carson power past Mansooj to win the Scottish Equitable Gimcrack Stakes.

Picture: JOHN CROFTS

○ **ON THE TURN: The field goes away from the stands at Chester.**
Picture: GEORGE SELWYN

between them and were a credit to their shrewd buyers and trainers.

Among the jockeys Mark Birch, Cock of the North for the fourth time with 53 winners, David Nicholls, John Lowe and Kevin Darley proved their worth again. The North can almost claim George Duffield as one of its own, and it was galling that an injury sustained while playing football ended his chance of reaching his first 100 winners in a season.

The most amazing achievement among the jockeys belonged to Stuart Webster, who shed 7lb in as many hours to partner Doon Venture in a Catterick seller and then gave him a fine winning ride.

Few would find it easy to disagree with Pat Rohan's opinion that the best lightweight jockeys

are to be found in the North. John Lowe, who can do 7st 7lb, and Lindsay Charnock, whose minimum is a pound more, are among the strongest finishers around.

Apprentices found opportunities to get established far from easy, though for the first time a girl — and a mother at that — Kim Tinkler, showed the lads the way home, topping the Northern-based apprentice list with 18 winners. Most of her successes were for the syndicate company of Full Circle Thoroughbreds, whose horses are trained by her husband Nigel and managed by her father-in-law Colin senior. However, she still had to go out and show she could deliver, which she did with telling effect.

Along with Julie Bowker, she hid behind a seemingly fragile frame toughness and enough talent to make an impression in what is still regarded as a man's game.

Some may argue it is too tough on the horse, statistics revealing that many jockeys fell foul of the offence of "excessive use of the whip". But in this respect it seems there may be one law for the rich and one for the poor, with some of the top riders getting away with more than the lesser lights.

The likes of Redcar, Beverley and Hamilton are rarely billed as the day's principal meeting but some of those personalities from south of the Trent have the fondest memories of them.

Redcar earned its niche in the racing history of the Royals when providing the stage for Princess Anne's first success under Rules on Gulfland on 14 August. And having saddled his first winner on the Flat at Lingfield Park, Michael Dickinson had to set his sights further afield to increase his score, his three other successes being at Beverley, Hamilton and York.

Five-year bans on trainers David Moorhead and Stephen Wiles were among the more unsatisfactory features of the Northern Flat season, while the fiasco before the Portland Handicap, when technical failure necessitated dispatch by flag and led to a false start, did not boost the image of the one of the country's major pastimes.

Still, there was much to remember with relish, and while the North might have to survive on little fish, hope springs eternal.

Things were rather better on the jumping scene, though the autumn death of girl jockey Jayne Thompson after a fall at Catterick Bridge cast an enormous shadow, coming so soon after amateur Michael Blackmore's death after a similar accident over hurdles at Market Rasen on 10 May.

On the credit side, the indomitable Arthur Stephenson, who fears none of his Southern-based contemporaries, carried the flag highest. He ended the 1985-86 season fourth in the prize-money list but second-best for number of

○ WHOA BOY!: False start to the Portland Handicap at Doncaster.
Picture: ALAN JOHNSON

○ JAYNE THOMPSON: Her death after a hurdles-race fall at Catterick Bridge, was the first fatality for a girl jockey.   Picture: ALAN JOHNSON

winners. His score of 73 was bettered only by Martin Pipe, but they averaged a mere £1,713 per win.

The South still holds the call in prize money and overall stable strength, but while the financial gap has narrowed in recent years, jumping is still the poor relation countrywide. Top National Hunt trainer Nick Henderson earned a little over £168,000 in win money, while Michael Stoute led on the Flat with more than £1.25m.

The Cheltenham Festival brought the North little winning cheer, with only Jobroke (later sold to the USA) successful in the County Hurdle. But Monica Dickinson did wonders to produce Wayward Lad to run a fine second to Dawn Run in the Gold Cup. And there are few who would disagree with Timeform's magnificent book Chasers and Hurdlers 1985-86, which gives him a place in steeplechasing's Hall of Fame.

Jobroke also saved the North from a whitewash at Liverpool, though John Wilson's Young Driver made a brave attempt to win the Seagram Grand National for Scotland.

Ridley Lamb, stable jockey to Arthur Stephenson, was the most

● **WELL DONE, DAD: David Tuck shows his delight at jockey-father Phil's efforts in equalling the record for consecutive jumping winners.**
Picture: PHIL O'BRIEN

successful Northern rider, with 47 winners, and he went on to join a select band who have topped the 500 mark over the sticks.

It was another season of contrasts for the ever-popular Jonjo O'Neill. He won the Gold Cup on Dawn Run, had several serious falls, and on 1 May announced his retirement from the saddle to start training. The following month came the news that sent shock waves beyond the

racing world, that he was fighting cancer.

Others to retire from riding, for a variety of reasons, were Tony Charlton, Alan Brown, Ronnie O'Leary and Gerry Kelly (all four to go training), and Chris Pimlott.

But new partnerships have sprung up. Phil Tuck and Gordon Richards made a great start to their association, and Peter Easterby and ex-Irish amateur Lorcan Wyer look as formidable.

Richards quickly helped Tuck etch his name in the record books alongside Johnny Gilbert by equalling the latter's 27-year-old record of ten consecutive winners under National Hunt Rules.

With Stephenson and Lamb, Dickinson and Graham Bradley, Denys Smith and Chris Grant, Jimmy FitzGerald and Mark Dwyer in the North's line-up, this is one area where the South does not have things all its own way.□

○ NORTHERN LIGHT: Chime Time, who did his connections proud before being sold to the United States.

Picture: ALEC RUSSELL

● **FAMILY AFFAIR:** A gathering of the Maktoum family and their associates at Royal Ascot.
Picture: GERRY CRANHAM

CHAPTER 14

Owners

by GEORGE ENNOR

○ **EXPENSIVE LUXURY: Sheikh Mohammed topped the list of winning owners with £830,121 in first prizes.**
Picture: TONY EDENDEN

Owners

by GEORGE ENNOR

IT MAKES IMPRESSIVE reading to see that the leading owner in 1986, Sheikh Mohammed of Dubai, had the winners of 119 races worth £830,121 during the season.

That is the sort of money which most of us will never see in a lifetime and the idea of having a horse or horses capable of earning such sums is beyond belief. But the whole exercise should be put into proper financial perspective. It will then become apparent that even for someone as successful as Sheikh Mohammed, owning race-horses is an expensive luxury.

Assuming he had 200 horses in training, and many of his trainers charge fees in the region of £200 per week, the bill comes to £40,000 every seven days. On top of that there are the not inconsiderable considrations of fees to vets, blacksmiths and jockeys, as well as for gallops.

Add to those mounting figures the gloomy fact that most horses never win a race, and it is easy to see why anyone entering into ownership of racehorses needs

○ **HAMDAN AL-MAKTOUM: Collects the Vernons Sprint Cup for his brother.** Picture: PROVINCIAL PRESS

○ **KHALID ABDULLAH: Narrowly beaten into second place.** Picture: GEORGE SELWYN

With wins in the St James's Palace and Queen Elizabeth II Stakes, both over the old mile at Ascot, Sure Blade more than did his bit. There was also the two-year-old Ajdal, whose hat-trick win in the Dewhurst Stakes might not have been achieved with the authoritative fluency many had expected, but he did win and beat some useful youngsters in the process.

Others who did well, though in some ways perhaps not so well as at one time had been hoped, were All Haste, Bonhomie and Verd-Antique, and if Henry Cecil's predictions are on the mark we may well see better things from Verd-Antique in 1987.

Sheikh Mohammed held pole position by just under £27,000 from Khalid Abdullah of Saudi Arabia, the shy, almost reclusive owner of the Horse of the Year, Dancing Brave. Though Dancing Brave lost the Derby in controversial circumstances and ended his career on a disappointing note at Santa Anita, he was still a colt of huge talent and one who generated excitement to match. His biggest win in England came in the King George VI and Queen Elizabeth Diamond Stakes, but the 2,000 Guineas and the Eclipse are hardly prizes to be sniffed at. His win in the Arc, as with all overseas events, is not relevant to these figures.

When Abdullah first hit the British scene, he, like the Maktoums, did so in a fairly small way, with a few horses trained by Jeremy Tree. Tree did not send out a major Abdullah winner in 1986, but all involved with Bellotto have high hopes for next season.

Guy Harwood, Dancing Brave's trainer, had a notable year with horses carrying the Abdullah green, pink and white colours. Backchat, Sarfraz, Primary and Bakharoff were members of a very useful Abdullah reserve squad at Pulborough. And from Barry Hills' Lambourn stable there were two fine wins for Rejuvenate in the Park Hill and Musidora Stakes.

boundless optimism and a deep pocket.

For men like Sheikh Mohammed financial problems hardly seem immediate, with the oil riches of the Persian Gulf state behind them. Not everyone approved, or maybe still approves, of the strong Middle Eastern presence in British racing, but there can be no doubt that the appearance of men like the Maktoums has been a major boost for racing in these islands, and no-one can begrudge Sheikh Mohammed his position at the top of the tree.

Though not the senior of the three brothers who have principally signalled the family's arrival, he can rightly be described as their front man. He first came on the scene in the late 70s and in a small way. In those days

his racing colours were blue, as now are those of his brothers Hamdan and Maktoum Al-Maktoum, instead of the present maroon he favours, and his first winner in England was the fast filly Hatta, successful in four races, including the 1977 Molecomb Stakes at Goodwood.

Now big-race success is the norm, and though in 1986 he had nothing to follow the fillies' Triple Crown glory of Oh So Sharp and the universally-hailed feats of Pebbles, it was not a bad year. His star was that fine filly Sonic Lady, whose Irish 1,000 Guineas success does not qualify for British statistics, but whose victories in the Sussex, Coronation, Child and Nell Gwyn Stakes made a major contribution to her owner's top placing.

○ **SWEET SMILE OF SUCCESS: The Aga Khan had a fine season climaxed by Shahrastani's dual Derby success.**
Picture: DAVID HASTINGS

Rumours once had it that the Aga Khan was not overkeen on maintaining a family tradition begun by his grandfather, the man who adopted the phrase "speed, speed and more speed", and was such a dominant figure in the years on either side of the second World War. However true that might have been, it is not the case now, and in the dual Derby hero Shahrastani he had a more than worthy successor to the talented but luckless Shergar.

Shergar's one crop of runners sired before his dreadful abduction and death are not going to be conclusive enough to judge how

O A TOAST: To St Leger winner Moon Madness from winning jockey Pat Eddery and owner Lavinia, Duchess of Norfolk.
Picture: JOHN CROFTS

well he might have done as a stallion, but we can at least hope that Shahrastani has every chance. He was easily his owner-breeder's chief moneyspinner, but with Shardari and Dihistan in the squad as well, there was strength in depth.

Shardari ran the race of his life against Dancing Brave in the King George and totally deserved his success in the Matchmaker International at York, while Dihistan's ability to win the Hardwicke and September Stakes suggests he must have been the best British-trained horse for many a day to act as a pacemaker, as he did at York and Ascot.

Other notable winners in the red and green colours of the Aga Khan

and trained by Michael Stoute were Tashtiya, Lisana and Kazaroun, while from Fulke Johnson Houghton's stable Kadial, Samanpour and Najidiya did their bit.

It is rare nowadays for a man to make the top rank among owners when a single horse carried his colours successfully, in the same way that winning the Grand National is no longer the automatic passport to the top of the jumping owners' table. But Harry Ranier, in whose name the Oaks and 1,000 Guineas heroine Midway Lady ran, finished fourth on the list after that fine filly, whom he owned in partnership with the Kinderhill Corporation of New York, collected £221,196 for those two brave wins.

That is a long way behind the £677,547 which put the Aga Khan into third place, but it is a very creditable sum by any standards and who knows how much bigger it might have been had not injury ended the filly's racing career after her runs at Newmarket and Epsom.

Just below Ranier, who was also Midway Lady's part-breeder, came Sheikh Maktoum Al-Maktoum, who won 25 races worth £218,866. Green Desert, hero of the July Cup and Vernons Sprint, and beaten only by Dancing Brave in the 2,000 Guineas, was his most notable runner in 1986, but Dusty Dollar chipped in with the Sun Chariot Stakes and Maysoon obliged in the Fred Darling.

O HAPPY FAMILY: Robert Sangster, who had mixed fortunes in 1986, at his 50th birthday celebrations with his wife Susan and mother Peggy

Picture: DAILY MAIL

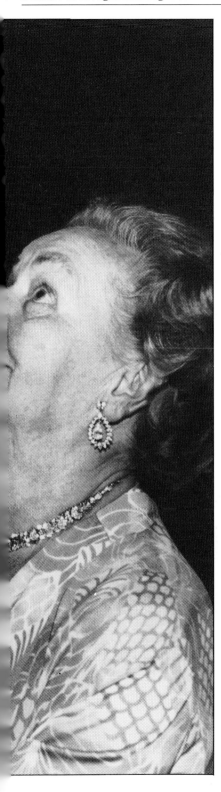

Robert Sangster was at major pains late in the year to dismiss any idea that the wheel had come off the carriage which sustains his worldwide bloodstock empire. And though the winners of 26 races worth £205,177 were not enough to make him leading owner for the sixth time in the last ten years, it was far from being a season of total disaster.

The Irish side of the operation, with Vincent O'Brien's team under a cloud for much of the year, made no impression on those figures; there was no winner from Ballydoyle in England in 1986. Instead the well-known Sangster silks were carried to victory by useful performers such as Santiki, Field Hand and Conquering Hero.

The biggest disappointment, at least for those outside the Sangster circle, was the performance of horses from his new private stable at Manton, run by Michael Dickinson. They claimed just four wins and 14 other placings from 55 runners, and late in November came the news that Dickinson had been relieved of his post, though the move was attributed to a personality clash.

In terms of numbers Sheikh Hamdan Al-Maktoum was not far behind Khalid Abdullah, with the winners of 77 races compared to the Prince's 80, but the fact that Sheikh Hamdan collected barely a quarter of the Abdullah earnings indicates there was nothing very special among them.

Another member of the Saudi Royal family — Prince Khalid is one — is Fahd Salman, who saw his principal trainer Paul Cole make such a bright start from his new base at Whatcombe. Prince Fahd finished eighth on the list with the winners of 37 races and £190,654. The consistent and hard-working Nisnas, successful in the Voltigeur and Alycidon Stakes, was one of his best standard-bearers, and there was useful back-up from the Chester Vase winner Nomrood, the regular European raider Sarab, Pochard and Otabari.

Time was when the list of leading owners was dominated by those based in this country, though it should be pointed out in qualification of that statement men such as the Aga Khan and Marcel Boussac acquired a significant amount of British prize money 50 years ago and more.

But with Robert Sangster no longer full-time resident in Great Britain, the only one of the top ten owners of 1986 who can justifiably be called British-based is also the only woman on the list. Lavinia, Duchess of Norfolk had a rare money-spinner in Moon Madness, who made great strides in four months. Having started in maiden company, he gave his owner-breeder Classic victory at her first attempt when he romped away with the St Leger at Doncaster in September. Moon Madness contributed six of the eight wins which netted £147,935 for the Duchess, with Entrancing and Mister Wonderful adding to her tally.

British racing has been grateful for large-scale American support for many years, and there have been few, if any, owners from that country for whom success is greeted with greater pleasure than that most generous of anglophiles, Paul Mellon. In the year his marvellous racehorse and notable sire Mill Reef died, Mellon made the top ten with the winners of 18 races and £152,317.

Star of his team was the fine two-year-old filly Forest Flower, though she was well supported by English Spring, Land of Ivory and Highest Praise. Nothing finished in front of Forest Flower in her five races in England, and the decision to disqualify her from first place in the Cheveley Park will remain controversial.

Whatever one's views on that incident, there is no doubt Forest Flower made a major mark on the British scene during 1986. To what extent she will do so in her second season remains to be seen, but while that is unpredictable, it seems safe to forecast that some of those who hit the high spots as owners will be back in 1987. □

● **TWO TOPPERS:** Another fine year for Newmarket trainers Luca Cumani (left) and Michael Stoute.
Picture: GEORGE SELWYN

136

CHAPTER 15

Trainers

by LAWRENCE WADEY

○ **TOP TEAM: Michael Stoute, the season's leading trainer, his wife Pat and stable jockey Walter Swinburn.**

Picture: ALAN JOHNSON

Trainers

by LAWRENCE WADEY

FROM NEWMARKET'S expansive heathland to the more tranquil, rolling downs of West Sussex, Michael Stoute, Henry Cecil, Guy Harwood and John Dunlop provided the heartbeat which sustained Flat racing in 1986.

Between them the Big Four took 39 of the 103 British Pattern races, plus 17 from abroad; they won nearly 15 per cent (409) of all races run in Britain, and amassed £3,361,876 in winning prize money.

One man towered above the rest. From 76 domestic winners Michael Ronald Stoute piled up a record-breaking £1,270,273, over £300,000 clear of Guy Harwood, to add a second trainers' championship to the one secured in 1982. He was a triple champion. The victories of Sonic Lady in the Irish 1,000 Guineas, Shahrastani (Irish Derby) and Colorspin (Irish Oaks) were instrumental in giving Stoute his first Irish trainers' title, and the

International Racing Bureau's Derby Award as leading British trainer overseas (£960,531 win and place).

If that is not enough, of his 76 domestic wins, paradoxically his lowest total since 1978, 20 were gained in Pattern company, double that of any other trainer.

For many, Stoute's production of Shahrastani to win two Derbys will be the highlight. Failing that it might be the foresight to repeat his

1982 trick with Marwell, by bringing Green Desert back in distance to win the July Cup, or, perhaps, the rekindling of Shardari's enthusiasm.

But perhaps Stoute's two finest achievements in 1986 came elsewhere.

The first centres on how he taught Sonic Lady, a head-strong, hard-pulling filly, to settle and won six Pattern races with her. She held her form from the Nell Gwyn Stakes at Newmarket in April to the Prix du Moulin de Longchamp in early-September. It was a training feat rivalled only by Harwood's exemplary handling of Dancing Brave.

The second was Stoute's willingness to take on the world. Not for him any whingeing about Lasix, rather the acumen to use it in Maysoon's bid for the Arlington Million. Nor any griping about a later date for this year's Breeders' Cup series, instead the determination to learn from 1986 reversals and turn them into success.

For Henry Cecil, it was never going to be easy to follow his

O HENRY CECIL: Less afraid to travel.   Picture: TONY EDENDEN

monopoly of 1985 — 132 winners, four out of five Classics, and in Oh So Sharp the first filly to win her Triple Crown since Meld in 1955. And in many respects he was hoist with the petard of his past excellence during 1986.

That he trained most winners (115) will be small compensation. A modest (for him) six Pattern victories at home were backed up by three in Europe, though Star Cutter in Italy and El Cuite in Italy and France seem to indicate he is quietly shedding his reluctance to travel.

Guy Harwood finished runner-up to Stoute for prize money and to Cecil for winners, but in one respect he eclipsed both, since in Dancing Brave he trained a colt to rank with the greats. His season had already spanned eight months, in which time he had been asked for his best in the 2,000 Guineas, Derby, Eclipse, King George and Arc, before he even set foot in the United States for the Breeders' Cup.

Harwood's was not simply a one-horse season, far from it. Those who saw Bakharoff's coltish

O JOHN DUNLOP: Back in the big time.   Picture: ALEC RUSSELL

O GUY HARWOOD: Second for winners and prizes but tops with Dancing Brave.   Picture: DESMOND O'NEILL

O ON HIS OWN: Champion trainer Michael Stoute in typical pose as patrols the Newmarket gallops on his hack.
Picture: GERRY CRANHAM

demeanour before the Lingfield Derby Trial, and also the mulish display of Primary, must still wonder how they were placed to win at all, let alone in the Group Two Geoffrey Freer Stakes and the Tote-Ebor, Europe's richest handicap.

Add to these the Pattern successes of Zahdam, Phardante, Cliveden and Allez Milord — the latter's effort in the Japan Cup another shining example of his trainer's ability at maintaining a horse's form — and it was a season to remember down Pulborough way.

John Dunlop, whose stable was ravaged by the virus in 1985, with just 67 winners, bounced back to win his fourth British Classic, with Moon Madness in the St Leger, saddled the first two home in the Royal Hunt Cup, and had significant success abroad with Tommy Way. One late-October

Saturday, at Doncaster, his season was made complete when, for the first time since taking out a licence in 1966, he achieved a century of winners in a season as George James and Cash Asmussen snatched a two-year-old maiden race.

Tight as it was, the Big Four's grip on the season was not unwavering. For instance, Ben Hanbury, despite an otherwise disappointing year, gained his first Classic success, when Midway Lady got up in driving finishes to both the 1,000 Guineas and the Oaks.

As a yard to follow, Luca Cumani's is a far safer haven. For the third consecutive year a level stake on all his runners (304) showed a healthy profit (26 points). And for the fifth year running he increased his number of winners in the season, moving on to 67 in 1986. His remarkable performance

as a trainer is epitomised by his big handicap record. He successfully laid out Dallas to collect both the Britannia Stakes and the Cambridgeshire, while Chinoiserie gave him a hat-trick in the competitive Extel Stakes.

Dick Hern's three-year-olds were in fine form in July, when eight winners returned an 18-point level-stake profit, and his seven domestic Pattern wins were bettered only by the might of Stoute and Harwood, confirming the West Ilsley trainer is still a man to be feared come the big occasion.

At a time when loyalty is all too often at the behest of finance, Hern stood up in support of his retained jockey Willie Carson, and lost some of Khalid Abdullah's horses for this year. But they were mainly the owner's second string and will be amply compensated by the extra intake from the Maktoums.

Richard Hannon showed he too can be equal to the big occasion given the right horse. His score of 56 was a personal best and included two Pattern victories from Don't Forget Me and one from Singing Steven. Combined they cost 22,200gns.

As the North versus South schism continued, Northern success stories remained an endangered species. Without a single representative in the top 12 trainers by prize money, the North had three Pattern wins — Mel Brittain's Grey Desire (now retired to stud) in the Duke of York Stakes, Sally Hall's Hallgate in the Diadem, and Mick Easterby's Wiganthorpe in the Gimcrack.

Only Peter Easterby, with 49 winners the Glen International Northern Trainer of the Year, made any sort of impression in the numbers game.

Perhaps the brightest spot in an otherwise bleak and all too familiar story for the North was the appearance of Nigel Tinkler on the 29 mark, more than twice his previous best. This year Tinkler has also doubled his string to fifty horses.

It is comforting to know that the bookmakers are not right all the time. As they sounded the bell for the season, in the blue corner, at a shade of odds-on to train more winners, they stationed Michael Dickinson, newly installed as

Robert Sangster's private trainer at £14m Manton. In the red corner was the street-wise Lester Piggott, steeled by many such encounters and odds against in a two-horse race for one of the few times in his life.

For Dickinson the season could hardly have been worse. Bolivia, his first runner, finished tailed off in the mud at Folkestone. Four winners and six months later he was sacked. The official statement issued by Sangster made reference to "fundamental differences of opinions."

Soon after, jump jockey Graham Bradley reflected on the fate of his mentor Dickinson: "I'm sure it was the money and the pressure for

O MIXED FORTUNES: Michael Dickinson, seen with Steve Cauthen, started the season with high hopes and ended it without a job.   Picture: GEORGE SELWYN

O OUT: Stephen Wiles was disqualified from training for five years. Picture: ALEC RUSSELL

O IN: Barry Hills took over from Michael Dickinson. Picture: ALAN JOHNSON

instant success that was really behind the break."

Put another way, he was saying it would have been hard to imagine a split if Dickinson had ended the season with 20 winners and the ante-post favourite for the 2,000 Guineas.

No sooner had Dickinson been swept aside, Barry Hills was proclaimed the new master of Manton. And Hills made no bones about his ambition, declaring his intention to be champion trainer.

Piggott, so long the punters' friend in the saddle, continued in that vein as a trainer. After a brief flirtation with a Guineas riding comeback, he settled down to send out a highly creditable 30 winners. And when Cutting Blade won the Coventry Stakes, he triumphed with his first runner in a Pattern race or at Royal Ascot. On one Sunday out of the country, his three runners won at Ostend.

Of the other new boys special mention goes to Lord John FitzGerald, like Piggott successful with his first Pattern and Royal Ascot runner. Sizzling Melody later added the Group Two Flying Childers to the Group Three Norfolk Stakes.

Michael Blanshard, Paul Felgate, Rod Simpson and Robert Williams also had first-time Pattern successes, when Lemhill took the John Porter, Gemini Fire the Molecomb, Brunico the Ormonde and Dominion Royale the Nishapour Stakes respectively.

By contrast Frankie Durr, who three seasons ago sent out 57 winners, suffered a lamentable time with only one more victory than Michael Dickinson. But if Durr thought things were bad he could spare a thought for those who did not make it to the end, for instance Chris Bell, who threw in the towel when Rotherfield Greys, his star sprinter, was removed from the yard.

There are others missing this year, notably Michael Albina, who left Newmarket for the United States, and Arthur Balding, who relinquished his position as Britain's senior trainer to hand over to his son John. Out of circulation too is Stephen Wiles, banned for five years after getting embroiled with Ken Richardson, the central character in the Flockton Grey escapade. But with the arrival of such as William Haggas and Claude Charlet at Newmarket, and John Wainwright in the North, there is no shortage of replacements ready to take up the battle again in 1987. □

O FAST STARTER: Lord John FitzGerald, who saddled Sizzling Melody to win at Royal Ascot in his first season as a trainer.
Picture: GERRY CRANHAM

● WALKING TO WORK: Steve Cauthen and Walter Swinburn off to find the action. Picture: DAVID HASTINGS

CHAPTER 16

Jockeys

by J A McGRATH

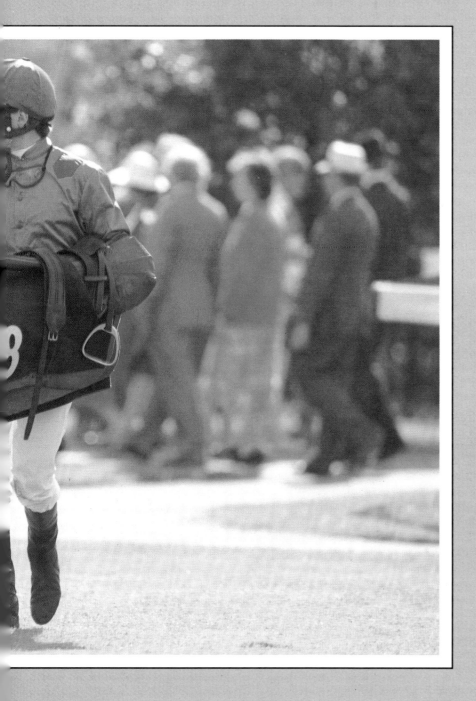

○ DERBY DAZZLER: Walter Swinburn won his second Epsom Derby, on Shahrastani, in another star-studded season.

Picture: TONY EDENDEN

Jockeys

by J A McGRATH

TAKE A TOPIC such as jockeys and immediately racing ranks are divided. Some sing their praises and leave one wondering whether the horse is no more than an extravagance; others regard jockeys as one of the game's necessary evils and say the horse wins despite the rider.

No-one could use the latter argument, and get away with it, about Pat Eddery, Steve Cauthen and Walter Swinburn, who strode the stage like giants in 1986.

Eddery, 35 the day after St Patrick's Day, demonstrated the wizardry, and agility, normally associated with a leprechaun, and rarely had a moment in the shade.

Like all jockeys, Eddery suffered disappointments. But analysing his record is more a task of grading varying degrees of success than contrasting highs and lows.

And when his pursuits in the saddle did not dominate the news, behind-the-scenes moves which led to a major shift in his allegiances from Vincent O'Brien to Khalid Abdullah soon grabbed the headlines.

Success at Ballydoyle proved to be elusive in 1986, but even so, few would have envisaged in the middle of the season Eddery answering the call from Abdullah, who had sought first claim on his services for some time.

Eddery's unforgettable win on Dancing Brave in the Prix de l'Arc de Triomphe in October put the seal on the new partnership and highlighted the intense rivalry between the Irishman and Greville Starkey. Starkey was nursing a back injury when Dancing Brave faced up to the grudge battle with Derby winner Shahrastani in the King George VI and Queen Elizabeth Diamond Stakes at Ascot in July. Eddery proved an able deputy.

Waiting for what seemed an eternity, Eddery sat poised on the inside near the rear of the field. Then when fully balanced in the home straight, he made his move.

○ PAIR OF ACES: Steve Cauthen lost his jockeys' title in 1986 but still did his boss Henry Cecil proud.   Picture: TONY EDENDEN

It was quick and ruthless and put paid to the opposition in a matter of strides.

Starkey had missed his chance to avenge the controversial defeat of Dancing Brave in the Derby, where he came storming up the centre of the course in the dying stages only to see his final, desperate surge of power peter out a short distance from the winning post. He had to settle for second to Shahrastani.

Starkey was all but crucified in the Press over the ride. "Starkey nightmare!" screamed one headline. "Aga Khan joy spells misery for Greville", and "It's too late for sad Starkey" were others.

The critics contended that Starkey should not have been back so far. However, subsequent wins in the King George and Arc, where Eddery too elected to wait at the rear of the field, seem to lessen the case for the prosecution. The saying goes that with hindsight you have 20-20 vision. The benefit of such assistance says that Starkey's crime in the Derby was, quite simply, to be beaten.

After the King George, Starkey was back on Dancing Brave in the Scottish Equitable Select Stakes, over a mile and a quarter at Goodwood in September. They won by ten lengths, but the reunion was short-lived because Eddery stepped forward to take the ride in the Arc on 5 October. Again, he waited and waited at the back of the bunch. It was only after Bering sailed past him on the outside that he launched Dancing Brave on his final challenge.

"I didn't want to come too soon because he's inclined to idle once he gets to the front," Eddery said after the big race. Even for a rider with nerves of steel, it was a close, finely-judged thing, though he won by a length and a half in course record time.

Eddery, with 176 winners, won back the British jockeys' crown after an absence of nine years. He has always displayed a certain genius in the saddle but Lester Piggott, 16 years his senior, hogged the spotlight right up to his last

○ **UNDER ORDERS: Down at the start Richard Quinn, Steve Cauthen and Willie Carson get ready for the off.**
Picture: DAVID HASTINGS

season, even when his riding activities were more concentrated abroad. The disappearance of Piggott from the ranks did not spell instant improvement in Eddery as a jockey. It merely made the average observer more aware and appreciative of his talent.

Piggott settled into training at Eve Lodge, Newmarket, but at one stage he looked set for a comeback. With Eddery under suspension in early-May, Vincent O'Brien went looking for a top-class replacement and Piggott emerged on the scene, poised to ride not only O'Brien's Tate Gallery in the 2,000 Guineas but also Midway Lady for Ben Hanbury in the 1,000.

Piggott flew to Ballydoyle to ride Tate Gallery in a gallop. However, on 2,000 Guineas day, it was Tony Ives, not Piggott, who was legged aboard. Like most incidents in-

volving Piggott, there was a mixture of the something bizarre, sensational and mysterious about it all. In a short statement after the comeback bid had been aborted, Piggott said: "After consultations over the weekend I have, in order to honour commitments, abandoned plans to return to the saddle." Midway Lady went on to win the 1,000 Guineas, boosting the talented but long underrated Ray Cochrane into the top bracket. Cochrane was one of the star finds of the year.

While the season belonged to Eddery, his old adversary Steve Cauthen would probably not count 1986 as one to look back on with enormous relish. He lost his title, and although second with 149 winners, he had an on-going battle to contain his weight. At the end of the season, when all hope of the

championship had gone, Cauthen's weight soared. His worries came to a head when he rode 1lb over at 9st at Doncaster in October.

Cauthen has conquered British racing, having won two riding titles and all the English Classics. The critics who dismissed him lightly in the early part of his career in Britain have long since eaten their words. At the end of the year on a visit to Hong Kong, he vowed to beat his weight problems and to win back the championship.

He knows what it is like to fight back, using brain-power combined with grit and determination. When he landed in Britain, he sized up the situation and made important adjustments to his style, which ultimately led to his taking the jockeys' crown. Many would ask why jockeys in America, and indeed Australia, where stake money is so high right across the board, still come to Britain to try their luck. Cauthen and New Zealand-born Brent Thomson are two good examples to pinpoint.

Thomson, for instance, left a top-class job with Colin Hayes, many times champion trainer in Melbourne and Adelaide, to accept initially a retainer with Robert Sangster and then Barry Hills. He firmly believes the best horses and the best racing in the world are in Britain, and wants to be part of that scene. A quietly effective

rider, he won the W S Cox Plate, traditionally Australia's premier weight-for-age event, three times by the time he turned 20. He was three times Melbourne champion after a highly successful apprenticeship in New Zealand. In some ways, there is a similarity between Cauthen and Thomson, in that one feels they were looking to new horizons after conquering all in their part of the world.

Like Cauthen, Thomson has had his share of disappointments and heartache. His relationship with Sangster went smoothly enough

and the retainer link with Barry Hills was seen as a natural extension. But the Thomson-Hills partnership was on the rocks by the midsummer of 1986. Thomson, while keeping his options open, announced he would like to stay in Britain but only 0n condition that he could secure the backing of a stable. He had had a long-standing offer in Australia to consider, but added: "I have come a long way down the road to be turning back now."

He was referring to his aim to make it to the top in Britain, an

O DIAMOND LIFE: Maxine Juster, winner of the Orloff Diamond Stakes at Ascot, top race of the year for women riders.   Picture: GERRY CRANHAM

ambition that still burns fiercely inside the quietly-spoken, dapper Australian. Thomson's plans for the new season were clarified when Peter Walwyn announced that he would be using him throughout 1987.

The link was interesting, because Walwyn retained Thomson's manager Joe Mercer not long back, but it left Paul Eddery out in the cold. Paul, a promising young rider with 49 winners to his credit for the year, had formerly been with Henry Cecil. He broke away to ride No 1 for Walwyn in a move that revived memories of the glory days at Seven Barrows when Pat Eddery punched home the winners. But that was not to be, with the latest Walwyn-Eddery association ended quickly.

Walter Swinburn, the other star of the season, must be commended for his riding of Shahrastani. In the Derby, he bounced the colt away and had him perfectly placed behind the leaders throughout before going for home. He was able to hold on despite the late, whirlwind finish of runner-up Dancing Brave. In the Budweiser Irish Derby, Swinburn had few worries, as he appeared to be cantering as they raced up to the home straight.

With Michael Stoute's stable again in such brilliant form, Swinburn found himself with an embarrassment of riches. He had to choose between Sonic Lady and Maysoon in the 1,000 Guineas and after much soul-searching he plumped for Sonic Lady. Later events were to prove his judgement spot-on but on the Newmarket Rowley Mile on 1 May stablemate Maysoon, ridden by Yves Saint-Martin, put her nose ahead to take second behind Midway Lady, with Sonic Lady third.

At one stage, Swinburn found himself coming under pressure when it came to decide between stablemates in the same race. The 'knockers' had a field day. Colorspin, ridden by Pat Eddery, won the Gilltown Stud Irish Oaks

⭕ ROMPING ROYAL: Princess Anne broke her duck on Gulfland at Redcar.
Picture: ALAN JOHNSON

but the ground at The Curragh softened up significantly near the race and Swinburn could be forgiven for choosing stablemate Untold, who finished 15 lengths behind in third. Swinburn, who at a tender age has won races such as the Derby (twice), Arc and King

George, proved again he is not one to get flustered when the big races are run and won.

The riding ranks in 1987 will include Cash Asmussen, the Texas-born champion of France, who will be riding No 1 for Vincent O'Brien in place of Pat Eddery, and also for

○ **MUD PACK: All in a day's riding for Princess Anne.**
Picture: PRESS ASSOCIATION

Robert Sangster in England. The exuberant American quickly established himself at the top in Paris and is another fiercely ambitious competitor. He has always taken the opportunity to ride in Britain when possible, and gives the impression he too would like to do a Steve Cauthen and conquer further horizons.

On the amateur front, Tim Thomson Jones landed the title from up-and-coming Amanda Harwood and more-experienced Maxine Juster. Maxine won the Orloff Diamond Stakes at Ascot on Eve's Error. But the most significant amateur win was that of Princess Anne on Gulfland in the Mommessin Stakes at Redcar on 5 August. Victory was popular for the simple reason that despite several failures, she kept at it until she reached the winner's stall.

As for continuing her race-riding career, Princess Anne joked that she would, "As long as owners like Gavin (Pritchard-Gordon) do not mind having idiots riding their horses!" □

○ **SMILING NOW: But the partnership of jockey Brent Thomson and trainer Barry Hills ended in 1986.**
Picture: TONY EDENDEN

● **WINNING TEAM:** Leading breeder the Aga Khan with his trainer Michael Stoute and Derby winner Shahrastani.
Picture: MARK CRANHAM

CHAPTER 17

Breeders

by ADRIAN COOK

○ CRYSTAL CLEAR: The Aga Khan receives the Matchmaker International trophy from Barry Weisbord (left) after the success of his home-bred Shardari.
Picture: ALAN JOHNSON

Breeders

by ADRIAN COOK

FOR THE SECOND time in six seasons the Aga Khan headed the list of thoroughbred breeders in Britain and Ireland, consolidating his position as Europe's leading stud owner.

For the last 15 years he has also finished in the top 12 on the list of winning breeders' in France, even though since 1979 he has had many horses in training in Britain, numbering in total about 60 in 1986.

On the death of his father Prince Aly Khan in 1959, the Aga Khan inherited bloodstock interests which had been built up so successfully by his father and grandfather since the early 1920s. Between them they had headed the British owners' list on 14 occasions and the breeders' list nine times. They also enjoyed great success in France and either owned and/

○ TABLE TOPPER: Shahrastani, who put his owner the Aga Khan top of the breeders' list in 1986.   Picture: JOHN CROFTS

or bred many of the best and most influential horses of the period.

Between 1924 and 1959 they bred 17 British Classic winners and owned 20, and were associated with such greats as Mumtaz Mahal, Nasrullah, Blenheim, Bahram, Mahmoud, Alibhai, Khaled, Migoli, Masaka and Petite Etoile.

From the mid-1950s their racing interests were centred on France, although they continued to own studs in Ireland, and after 1966 the present Aga Khan ceased to have horses in training in Britain. However, following the purchase of the Dupre and Boussac bloodstock in 1977 and 1978 respectively, and the expansion of the Aga Khan's broodmare band to its present size of about 200, the decision was taken to return to a British stable.

Shergar was among the second batch of horses sent over and his exploits in 1981, when he won the Derby, Irish Sweeps Derby and King George VI and Queen Elizabeth Diamond Stakes made the Aga Khan leading breeder that year. In the next four seasons he figured in the top dozen breeders thanks to such good winners as Khairpour, Vayrann, Karadar, Borushka, Baynoun, Kirmann, Dafayna and Shernazar.

His big winners trained in France in the 1980s have included the local Derby winners Darshaan and Mouktar, Arc heroine Akiyda, French 1,000 Guineas winner Masarika, as well as Akarad, Shakapour, Sharaya, Sumayr and Kozana. Aga Khan-breds have also earned over a million dollars in the United States in both 1984 and 1985, largely as a result of Breeders Cup Turf winner Lashkari and Grade One winners Nassipour, Yashgan and Sharannpour.

Even by these standards 1986 was an outstanding year for the Aga Khan, who bred ten individual Pattern-race winners in Europe. His 1979 French Derby winner Top Ville (sold to Sheikh Mohammed in 1985) also consolidate his position as one of Europe's premier sires.

In Britain and Ireland horses bred by the Aga Khan earned, incredibly, more than £1,100,000, headed by the dual Derby winner Shahrastani and the Matchmaker International winner Shardari, but also including Dihistan, Kazaroun, Tashtiya, Dolka, Riyda, Samarid, Altiyna, Kabiyla and Kadial.

In France his representatives included the Prix du Conseil de Paris winner and French Derby second Altayan, Prix Vermeille winner Darara, Grand Criterium winner Danishkada and other Pattern-race winners Anazid and Sharaniya.

Unlike so many of the new forces in racing he does not buy youngsters at public auction — the champion French 1976 juvenile Blushing Groom, purchased as a foal, was one of the last — but relies on the produce of his own studs for his success.

His operation is strictly commercial, however, hence the sale of Blushing Groom and Shahrastani to the United States, although he retained an interest in each. The sale of Blushing Groom provided him with the access he needed to the best US sires to keep his studs at the top of the breeders' list and gave him Shahrastani.

He also stands stallions at his studs in Ireland and France, and his operations have survived the kidnapping of Shergar in 1983. His team in 1986 comprised Darshaan, Mouktar, Nishapour, Akarad, Lashkari and Vayrann, but this year Shardari's arrival in Ireland has resulted in the unusual move of standing a stallion (Nishapour) in England.

The collation of breeding statistics has been made almost impossible by the spread of internationalisation in racing and breeding in the last decade, with owners such as the Aga Khan, Robert Sangster, Stavros Niarchos and the Arabs having horses in training in several different countries.

The problem does not end there, as the names of their bloodstock operations may vary from country to country. So some of the Aga Khan's US-breds are listed under Herkimer Ltd, while the Niarchos US operation goes under the name of Flaxman Holdings Ltd.

The breeder may also decide to change the name of his operation. Sheikh Mohammed currently has horses bred by him under the guises of Dalham Hall Stud Ltd and Aston Upthorpe Stud Ltd, as well as his own name.

Then, like Robert Sangster, a breeder may operate under his

● **QUIET TIMES: Robert Sangster, seen with his wife Susan at Royal Ascot, had to give way in the list of breeders.**
Picture: DAVID HASTINGS

own name or that of his stud, in Sangster's case Swettenham, or be involved in a variety of other partnerships, such as those of the Coolmore complex in Ireland.

At least these are fairly well known, but in 1986 European Pattern-race winners were bred by such as Dolldreams Ltd, T & T Investment Co, and Bras Partnership, while the Stud Book is filled with the names of various companies which mean little except to those most closely involved.

For the foreseeable future the breeders' table seems sure to be a battle between the long-established stud of the Aga Khan and the newer forces of Sangster, Khalid Abdullah and the Maktoum family, which still has a long way to go to match the consistent success of its operation.

It was a quiet year in Europe for Sangster, both as an owner and as a breeder. Authaal, Acushla and Field Hand were his principal

successes on the breeding front, the last-named the result of a cheap mating between Crofter and Sangster's first mare Audrey Joan. And although Abdullah had an outstanding year with his $200,000 purchase Dancing Brave, the only Pattern-race winner bred from his top-quality broodmare band was Rejuvenate, Group-race successful in the Musidora Stakes and Park Hill Stakes.

Sheikh Mohammed's Dalham Hall Stud Farm topped the breeders' list in 1985, thanks to the Triple Crown winner Oh So Sharp, but although he was again leading owner, the only 1986 European Pattern-race winner bred by him was the German Group Three winner Singletta.

However, with the Sheikh's broodmare band increasing from about 30 in 1983 to around 100 in 1986, and similar increases in the size of operation by his Dubai brothers Hamdan Al-Maktoum and Maktoum Al-Maktoum, they are

sure to have a profound effect on development of the thoroughbred in years to come.

Of the 138 Pattern races run in Britain and Ireland in 1986, 51 winners carried the suffix USA, and three the suffix FR. The remaining 84 were won by horses bred in Britain or Ireland. However, taking only the winners of the most important races, the balance shifts noticeably in favour of the American-breds. They won 16 Group One races as compared to Europe's 13, two of which were won by French-breds.

Success of the American-breds in top British races means that several Americans are near the top of the breeders' table, some responsible for only the occasional winner. Such is the case of the leading European specialist miler Sonic Lady, bred by J Allan Mactier of Ponca Hills Farm, Kentucky.

He bought her dam, the Child Stakes ⁄ winner Stumped, for

110,000gns at the 1980 Newmarket December Sales. From the family of Lavant, which was not admitted into the General Stud Book until 1969, Stumped proved her worth as a broodmare with Sonic Lady, who fetched $500,000 as a yearling.

A similar case is that of the Glen Oak Farm of Victor Green which from a handful of mares produced Dancing Brave. However, although Green is listed as sole breeder in the US Stud Book, Dancing Brave was bred as the result of a foal-share agreement with Gainesway Farm, who stand Dancing Brave's sire Lyphard.

Glen Oak Farm was based in Kentucky at the time of the birth of the King George winner but has since been sold to Allen Paulson, although Green retained the name for his new West Virginia operation. Green had purchased Dancing Brave's dam for just $11,000 as a yearling and saw her win nearly $350,000 on the track. He sold her privately in 1986 year to Khalid Abdullah.

In contrast to Green's operation, Gainesway is one of the largest US farms, which stood more than 40 stallions in 1986 and generates over $100m in annual stud fee income.

Other important American-bred winners produced in partnership included Midway Lady, by Ed Seltzer and the Shadowlawn Farm of Harry Ranier, and the sprinters Green Desert and Gwydion by Eaton Farms Inc and Red Bull Stable.

Nelson Bunker Hunt, who with Edward Stephenson bred the Champion Stakes winner Triptych and her sister Barger (winner of the Prix Vanteaux), was solely responsible for other European Pattern winners in Swink, Reloy and Rosedale, plus the US Grade One winners Dahar and Estrapade.

Minstrella's three Group One successes earned about £220,000 for her owner-breeder Edwards Evans, who also enjoyed success in the United States with a pair of Graded stakes winners in Scoot and

○ FINE FILLY: Stable girl Amanda Honeywell and Midway Lady, a triumph for US partnership breeding.   Picture: LAURIE MORTON

● BLOOMING GOOD: Forest Flower, who played her part in another excellent international season for breeder Paul Mellon.

Picture: TONY EDENDEN

● **ONLY THE BEGINNING: Forest Flower is first past the post ahead of Minstrella in the Tattersalls Cheveley Park Stakes but breeder Paul Mellon lost the glory later.** Picture: TONY EDENDEN

Dismasted. Evans' father Thomas, who races under the name of Buckland Farm, bred, raced and stands the 1981 Kentucky Derby winner Pleasant Colony.

Minstrella's great rival Forest Flower carries the familiar colours of Mill Reef's owner Paul Mellon, who had an excellent year in the United States and Europe. Besides Forest Flower and English Spring, Mellon bred the Group One Premio Roma winner Fire of Life, as well as the US Grade One winners Dangers Hour and Dance of Life.

Big-race wins are also nothing new to the Firestones, who have large strings of horses in training on both sides of the Atlantic. They gained easily their most important success of 1986 with the home-bred Flash of Steel, winner of the Airlie/ Coolmore Irish 2,000 Guineas and now at the Irish National Stud.

Other well-established breeders to find success at the highest level were Dick Hollingsworth, with his staying king Longboat, and Louis Freedman's Cliveden Stud, with Reference Point. It was a red-letter year for the Norfolk family thanks to Lavinia, Duchess of Norfolk's St Leger hero Moon Madness and the Pattern winner Mister Wonderful, and to Lady Sarah FitzAlan Howard's top overseas winners Efisio and Mountain Bear.

Two newer studs to notch an impressive record were Bob Cowell's Chevington Stud, with the Yorkshire Oaks winner Untold, and Egon Weinfeld's Meon Valley Stud, which had another top-class filly in Colorspin. And the Binet's Kilfrush Stud followed up its 1985 success with French 2,000 Guineas winner No Pass No Sale by breeding the leading sprinter and Breeders' Cup Mile winner Last Tycoon, plus the Group-race winning juveniles Grand Chelem and Wiganthorpe.

Another stud whose success came both here and on the Continent was Peter Goulandris's Hesmonds Stud, breeders of the good fillies Maysoon, Three Tails, Mountain Memory and Iosifa. Goulandris's Petra Bloodstock Agency also bred the good French-trained trio Secret Form, Liastra and Highest Honor.

One the most successful domestic breeders in 1986, Peter Clarke of Cookstown House Stud, dispersed his mares at the end of the year, but the exploits of Phoenix Champion Stakes winner Park Express helped him go out on a high note.

And 1986 was also the end of an even more significant era with the December Sales dispersal of the mares from Jim Joel's famous Childwick Bury Stud. The Joels bred such Classic winners as Humorist, Royal Palace, Fairy Footsteps and Light Cavalry there.□

● **RUNNING FREE:** Sharpo, champion sprinter who became leading first-season sire.
    Picture: GERRY CRANHAM

CHAPTER 18

Sires

by ADRIAN COOK

○ GRAND OLD MAN: Northern Dancer had eight of his sons packed into the top 20 sires in Britain and Ireland in 1986.
Picture: JOHN C ENGELHARDT

Sires

by ADRIAN COOK

THE INFLUENCE of American breeding in general and Northern Dancer in particular was felt more strongly than ever on British and Irish racetracks in 1986, when for the fourth time in five years the champion stallion was either Northern Dancer or one of his sons.

On this occasion Nijinsky took the honours, and for the first time he headed both the British and Irish sires' tables. But it is appropriate to dwell first on Northern Dancer, who dominated the British list to such extent that eight of his sons figured among the top 20.

Fourteen of the 29 Group One winners in Britain and Ireland were sired by Northern Dancer or one of his sons, and only the head of Mashkour prevented an Epsom Derby 1-2-3 for his grandsons, although the first four were all bred in the United States. And despite some expensive failures in his two previous crops, the signs are for further glory. Four-times champion British and Irish sire, Northern Dancer served notice that he is still a force to be reckoned with when his two-year-old son Ajdal won the Dewhurst Stakes.

Of the top 20 sires in 1986 only eight are based in either Britain or Ireland. Seven stand in America, one is in South Africa and the remaining four are dead. Names surprisingly missing from the list are Habitat, who dropped out of the top 20 for the first time in a long and honourable stud career after 13 consecutive seasons, and last year's runner-up Shirley Heights, whose only Pattern-race success in 1986 was recorded in France.

After eight consecutive years in the top 20, Nijinsky recorded his lowest positions in the British sires' list in 1984 and 1985, although with such international stallions one has also to study the statistics in France and the United States for the overall picture.

The 1970 Triple Crown winner achieved the unique feat of siring the winners of Derbys at Epsom, The Curragh and Churchill Downs, and he has now bred ten winners of Classic races in England, Ireland, France, Italy and the United States. Shahrastani, his third European Derby winner, following Golden Fleece and Caerleon, amassed all but £73,000 of Nijinsky's earnings of £684,000, and those alone were enough to assure his sire of the title.

For much of the year Nijinsky also headed the US sires' list, for besides Ferdinand, the Kentucky Derby winner, his representatives included the winners of Graded stakes Dance of Life, Duty Dance, Fred Astaire, Gallant Archer and Val Danseur.

Leading domestically-based sire was the Irish National Stud's Ahonoora, who retired at a bargain basement fee of IR£2,250 in 1980 but whose services will cost IR£20,000 in 1987 as a result of his outstanding success with ordinary mares. Blistering speed was the

hallmark of Ahonoora but many of the progeny of this son of Lorenzaccio, the Champion Stakes winner, stay much better than he did, a notable example being the top-class filly Park Express.

Ala Mahlik, the 1,000 Guineas fourth, the smart Irish three-year-old Nashamaa and the high-class juvenile Don't Forget Me were other notable progeny by Ahonoora, whose earlier winners included the good fillies Park Appeal, Ahohoney and Princess Tracey.

Lyphard enjoyed his best season in Britain and Ireland thanks to Horse of the Year Dancing Brave, whose British earnings of £514,000 singlehandedly assured his sire of third spot, although he had other useful performers in Imperial Frontier and Wuthering Heights. Dancing Brave's Arc success, backed by smart performers such as Lesotho, La Grande Epoque, Tenue de Soiree and Cadeaux d'Amie, also ensured Lyphard a high ranking in France, where he was champion sire in 1978 and

O RUNNING HIGH: Lyphard had his best season in Europe and did well in the United States. Picture: 'Z'

1979, and earned him the position of leading US sire in Europe for 1986.

Manila's six Graded stakes wins in the United States, rounded off by his famous victory in the Breeders' Cup Turf, took Lyphard to the top of the US sires' list in November. Dahar and Ends Well were other major winners for him there.

Unlike Nijinsky and Lyphard, Alleged has not made much impact in the United States, but he enjoyed his second consecutive outstanding year in Europe. His daughter Midway Lady, who landed the 1,000 Guineas and Oaks double, followed up the 1985 Classic successes of Law Society and Leading Counsel, and there were European Pattern-race wins for Kazaroun, Laluche, Nemain, Nomrood, Sharaniya and Wise Counsellor. So many of Alleged's progeny are in training on this side of the Atlantic that he even finished equal seventh on the British and Irish sires' table for races won, with 31 successes.

Nureyev was exported to the United States after one season at stud in France which yielded ten stakes winners, including smart Theatrical. His oldest American-conceived progeny were three-year-olds of 1986 but the move seems to have done him no harm. His most important British-trained winner was the outstanding miler Sonic Lady, successful in six Pattern races in three countries, including the Irish 1,000 Guineas and Swettenham Stud Sussex Stakes.

Nureyev's other three-year-olds included the French Pattern-race winners Lead On Time and Only Star, while his juveniles included the leading French two-year-olds Miesque and Fotitieng, and the highly promising Gayane and Stately Don.

Following Nijinsky, Lyphard and Nureyev, the fourth son of Northern Dancer in the top six is the 1977 Derby winner The Minstrel, who ended the year as leading sire of two-year-olds thanks to his brilliant daughter

Minstrella. Bakharoff and High Competence also gave him good wins in Europe while he enjoyed his best year so far in the United States with important successes from Palace Music, Treizieme, Laser Lane and Silver Voice.

Kris, champion sire of 1985, dropped to seventh but enjoyed another excellent season, with Flash of Steel becoming his second Classic winner following Oh So

Sharp. Sure Blade also proved himself a high-class miler with wins in the St James's Palace and Queen Elizabeth II Stakes, while there were tip-top efforts from Dusty Dollar, Fitnah and Putting, and his juveniles included the promising pair Nettle and Scarlet Blade.

Riverman enjoyed easily his most successful season here in 1985, when he finished fifth in the

○ ABSENT FRIEND: Nureyev went to the US after one stud season in France but he excelled in 1986.   Picture: LESLEY SAMPSON

table thanks to the top performers Rousillon and Triptych. The latter's string of courageous performances in 1986 ensured Riverman a high position again, with her earnings of about £260,000 providing the bulk of his earnings. This dual French champion sire had several other smart French-trained performers, including Barger, Admirable Micol, River Memories, Riverbride, and Riverjoy, as well as the smart US winners Minneapple, Pillaster and Rivlia.

Welsh Pageant, who died in 1984, finished in the top 20 for the seventh time. The major domestic earner of this high-class mile to mile-and-a-quarter performer was the staying king Longboat. He was also represented by the high-class gelding Teleprompter, Gallinule Stakes winner Welsh Fantasy, the smart Rhondaling and Brave Owen, and the United States Grade One winner Mountain Bear.

In tenth place came Mill Reef, who had to be put down in February 1986 at the National Stud. Champion sire in 1978, he finished in the top ten for the sixth time and proved himself an outstanding stallion. The success of Reference Point in the William Hill Futurity raises hopes that he has sired another outstanding performer of the calibre of such as Shirley Heights, Acamas, Fairy Footsteps, Glint of Gold, Diamond Shoal, Wassl and Lashkari.

Other leading prospects by Mill Reef for 1987 include the fillies Milligram and Canadian Mill, while there were major successes in 1986 for his daughters Fleur Royale, Gull Nook and Mill on the Floss and further afield for his sons Big Reef and Marooned.

Thatching has steadily improved his position in the sires' table from 60th in 1984 to 36th in 1985 and 11th in 1986, when he also finished equal second in terms of races won and individual winners. But it was not only quantity which helped him to his high position. His winners included the good juveniles Wiganthorpe, Mansooj

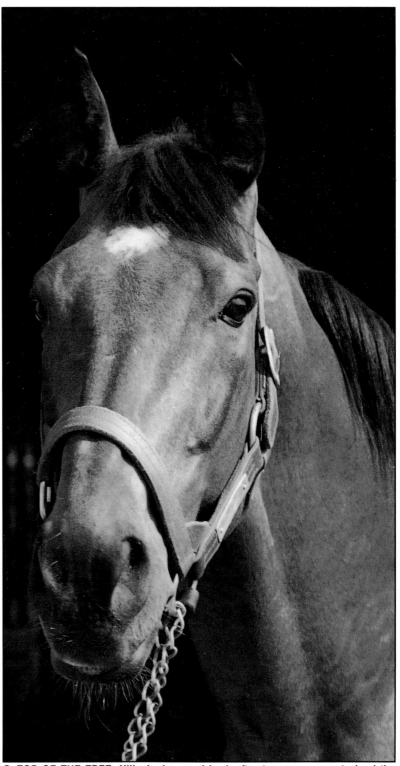

O TOP OF THE TREE: Nijinsky bounced back after two poor years to lead the way in Britain and Ireland.   Picture: LESLEY SAMPSON

and Darcy's Thatcher and three-year-old Rustic Amber, while in the United States his daughter Aberuschka was a smart Graded stakes winner.

Northfields was exported to South Africa in 1983, so his last European crop are now three-year-olds. 1986 was the eighth occasion on which he finished in the top 20. The pick of his runners were Scottish Reel, Nordica and Mr John, while he tied for second place with Thatching for races won and individual winners.

The wisdom of Sheikh Mohammed's purchase of Top Ville for his Dalham Hall Stud in 1985, when it seemed likely the 1979 French Derby winner would be sold to the United States, was further emphasised in 1986. The son of High Top figured high on the sires' list on both sides of the Channel, thanks to the Group One winners Shardari, Darara and Saint Estephe, as well as such other smart performers such as Un Desperado, Iosifa, and Top and Lady.

O DANZIG: New star on both sides of the Atlantic. Picture: 'Z'

The seventh US-based sire in the top 20 is the lightly-raced Danzig, who has proved a revelation on both sides of the Atlantic with his first three crops, though he was not sound enough to prove his ability in stakes company after easily winning his first three starts. His first crop included Chief's Crown, the 1984 US champion juvenile, and other Grade One winners Stephan's Odyssey and Contredance. He has had four more winners in the top

grade in the States with Danzig Connection, Lotka, Polish Navy and Qualify, and since the flow of top winners show no signs of abating, he is probably the hottest property on the US stud scene.

In 1986 Danzig had his first Group One winner in Europe when Green Desert took the July Cup, while the smart Irish filly Polonia provided further evidence that this son of Northern Dancer is also going to be a major force on this side of the Atlantic.

Be My Guest, champion sire in 1982 when his first crop were three-year-olds, has had rather erratic results since, finishing only 33rd in both 1983 and 1985 but sixth in 1984 and 15th in 1986. His three-year-olds included the high-class French colt Double Bed and the smart winners Eve's Error, Riyda, Santiki and Top Guest, while among his juveniles were the undefeated filly Invited Guest and the promising French colt Grand Chelem.

Bustino has not quite lived up to the high hopes held for him when he retired to stud, probably because his stock need time and distance, but he made the top 20 for the third time in 1986. His mainstays were the high-class older horses Bedtime and Supreme Leader, but Rakaposhi King, Paean and Startino all showed smart form.

Mummy's Pet, who was put down in September, was a prolific sire of winners and in 1986 his progeny helped him to top the lists for individual winners and races won, with 27 winners of 43 races. He has finished in the top 30 for the last eight seasons, with a career best sixth in 1983. This time he had a quartet of smart three-year-olds in Mister Wonderful, Moonlight Lady, Mummy's Favourite and Treasure Kay.

The eighth son of Northern Dancer to make the top 20 is the 1977 champion juvenile Try My Best, who has got over the fertility problems which blighted the start to his stud career. His outstanding performer was the leading sprinter

Last Tycoon, who went on to prove his versatility by winning the Breeders' Cup Mile and has joined his sire at the Coolmore complex.

The presence of Shergar in 19th place with only one crop to represent him confirmed the loss that European breeding suffered when he was abducted from the Ballymany Stud in 1983. The 14 winners from that crop include the runaway Irish St Leger winner Authaal (at IR3,100,000gns the European record-priced yearling), the Pattern-race winning fillies Maysoon and Tashtiya, the stakes winners Dolka and Tisn't, and the Pattern-race placed Sherkraine and Shibil.

The top 20 is completed by Persian Bold, who has enjoyed greater success overseas than at home and tops the list of British and Irish sires by worldwide earnings with a total of over a million pounds. In the United States his progeny have done especially well, with Persian Tiara, Kings Island, Bold Arrangement, Pennine Walk and Bruiser his major earners, while he has also been represented by an important winner in Japan.

On the domestic scene Persian Bold's son Pennine Walk was one of the best milers in training while the juveniles Inanna, Baba Karam and D'Azy also did well.

The leading first crop sire of 1986 was Sharpo in terms of individual winners, races won and prize money earned. He had 11 winners of 19 races worth £127,000 and was also placed third among all sires of two-year-olds in terms of prize money.

His winners included the Coventry Stakes scorer Cutting Blade, Middle Park and Prix de la Foret second Risk Me, Irish stakes winner Keen Cut, Pattern-race placed Rumboogie and the smart Print. However, had it not been for the disqualification of Forest Flower in the Tattersalls Cheveley Park Stakes, the title would have gone instead to the US-based Green Forest, sire also of the French Pattern winner Indian Forest. □

⊙ SAME AGAIN: For the second year running Alleged made an impact.   Picture: 'Z'

● CHATEAU CHANTILLY:
Bering, France's champion three-year-old colt, on his way to winning the Prix Jockey-Club Lancia.
Picture: DAVID HASTINGS

CHAPTER 19

France

by DESMOND STONEHAM

O POWER BOOST: Bering proves himself the French champion in the Prix du Jockey-Club Lancia. Picture: P BERTRAND

France

by DESMOND STONEHAM

IT WAS A REFLECTION of sorts on French racing in 1986 that the greatest credit must be given for achievements outside the country. They belonged to Robert Collet, who trained Last Tycoon to win three races in the Grade or Group One category, but none in France.

At home Collet had a somewhat moderate season. But elsewhere this most popular professional saddled Last Tycoon to win the King's Stand Stakes and William Hill Sprint Championship in Britain and Breeders' Cup Mile at Santa Anita.

The decision which Collet made in August to remove Last Tycoon from further sprints was most carefully thought out. At the time he said: "I've already crushed the top English sprinters with Last Tycoon on two occasions, so there's no point in taking them on again in the Abbaye."

Instead Collet, 36, completely changed Last Tycoon's training pattern so that he might stay the mile at Santa Anita. He even took the three-year-old son of Try My Best down to Evry on a filthy afternoon to work him on the inner track, which resembled the California circuit.

As the record book now shows, Last Tycoon and Yves Saint-Martin fully justified Collet's confidence when they defeated Palace Music and a good field in the Breeders' Cup Mile.

With Last Tycoon retired to the Coolmore Stud, he may have another colt with which to hit the headlines in 1987. He wrapped Grand Chelem, winner of the Prix des Chenes, in cotton wool as a two-year-old. But next season there is every probability that Grand

Chelem will be aimed at the General Accident 2,000 Guineas.

Criquette Head was leading trainer in France for 1986 and her father Alec the top breeder, mainly thanks to the family-owned Bering, whose only defeat was handed out by Dancing Brave in the Trusthouse Forte Prix de l'Arc de Triomphe.

Bering and Gary Moore had never been extended in four races before the Arc. Their greatest moment came when in winning the Prix du Jockey-Club Lancia (French Derby).

Conditions for the Arc were not exactly in favour of Bering. There was a lack of early pace and not enough cut in the ground for the son of Arctic Tern. Also, in the opinion of Moore, "Bering had had such easy races during the year that he could have even been a little short of experience compared to Dancing Brave." Bering lost nothing in defeat and has now been retired to stud in Kentucky.

Criquette Head's other star during 1986 was the gallant Baiser Vole. Discarded by stable jockey Moore, she revelled on the firm ground to win the Dubai Poule d'Essai des Pouliches (French 1,000 Guineas) to give replacement jockey Guy Guignard his first Classic win.

Francois Boutin had an extraordinary season, winning a small number of races but no fewer than six out of a total of 25 in the Group One bracket. His main winners were Baillamont (Prix Ganay and Prix d'Ispahan), Lacovia, who was spectacular when taking both the Prix Saint-Alary and Prix de Diane Hermes (French Oaks), and the top-class two-year-old filly Miesque, who picked up the Prix de la Salamandre and Prix Marcel Boussac.

It was a great pity that Lacovia could not take part in the Arc de Triomphe, as she might have given Dancing Brave a fright. But the daughter of Majestic Light broke down when finishing third behind Darara and Reloy in the Trusthouse Forte Prix Vermeille. Boutin commented: "It was only her great courage which enabled her to finish third."

Owned by Geneva-based Gerry Oldham, Lacovia will be covered for the next two years by Lyphard, sire of Dancing Brave and

O **BOUTIN'S BEAUTY: Lacovia lands a spectacular win in the Prix de Diane Hermes.** Picture: JOHN CROFTS

O **LUCKY FOR ONE: Guy Guignard takes an unexpected chance on Baiser Vole to win the Dubai Poule d'Essai des Pouliches.** Picture: P BERTRAND

Breeders' Cup Turf winner Manila.

Boutin hopes Miesque may go on to avenge the disappointment suffered at Newmarket in the 2,000 Guineas by her sire Nureyev's disqualification after passing the post first at Newmarket. She has the best qualities of her sire, particularly instant acceleration.

It was also a memorable season for American Cash Asmussen, 24, who was champion jockey for the second consecutive season. He was so confident of his championship that he quit France for his Texas home in early-November.

Asmussen came across the Atlantic in 1982 when he signed a contract with Greek shipping magnate Stavros Niarchos. Probably the best horse he has ridden in five years in France is Northern Trick, who shattered her field in the Prix de Diane before winning the Prix Vermeille.

For part of 1986, Asmussen was attached to the Chantilly stable of Mahmoud Fustok, and their early-season success was impressive to say the least. By the beginning of June, Fast Topaze had taken the Dubai Poule d'Essai des Poulains (French 2,000 Guineas) and Prix Lupin, and Magical Wonder the Group One Prix Jean Prat Ecurie Fustok.

But at the end of July, Asmussen virtually severed his ties with Fustok when signing a contract for 1987 with Robert Sangster, which means he will ride for Vincent O'Brien at Ballydoyle and Barry Hills at Manton.

Neither of his new stables reached great heights in 1986; it is to be hoped Asmussen will not regret his departure from France, where he could have been champion jockey again in 1987.

Pat Eddery's contract with Khalid Abdullah, whose many horses trained in France are largely with Andre Fabre, will be here nearly every Sunday during 1987 and can expect also to be a frequent midweek visitor.

Patrick Biancone began the 1986 season with great gusto but his stable ran out of steam by June.

O FAST STARTERS: Fast Topaze continues a brilliant early season for Cash Asmussen and Mahmoud Fustok by winning the Dubai Poule d'Essai des Poulains.
Picture: JOHN CROFTS

He ended with two Group One wins, through Air de Cour (Prix du Cadran) and Sakura Reiko (Prix Morny).

After Pradier had run poorly in the Prix du Jockey-Club, owner Daniel Wildenstein decided to dispense with the services of stable jockey Eric Legrix, and Biancone signed up Hong Kong-based Tony Cruz for 1987. Legrix did little wrong, but it must be doubted if Wildenstein recovered from the defeat of Sagace, who was ridden by Legrix when disqualified after "winning" the Arc de Triomphe in 1985.

Legrix partnered Sakura Reiko to victory in the Prix Morny but was replaced on the filly when she ran in the Prix de la Salamandre and the Prix Marcel Boussac. Sakura Reiko did no better in the hands of Yves Saint-Martin.

The first Group One two-year-old event of the season was the Prix Robert Papin, which went to the brilliantly fast Balbonella, trained in the provinces at Pau by Francois Rohaut.

Bought in at the 1985 Deauville sales as a yearling, Balbonella was purchased by the Maktoum family after the Papin but managed only fourth place behind Sakura Reiko, Shy Princess and Miesque in the Prix Morny. Balbonella's new trainer Criquette Head decided to

Jentzsch had an amazing season in France with two Group One victories. He saddled Acatenango to win the Grand Prix de Saint-Cloud in the hands of Steve Cauthen, who also took the Prix du Haras de Fresnay-le-Buffard Jacques le Marois with stablemate Lirung. But Lirung lost his milers' title in the Prix du Moulin de Longchamp Ecurie Fustok. Here he was third behind the top English filly Sonic Lady, and Thrill Show, who went on to win a division of the Hollywood Derby.

Michael Stoute was one of five English-based trainers to win Group One events in France during 1986. Their finest day came on 5 October, when Dancing Brave captured the Arc de Triomphe, to give Khalid Abdullah and Pat Eddery their second consecutive win after the award to Rainbow Quest in 1985. The same afternoon Eddery rode Double Schwartz to win the five-furlong Prix de l'Abbaye de Longchamp.

English domination lasted to the final day at Longchamp, when Richard Quinn and the brave Sarab held on to beat travelling-companion Risk Me in the Prix de la Foret. And later that afternoon, Henry Cecil, not the most avid traveller, saddled El Cuite to win the Prix Royal-Oak (French St

retire her for the season, and the daughter of Gay Mecene will be trained to stay a mile this year.

For the second consecutive year, fillies effected a clean sweep of the major two-year-old races in France, as Danishkada made all in the Grand Criterium. She was the fourth consecutive filly to win France's top two-year-old event. Danishkada is trained by Alain de Royer-Dupre and owned by the Aga Khan, who headed the owners' list in 1986. The same connections were also involved with Darara, who scampered away with the Trusthouse Forte Prix Vermeille. The filly was then supplemented for the Arc but did not have much luck in running, finishing sixth.

The German trainer Heinz

○ SOME CONSOLATION: Eric Legrix won the Prix Morny on the grey Sakura Reiko but later lost his job.   Picture: GEORGE SELWYN

Leger) in the hands of Steve Cauthen.

A new name on the Pattern roll of honour was that of Jonathan Pease, a rather shy Englishman based at Chantilly, who trained Swink to win the Grand Prix de Paris. Pease was responsible for two horses belonging to Nelson Bunker Hunt — Swink and Reloy, who after picking up the Prix de Royaumont, finished second to Darara in the Prix Vermeille.

Biggest tragedy of the year came when Dawn Run broke her neck in the Grande Course des Haies d'Auteuil (French Champion Hurdle). The pride of Ireland was killed outright, leaving her French jockey Michel Chirol to bemoan, "I was sure to win".

In any other circumstances the Grande Course would have been remembered as one of the great international events of the year, with runners from England, Ireland and the United States. Instead, the fact that French horse Le Rheusois hung on to beat the American champion Flatterer, who excelled in the hands of English jockey Richard Dunwoody, seemed almost incidental.

The finances of French racing remained static during 1986, with tote turnover being increased fractionally but below the domestic inflation rate. Enormous efforts have been made to attract more people to the sport, but as one veteran punter said: "Nowadays, if a girl drops a handkerchief, she is

O SONIC BOOM: Another smashing win for British trainers as Sonic Lady takes the Prix du Moulin de Longchamp.

Picture: JOHN CROFTS

picked up, put on the back of a motorbike, and probably makes love to her companion the same day. When I was young, it took three weeks to reach the same goal — and we often took our girl friends racing."

On a more serious note, the French have so many other attractions, and horse racing is not one of the nation's favourite sports. Most weekends, the more privileged part of the population jump into their cars to hurry off for a break at the family's secondary residence.

To attract more interest in racing, the Pari-Mutuel have announced a new bet, the Quarte Plus, which asks the punter to find the first four past the post in an event of quality. The Pari-Mutuel is being modernised throughout France in the 6,000 or so cafes which serve as betting shops. This new machinery, together with new ideas, is considered important as there is a possibility that under European law, bookmakers could operate in France in the year 1992, so bringing about the downfall of the last bastion of the tote monopoly.

For those looking to make either the bookmaker or the machine pay in 1987, Danishkada is a candidate for the French 1,000 Guineas and Miesque for the English equivalent. Although French colts achieved little as two-year-olds, it should be worth keeping an eye on Grand Chelem. □

● **RAIDER OF THE ARC:**
Dancing Brave in full flight as
he trounces a superb field in
the Prix de l'Arc de Triomphe.
Picture: GERRY CRANHAM

CHAPTER 20

Arc de Triomphe

by TIM RICHARDS

○ **MOMENT OF TRIUMPH: Khalid Abdullah receives the Arc trophy for Dancing Brave's win.** Picture: DAVID HASTINGS

Arc de Triomphe

by TIM RICHARDS

NOT MANY racehorses make the correspondence columns of *The Times*.

But Dancing Brave, by virtue of his spectacular victory in the THF Prix de l'Arc de Triomphe, followed by his controversial defeat in the Breeders' Cup at Santa Anita, was the subject of letters to the Editor of that distinguished paper.

John Hislop, owner of the great Brigadier Gerard, hit out at the unfairness of racing in the United States, where horses run with the assistance of medications which are not permitted in Europe.

And Peter Knight, of St James's, wrote: "Occasionally a racehorse captures the imagination of a far wider public than those who patronise the sport. Dancing Brave was such a horse (Brigadier Gerard was another).

"The connections of Dancing Brave have more than honoured their obligations to the sport by running him on five racecourses in the United Kingdom as well as delighting a huge crowd in Paris."

Indeed, that is just why Dancing Brave made those unusual appearances on the letters pages of *The Times*; he entertained; he lit so many fuses of fun for so many people that his name galloped beyond the racing pages to spread the great gospel of the game.

His spectacular triumph in the Prix de l'Arc de Triomphe could not have been better stage managed. Because for the first time in its 65-race history the Arc was being screened live on television to 17 different countries throughout the world.

Another first was Channel 4's 35-minute show transmitted throughout Britain in place of the BBC's annual ten-minute Arc slot.

The world was watching and it was as if Dancing Brave and Pat Eddery realised it. The instant Eddery took a pull just inside the two-furlong from home marker they had us all thinking: the cheek of it!

There were the best horses from Europe, Bering, Acatenango, Shahrastani, Darara, Shardari,

Nemain and Baby Turk stretching desperately for the line.

And what did Eddery do?

With almost casual impudence, the Irishman checked Dancing Brave, steering him in behind French Derby hero Bering, the horse they believed in France was invincible in the Arc.

Unknown to Eddery, his split second flash of confidence signalled worldwide the message we had all been waiting for: Here comes the Champion of Europe.

Eddery rode him like a champion and Dancing Brave responded with the wizardry and authority the 10,000 British race fans had crossed the Channel to witness.

When Eddery produced Dancing Brave with his now famous supercharged overdrive he cut down Bering and the rest as if they were part of the worst instead of one of the best Arc fields in the history of the race.

Unknown to the crowd, bustling for a closer glimpse of the Brave, his victim Bering had displayed enormous courage by finishing on three legs.

His trainer Criquette Head revealed four days later that Bering had fractured a shin bone.

Her feeling for France's great sporting occasion concealed the bitter disappointment when she told me: "In no way am I wanting to make excuses. Bering is a good horse and we know that Dancing Brave is a very good horse."

For your correspondent it was the first live Arc. There could not have been a better baptism.

How lucky can you get to see history being made and printed indelibly alongside that other unforgettable day?

The code was different but the emotions ran even higher at Cheltenham last March when Dawn Run and her courageous partner Jonjo O'Neill completed the unique Champion Hurdle-Cheltenham Gold Cup double.

It was difficult not to feel for Greville Starkey, who set out on Dancing Brave at the beginning of

his three-year-old career.

After Starkey's controversial Derby defeat on Dancing Brave, the ride was virtually handed to Pat Eddery on a plate because of his injury before the King George.

Since then Eddery has been signed up with a mind-boggling contract as Khalid Abdullah's first jockey worldwide.

But even so both Guy Harwood and Khalid Abdullah took time off from the celebrations to spare a thought for Starkey.

Abdullah admitted: "Starkey would have won on Dancing Brave today."

And Harwood said of his longstanding stable jockey: "I wish Greville had ridden Dancing Brave. I have enormous sympathy for him."

At first the fined-down frame of Starkey sitting in the jockeys room cut a lonely figure in the Arc aftermath.

But after the introductory: "Bad luck, Grev" from eager members of the Press Britain's senior jockey held court from behind a brave smile.

"It's only money," laughed Starkey, winner of the 1975 Arc on Star Appeal. "And after this Pat's got more than me!"

He added: "There is no question, it is the best Arc I have ridden in and I knew 'The Jet' would win because I had been with him the week before and he was tophole. Nothing can live with 'The Jet'."

Starkey posed the question: "How many Group One races have they won between them? (the answer was 11), and look what Dancing Brave did to them. He swept them aside so impressively."

Weeks later when the big race adrenalin had stopped racing through his Irish veins Pat Eddery took a level-headed look back at Arc day with all the cool, which has helped to hoist him on to the pedestal as number one successor to Lester Piggott.

"There was such a great build-up to the race and the field stood up to be better than in most years with so many top class horses.

"And to crown it Dancing Brave did his stuff in the style of the true champion that he is."

Dancing Brave had been a wholesale gamble on both sides of the Channel and gone off at 11-10 favourite.

Bookmakers back home were bleating because they reckoned they could not hedge their bets and influence the starting price as they do in the domestic market.

Indeed, some of the big firms said they had been caught with their pants down and taken such a striping from punters that they refused to offer Pari-Mutuel odds on the Breeders Cup in California a month later.

The bookmakers may have been wincing in public but, privately, I bet they were applauding Dancing Brave's triumph.

After all, Ladbrokes, Hills, Mecca and Coral are aware of the value of marketing and advertising.

And they know that, at the end of the day, there is only one winner when the pulse of two racing nations quickens with all the expectancy of a race like the 1986 Arc. That winner is racing itself.

There was no disguising the feelings of Louis Romanet, Director General of the Societe d'Encouragement – the French Jockey Club.

Sitting in his office at Longchamp with all the drama of the Arc only hours old Romanet beamed from behind his glasses.

He told me: "We are trying to sell French racing with bigger television coverage throughout the world.

"In 1987 I am hoping we will be able to promote an hour long programme from Longchamp.

"If we can have another race with a result as perfect as this we must be well on the way to selling our commodity."

Perhaps then even France's stuffy newspaper *Le Monde* may permit a line or two of reflection on the passion found in Paris on the first Sunday in October. □

● **TRUE GRIT: Flash of Steel runs on under pressure to beat Mr John in the Airlie/Coolmore Irish 2,000 Guineas.**
   Picture: GERRY CRANHAM

O NO DOUBTS: Shahrastani holds centre stage with an easy win in the Budweiser Irish Derby.

Picture: PRESS ASSOCIATION

Irish Flat

by TONY O'HEHIR

IT WAS A SEASON to forget for Irish trainers on the Flat in 1986, when English raiders enjoyed their best year in Ireland and Michael Stoute led the way as champion with a hat-trick in the Classics.

Shahrastani's eight-length win in the first Irish Derby sponsored by Budweiser was the jewel in the crown as Stoute became the first trainer to win three Irish classics in the same year since Vincent O'Brien in 1977.

Budweiser's arrival on the scene, and their welcome contribution of

IR£250,000, made the 28 June event the richest ever staged in Ireland. And until the Prix de l'Arc de Triomphe in October it was the biggest prize contested in Europe.

Shahrastani's first-place pick-up of IR£299,800 was almost IR£131,000 more than Law Society earned when he won the last Joe McGrath Sweeps Derby in 1985. In those circumstances it needed a performance worthy of the occasion, and the Epsom Derby winner delivered the goods.

He went to The Curragh with

something to prove. He got less credit for his Epsom success than he deserved. Instead, that race was widely regarded as one Dancing Brave should not have lost.

Dancing Brave missed the Irish Derby, but though subsequent events at Ascot and Longchamp showed him to be Shahrastani's superior, on that hot, humid day in June even Guy Harwood's brilliant star might have found the Aga Khan's colt difficult to beat.

Once Walter Swinburn sent Shahrastani past Bonhomie almost

two furlongs out the contest was over. The winning margin had been equalled only by Assert in recent times. It was a brilliant performance by a colt obviously at his peak.

Mashkour, only three lengths behind Shahrastani at Epsom, was beaten out of sight, finishing ten lengths adrift. And it was a bad result for the home-trained colts, none of which finished in the first four. That last happened in 1967, when Ribocco was the winner.

The home brigade fared little better in the other big races and managed to keep only three of the nine Group One prizes in this country. The visitors' haul from all races, win and place, topped IR£1.3million.

Stoute led the money list. His Classic haul, through Sonic Lady, Shahrastani and Colorspin, plus Samarid's win on Derby day, were enough to topple Dermot Weld, who had the highlight of his season at The Curragh in May, when Flash of Steel won the Airlie/Coolmore 2,000 Guineas.

Weld's first Classic-winning colt, now standing at the Irish National Stud, revelled in the heavy ground and beat Mr John threequarters of a length. Confirmation of his win was delayed until the Turf Club Stewards dismissed an appeal by John Michael, Mr John's owner, who claimed that The Curragh Stewards should have disqualified Flash of Steel for hampering his horse in the last furlong.

Under pressure from Michael Kinane, Flash of Steel drifted to the right and Mr John did not have much room to manoeuvre. But both the Stewards on the day and those in Dublin thought he had enough room.

A week later a different panel of Stewards at The Curragh set a precedent for other countries when they allowed Sonic Lady to run in the Goffs 1,000 Guineas. The filly's passport had been left in Newmarket and the authorities agreed to accept a facsimile copy of the document, transmitted from the Michael Stoute stable to Turf Club headquarters, sited behind The Curragh stands.

That revolutionary step and a change of bridle helped Sonic Lady

O HOME WIN: Park Express keeps a major prize in Ireland by landing the Phoenix Park Champion Stakes.
Picture: CAROLINE NORRIS

○ NEW NAME: But a familiar winner as Shahrastani picks up the Budweiser Irish Derby.   Picture: GERRY CRANHAM

○ STROLLING PLAYER: Minstrella lands another major Irish prize, beating Polonia in the Moyglare Stud Stakes.   Picture: CAROLINE NORRIS

become Sheikh Mohammed's first Irish Classic winner. The new bridle enabled her to relax, which she had failed to do at Newmarket when finishing third to Midway Lady in the General Accident 1,000 Guineas. It worked perfectly and Sonic Lady burst clear of the pack in the last furlong to beat the fast-finishing Lake Champlain by two lengths.

Stoute was back for more in July when he sent two fillies for the Oaks. Swinburn preferred Untold to Colorspin, hardly surprising in view of their form behind Midway Lady at Epsom. But heavy rain overnight changed the picture dramatically. Untold failed to act in the softened ground and struggled home third, 15 lengths behind her stablemate and Pat Eddery.

Colorspin cruised past Fleur Royale a furlong out and won by three lengths. Success brought from Eddery the observation that he had never ridden an easier Classic winner.

The sight of a motionless Eddery was a sickening sight for Fleur Royale's jockey Christy Roche, but he was to gain his revenge in October in the Jefferson Smurfit Memorial St Leger. The field of six was the smallest for 28 years and Roche decided he had the machinery, in Authaal, to make almost all the running. His forcing tactics won the day and David O'Brien's colt, who was 15 lengths clear at halfway, won by five.

Authaal set a European record when sold as a yearling for IR3.Im guineas. He later developed a sand crack in his near-fore hoof, which had to be screwed, and his debut was delayed until July.

Most valuable prize won by an Irish-trained Flat racer during the year was the IR£261,500 by Park Express in the third Phoenix Champion Stakes in September. For her trainer Jim Bolger it was a career highlight in a year when he alone among Irish trainers won races in England. Park Express reversed the season's trend when she beat the visitors, who had a

O **LONE STAR: Polonia, Ireland's top two-year-old filly, on her way to victory at The Curragh.**

Picture: CAROLINE NORRIS

seven to six numerical advantage in the Phoenix Park race.

The French gave her most to do, with Double Bed and Triptych finishing second and third. Angel Cordero, on his first visit to Dublin, gave Triptych a lot to do

but it mattered not one iota to the largely partisan Sunday crowd, who rejoiced in a home win.

By the time the Bolger-Declan Gillespie alliance ended in August, John Reid had linked up with the stable's big-race runners and he

was aboard Paddy Burns' filly at Phoenix Park. It was the middle leg of a memorable Sunday treble of Group One races for Reid, who won the Heinz 57 Phoenix Stakes and Moyglare Stud Stakes on Minstrella.

If Shahrastani's Derby was the performance of the season, the Phoenix Stakes was the race of the year. Minstrella held her great rival Forest Flower by a short head on a day when The Park race at last justified its Group One status.

First run in 1902, the Phoenix Stakes became recognised as the two-year-old sprint championship in Ireland. Upgraded to Group One in 1980, it had its distance increased from five to six furlongs three years later.

Recent results had not been up to the required standard and it was decided to go for broke by doubling the value of the race to IR£200,000 in 1986, with a late supplementary stage introduced in an attempt to attract the best talent available. The gamble was successful, and so was the form of the race, since six

of the field later won Pattern races.

Minstrella was soon back, and in September she outpaced Polonia, Ireland's best juvenile, in the Moyglare. On the same afternoon Ireland's third and final Group One event for two-year-olds was exported when Lockton came late to beat Baba Karam by a head in the National Stakes.

Baba Karam had come close to achieving a fairytale win for record-producer turned trainer Denny Cordell. But this season Baba Karam will race for Vincent O'Brien, who had a quiet, virus-affected year. O'Brien won only two Pattern races, with Acushla and Wise Counsellor, and all but closed down Ballydoyle for three weeks in June.

Dermot Weld again trained most winners. His total of 95 was almost double that of his nearest rival

John Oxx, whose 50 was a career best.

A third consecutive jockeys' title for Michael Kinane was always on the cards, even if a visit to the seaside in August had almost disastrous consequences. Kinane, who rode 80 winners including five out of six at Phoenix Park in June, broke a wrist and a thumb in a fall at Laytown Strand races.

During Kinane's absence Weld's No 2, David Parnell, got the chance to fulfil his potential, ending the season with 29 winners and the job as Liam Browne's stable jockey in '87.

With 19 winners John Egan was apprentice champion for the first time, and he did well to finish second to Swedish girl Jenny Moller in the Long John Scotch Whisky European Apprentice series.

FIRST AMONG MANY: Sonic Lady leads the charge in the Goffs 1,000 Guineas, beating Lake Champlain (right).
Picture: ED BYRNE

No review of the Flat in Ireland would be complete without reference to one major change for the better in 1986, and one significant alteration which will become apparent this year.

On 29 April New Zealand-style starting stalls were introduced at Dundalk. Their use countrywide has put right the problem of ragged starts which existed at all but the major tracks.

Less welcome is the fact that Pat Eddery's contract with Khalid Abdullah means visits to his native country will be restricted this year. He rode 46 winners from 131 rides in 1986 and will be greatly missed by Irish racegoers, with whom he has been a great favourite. In their eyes his replacement at Ballydoyle, Cash Asmussen, has a hard act to follow. □

○ **PAYING DIVIDENDS: Authaal, Europe's most expensive yearling, lands the Irish St Leger.** Picture: CAROLINE NORRIS

● **BLACK VELVET: Stoute and champagne after Untold's win in the Yorkshire Oaks.**
Picture: GERRY CRANHAM

CHAPTER 22

Michael Stoute

by PAUL HAIGH

◯ I CAME, I SAW, I CONQUERED: Three faces of champion trainer Michael Stoute. Pictures: TONY EDENDEN

Michael Stoute

by PAUL HAIGH

WHATEVER THE CHALLENGES provided by Pat Eddery, Guy Harwood and the rest of those connected with Dancing Brave, 1986 can be regarded as Michael Stoute's year. In winning his second trainer's title he dominated the opposition for most of the season.

Shahrastani won the Derby for him, as Shergar did in his previous championship year of 1981. His horses won more money abroad than any other British trainer's. And at home, only a couple of years after Henry Cecil became the first to send out the winners of over £1m worth of races, Stoute cracked £2m, and at one point seemed likely to make it three.

Now the master of Beech Hurst and Freemason Lodge stables, Stoute came to England from Barbados when he was 19, already addicted to racing as a result of his police chief father's decision to buy a house adjoining the local course and a friendship with ex-jockey Freddy Thirkell.

He worked for bloodstock agents Kerr and Co. for a time, until Sir Eric Halliwell, a family friend from Ireland, who had lived next door to Pat Rohan, offered to put in a word. Stoute went to Rohan as assistant. In such ways is racing history made.

"I got a marvellous grounding with Pat in every aspect of training," says Stoute, who joined Doug Smith in 1969 when the ex-rider took over Lord Rosebery's horses after the death of Sir Jack Jarvis. Sleeping Partner and Crooner were two of the very good horses with which he was associated.

Stoute's training apprenticeship continued with Tom Jones between June 1970 and September 1971, before he became a public trainer at the end of that season. Since then his progress has been too consistently spectacular for luck to have had much to do with it.

In his second season he produced top-class winners in Blue Cashmere and Alphadamus,

bought for 9,000gns and 1,200gns respectively and a talking point for those who reckon great trainers are great simply because they get the most expensive horses. The big owners have come to Stoute as a result of his achievements, not as their precondition.

Last season's heroics did not exactly stun him. "It was very clear at the end of 1985 that we had a lot of strength in depth amongst the two-year-olds and also some high quality three-year-olds," he says. "But there are always some disappointments: horses that don't go on for various reasons, and you can never go into a season expecting to do well. When you have a horse like Shahrastani, for example, you're naturally hopeful, but you can't tell during the winter that he's going to be a Derby winner".

It was perhaps his handling of Shahrastani which best exemplified Stoute's brilliance in 1986.

His preparation for Epsom was immaculate. He might not have

reached the height of his three-year-old powers until the Irish Derby, but via his reappearance in the Guardian Classic Trial and what some thought to be an unimpressive victory in the Mecca Dante, he was coaxed into a condition and a state of mind that made him the one to beat on the first Wednesday in June. None of the opposition, however illustrious and whatever their excuses, was able to do it.

In the 1970s Greville Starkey was Stoute's first choice jockey. In the '80s it has been Walter Swinburn, and Stoute is well aware of the part played by his stable jockey - "still improving and getting stronger" - in the Derby triumph.

"If Lester had ridden Shahrastani in the Derby and won as Walter did I think he'd have got a hell of a lot of credit for it," says Stoute. "I think in hindsight we can say that Dancing Brave may simply not have been a left-handed horse - maybe after Santa Anita people won't be as critical of Greville as they have been - but you can't get away from the fact that Walter did everything right and rode a tactically superb race."

Shahrastani's climax at The Curragh, where on a line through Bakharoff he suggested he was superior to the much-lauded Prix du Jockey-Club winner Bering, was followed by the hangover of the King George VI and Queen Elizabeth Diamond Stakes, and not a few thought we might have seen the last of the racecourse efforts of this son of Nijinsky.

At Ascot Shahrastani had looked light and became uncharacteristically agitated during the preliminaries. After the race, it was found that he had "a respiratory problem" and it seemed unlikely that even Stoute could get him back to anything like his best. He did, however, and without being able to get a prep race into Shahrastani, who had been off the course since July and was "not an overgenerous worker" at home.

Stoute took him to Longchamp for the Prix de l'Arc de Triomphe

fit enough to look like a possible winner until that remarkable last half-furlong. Shahrastani proved at Longchamp that there had been no fluke about Epsom and that he definitely belonged in the same league as Dancing Brave, the horse who without him, would have been unbeaten in Europe. Stoute and his team gave him the opportunity to prove it.

But in 1986 the stable was running anything but a one-act show. Halfway through the season he began to look more than a little like Cecil B. De Mille.

Green Desert, a Dancing Brave victim in the 2,000 Guineas, was successfully converted into a tip-top sprinter. Shardari, after initial disappointments, showed himself to be the best four-year-old colt in Europe. And for fillies, may be Busby Berkeley was the man with whom to compare him. With Untold, Colorspin, Maysoon and Ivor's Image leading the bunch, Stoute's middle-distance fillies had such strength in depth that only Midway Lady prevented him from mopping up.

There was also Sonic Lady. Thwarted by Midway Lady and her own sense of occasion in the 1,000 Guineas, she went through five races unbeaten before the Breeders' Cup which included the Irish 1,000 Guineas, Coronation Stakes at Royal Ascot, Swettenham Stud Sussex Stakes and Prix du Moulin. At Santa Anita she alone of the British team looked like winning her race. But after she had taken the lead entering the short straight, her long season and the travelling got the better of her, and she finished in the ruck behind Last Tycoon.

To everybody's delight and some people's surprise Sonic Lady remains in training in 1987. Stoute might have had a lot to do with the decision. "I was all for it," he says. "I cannot understand those who criticize owners for retiring a top-class three-year-old colt, however nice it is to see more four-year-olds in training, because it just doesn't make economic sense not to. But

with a filly it's different because she can only have one foal a year."

Stoute is looking forward to training Sonic Lady in the 1987 season almost as much as he would have looked forward to training Shahrastani. "I think he would have been at full strength as a four year-old; he was a progressive horse," he says.

Sonic Lady's campaign in 1986 should be more relaxed. "We won't have a Classic programme to worry about," he reasons, "so we won't have to hurry her in the spring." If she continues the process of learning to settle, Sonic Lady may be tried at ten furlongs, otherwise her targets are likely to be the same as last autumn.

Stoute is undaunted by the November experience in California, and does not go along with those who saw the eclipse of the British as a serious argument against the growing conviction that horses running here are as good as, if not better than, any in the world. "It's been totally overplayed," he says, "because we have a very good record in International races. California is different. A lot was learnt at Santa Anita, though."

With the notable exception of Ajdal, the Stoute two-year-olds of 1986 were not regarded with the same awe as those of 1985. Their trainer, however, gives the impression there is more to know about them than has so far been made evident. "I couldn't go as far as to say they're as promising as the last lot," he says carefully. "But I would go as far as to say they're a little stronger than some people are aware."

Stoute likes being champion trainer, and does not mind admitting to a sense of rivalry with such as Cecil and Harwood. "I'm not paranoic about it," he explains, "but this is a competitive sport and obviously you're aware of who you've got to beat."

Had he ever expected to be champion trainer one day? Was it all planned? "Oh, yes definitely," he says. "Champion of Barbados." □

● ON THE ATTACK: At Talaq takes the Fosters Melbourne Cup.
   Picture: PATRICK McGRATH

CHAPTER 23

Racing Abroad

by ROBERT CARTER

O ENGLISHMAN ABROAD: Henry Cecil makes a rare foreign foray and wins France's Prix Royal-Oak with El Cuite.

Picture: JOHN CROFTS

Racing Abroad

by ROBERT CARTER

IT IS TEMPTING to see Britain at the centre of international racing, because British trainers have been so successful overseas, but in many ways that view is wide of the mark.

Britain, with a little over 3,000 races on the Flat each year and piddling prize money for all but a few events, is a small country in terms of racing the world over. But its advantages of excellent turf, top-class training conditions, conscientious care for horses, and traditional events carrying both high prestige and internationally competitive prizes have made its racecourses for the time being the chosen battleground of several groups of rich, foreign owners.

But the glorious illusion, by which the small-scale British scene can appear a match for the richer sport in the United States or even France, could be easily shattered. It requires only economic or political problems here or in countries from which these owners are drawn, perhaps simply the defeat of Mrs Thatcher at the polls, to drive away a significant number.

What would Flat racing be like then, in a country where many native owners have retreated to jumping rather than compete against people who are so immeasurably richer?

British racing would have become a backwater in the 1970s if the Jockey Club had not been able to attract Arab owners to compete with Americans and others on our soil. Instead, our sport could hardly be stronger than it is at present.

It makes sense to have a large string of horses trained in Britain only if the enterprise is run on international lines. There are 103 Pattern races to contest at home and our system, with its emphasis on handicaps, makes it difficult to place a horse, particularly an older one, which is just below Group-race standard.

In addition there are 226 Pattern races elsewhere in Europe, only a few of which are off limits to foreign raiders, offering opportunities that are obvious.

British trainers carried off 49 of those events last year — 15 in

Italy, 14 in Ireland and ten each in France and Germany. They included seven of the 12 Italian Group One races and six out of nine at that level in Ireland. The French were able to win four in Britain, thanks to Saint Estephe, Triptych and a double dose of Last Tycoon, but British raiders responded with victory in five of the 24 French Group One events.

Of course, there is little discernible pattern in the European Pattern, because each country guards its own interests too closely. But, whatever the system, someone will find a way of turning it to advantage and in recent years British trainers have exploited it most effectively.

Even Henry Cecil, who for long resisted the pressures to race outside Britain and Ireland, except with the occasional horse like Ardross, appears to have accepted the necessity. He won the Prix Royal-Oak and Gran Premio d'Italia, both Group One, with El Cuite, and the Premio Vittorio di Capua with Star Cutter. More travel may prove inevitable.

Michael Stoute, who won a mere £7,993 overseas in 1984, has shown the value of looking outside Britain. His stable was so full of talent in 1986 that he had no alternative. Ivor's Image, who was perhaps his fourth or fifth best three-year-old filly, won the Oaks d'Italia at Milan and Grade Two E P Taylor Stakes in Canada, and was a close fourth in the Prix de Diane. She ran only twice at home, each time finishing behind one of her stablemates. Her trainer collected ten of the 80 British wins abroad and 16 out of 167 places for total earnings of £960,531.

John Dunlop, who won the Derby Italiano and Gran Premio di Milano with Tommy Way, is one of the most internationally-minded British trainers. Foreign success has meant not only placing his horses to best advantage but also attracting new owners, like Paolo Tomei, who bred Tommy Way in Ireland and raced him until just before his Derby victory.

Italian owners have more good mares in the British Isles, particularly Ireland, than at home.

This means not only that they can breed to better stallions but also have moved valuable assets to secure countries, an important aspect of international racing. Tommy Way ran seven times in 1986, four in Italy, once in Germany, where he took the Group Two Hansa Preis, once in Japan, where he was down the field in the Japan Cup, and just once in Britain, first time out, when not ready to do himself justice and third at Haydock Park.

The Japan Cup was won by gallant Jupiter Island, better than ever at seven, who held off Allez Milord (the only British-trained Group One winner in Germany in 1986), to give Clive Brittain victory in a mammoth international prize for the second year running.

Brittain, who won the 1985 Breeders' Cup Turf with Pebbles, went close with Bold Arrangement to becoming the first British trainer to saddle a Kentucky Derby winner. That colt and Jupiter Island, who was a close third to Dahar in the San Juan Capistrano Handicap, earned £151,440 in the

O JUMPING JUPITER: Clive Brittain makes it pay on the other side of the world with Jupiter Island (nearside), who beats Allez Milord in the Japan Cup.

○ TURFED OUT: Manila beats Wiltshire-trained Damister by a nose in the Turf Classic at Belmont Park.

Picture: BOB COGLIANESE

United States. British horses failed to win a single American race in 1986, although Damister was within inches of triumph in the Turf Classic and brave Bold Arrangement was a little unlucky in the Derby. Nevertheless, they earned £482,317 from ten places and Brittain's near-miss will act as a pathfinder.

The present state of play is this. Owners based in Britain have weakened the standard of racing in America by buying so many top-quality yearlings. On the other hand, they have helped American breeders because their products are spread more widely and thus can win more big prizes. European races, and the Anglo-Irish variety in particular, offer such poor opportunities for older horses that all but the best and worst will be drawn back to the States, along with a significant number of European-breds.

American racing encourages competition between older fillies and mares, by providing them with a separate programme, and it also

has an insatiable demand for all horses of allowance standard. Anyone who thinks there are fewer Timeform-rated 90 to 120 horses around these days, is right. They have a far better chance across the Atlantic. British observers draw satisfaction from the successes of these exported horses, while Americans naturally relish the great improvement wrought by their trainers.

One of the strangest ambitions of recent years is that of the official Handicappers in Europe, who wish to extend their ratings worldwide. This inevitably means relying on a limited number of form lines, but the officials could be easily misled, as when making Long Mick fourth-best two-year-old in Europe in 1983 and best in France.

However improbable the line, someone will choose to accept it, as with the calls to give Manila his due after his victory, with Dancing Brave an unhappy fourth, in the Breeders' Cup Turf. Only dreamers can believe that a colt who defeated Damister by a nose and

Theatrical by a neck, at weight-for-age each time, can be said to lead the world.

Every country is hungry for champions, Britain as much, or more, than any other. There was a rush to acclaim Shahrastani as a second Shergar as soon as he won a race at Sandown Park with only three effective participants, while a cross-Channel victory in the Prix du Moulin was deemed enough to hail Sonic Lady as the best miler in the world.

The British view of the racing world scarcely stretches beyond the Continent. We have a limited understanding of the sport in the United States, as the events of Breeders' Cup day reminded us, and hardly any of racing in countries such as Japan or Australia, with its 20,000-plus races and where the level of prize money is far above our own.

Australians believed they had discovered a world champion in Bonecrusher, a four-year-old New Zealand-bred gelding. He was declared "the greatest horse to

○ **TALKING HORSE:** The fame of New Zealand-bred Bonecrusher spread throughout the racing world in 1986.

O ON TOP DOWN UNDER: At Talaq, fourth in the Epsom Derby, lands the Fosters Melbourne Cup.

Picture: MELBOURNE HERALD

cross the Tasman since Phar Lap" when winning the Tancred Stakes at Rosehill, Sydney, over Easter, a triumph he followed a week later by taking the AJC Derby at Randwick. Bonecrusher continued in great form and by 25 October, when he beat Waverley Star by a neck in the W S Cox Plate, his record stood at 13 wins from 24 outings, six in Group One class. He

was certain to start favourite for the Japan Cup and carried total Australasian confidence.

However, Europeans who noticed that he had been in receipt of two kilos when defeating the subsequent Melbourne Cup winner At Talaq by a length and a half in the Group One Underwood Stakes, at Caulfield on 25 September, must have raised an eyebrow. At Talaq

was rated 24lb behind El Gran Senor on the 1984 European Classification of three-year-olds and a mere 107 by Timeform the following year.

It was a disaster when Bonecrusher went down with a high temperature and had to be withdrawn a few days before the Japan Cup. That race is the only international event at present

⊙ OUTWARD BOUND: Bold Arrangement went close to victory in the Kentucky Derby
Picture: GERRY CRANHAM

likely to attract horses from Australia and New Zealand and would have provided invaluable comparison.

Meanwhile, Argentines believe they have "the best since Forli" in a three-year-old called El Serrano, who had won 11 of his 15 races to November, including the last seven on the trot. After winning the first two legs of the Argentine Quadruple Crown, the Polla de Potrillos and Gran Premio Jockey Club, he was sold to the Hickory Tree Stable of James P Mills, for whom he added the Gran Premio Nacional (Argentine Derby) on 9 November. Mr Mills, whose wife raced their home-bred Gorytus, is expected to test this South American champion, a son of the 1964 Greenham Stakes winner Excel, in the States in 1987.

This is good news for Americans but not for Argentine racing, which has been badly affected by economic conditions and runaway inflation, and cannot afford to keep its best horse at home. In the long run, Europe faces the same threat, simply because American owners compete for greater prizes and have a richer breeding industry and are thus justified in spending more money.

The great international stables, operated in the main by Arab owners, are able to exploit the best of both worlds, running their young horses in Britain before deciding on a stud career or further competition in the United States.

British racegoers are fortunate to have been treated to the best in recent years, thanks to the efforts of outsiders, but nothing lasts in this uncertain world. We had better enjoy the parade of stars while we can.□

● **PAY DIRT: Rounding the home turn at Santa Anita.**
Picture: GEORGE SELWYN

CHAPTER 24

USA

by DAN FARLEY

○ ANCHORS AWAY: Danzig Connection and Chris McCarron find their water wings to take the Belmont Stakes.

Picture: BOB COGLIANESE

USA

by DAN FARLEY

A REVIEW of any season in which some 75,000 horses run in well over 80,000 races for purses totalling more than $650m is not approached lightly. That is racing in the United States today, with over 8,000 days of sport carded annually. So the following is an attempt to skim the top off those horses and events which made the 1986 season what it was — long, interesting and unpredictable.

The Early Months

Quality winter racing in the States can be found in only two places, Santa Anita and whichever of the south Florida tracks, Gulfstream Park or Hialeah, is conducting the prized mid-winter dates of early-January to early-March.

People look for Classic horses from these two places. Some are putting the stamp of legitimacy on their previous season's campaign, others might be coming into their own, and then there is the return of the past year's stars.

On the West Coast the dominant figure among Classic hopefuls was Snow Chief. And in an interesting move trainer Mel Stute shipped the plebeian-bred colt to Florida, where he readily displayed equal superiority over his East Coast rivals, scoring a facile win in the

O WORM'S EYE VIEW: Snow Chief is an easy winner of the Preakness Stakes.

Florida Derby at Gulfstream. The colts' Classic would not lack for a solid favourite.

Among those in other divisions, the previous year's Belmont Stakes winner Creme Fraiche looked good in the handicap ranks, and Lady's Secret began the season where she would end it, in championship form.

Skip Trial's win in the Gulfstream Park Handicap and Turkoman's emergence as the best handicap horse in the East, with wins in the Widener and later the Oaklawn Handicap, were paralleled in the West by Greinton's brilliant victory in the Santa Anita Handicap. It was Greinton's first start after a four-month lay-off, and not long afterwards, his arch rival Precisionist evened the score between them in their eighth meeting, in the San Bernadino Handicap.

Colts Classics

Just as Snow Chief continued to dominate in the West, Badger Land, trained by the ever-present D Wayne Lukas, did so in the West. But in the Kentucky Derby (where Clive Brittain's Bold Arrangement put up a brave show for England by finishing second) it was the ageless team of trainer Charlie Whittingham and rider Bill Shoemaker which got the money and the glory with Ferdinand, giving his sire Nijinsky a Derby winner in England and the US in the same season.

Two weeks later, though, it was no contest as Snow Chief easily won the Preakness Stakes from Ferdinand.

The deciding match was not to come in the Belmont Stakes. Snow Chief went to Garden State Park to win the Jersey Derby, while Ferdinand moved on to New York for the last of the Triple Crown events, the Belmont Stakes, which for the fifth time in succession belonged to veteran trainer Woody Stephens. He won with Danzig Connection, also the first Classic success for jockey Chris McCarron.

After three Classics, the three-year-old colts were left without an undisputed leader. To make things worse, Snow Chief later sustained an injury that set him on the sidelines until the last week of the year.

O FERDINAND: Winner of the Kentucky Derby.
Picture: ASSOCIATED PRESS

The situation never improved, though there was brief brilliance from such as Ogygian and Meadowlake, and several major wins for Wise Times and Broad Brush over mediocre opposition.

The truth was that without Snow Chief and Ferdinand, who was also off the track until December, the division achieved little excitement and generated little authority, save for one other, whose performances on grass made him perhaps the best horse in the country. More about Manila later.

Fillies Classics

The three-year-old fillies had considerably more quality than the colts, but they too had their share of bad luck. Undefeated Tiffany Lass and Hidden Light met in the coveted Kentucky Oaks the day before the Derby, and Tiffany Lass barely maintained her status over the Lukas-trained duo Life At The Top and Family Style. Tiffany Lass did not race again during the year.

Hidden Light, winner of the Santa Anita Oaks, went on to add the Hollywood and Del Mar versions, but she too was denied her chance to shine brightest because of injury late in the season.

Team Lukas won several events in the division, which was no surprise, given the strength and depth of his stable, but again this was a category which could never establish a clear leader, despite subsequent wins by Irish-bred Valley Victory, Classy Cathy and others.

The others included a grey filly named Melair, undefeated and with a victory over colts (Snow Chief among them) in the one-mile Silver Screen at Hollywood Park.

Handicaps

The handicap division in the United States simply refers to older horses, not those of lesser ability, and here the New York Racing Association's triple crown of Metropolitan Mile, Suburban and Brooklyn Handicaps is both important and lucrative.

French-raced and American-bred Garthorn, trained by Bobby Frankel, took the Metropolitan, then went back home to California to prepare for the future undefeated on dirt in this country.

Roo Art, a rags to riches colt taken over by Lukas earlier in the year, surprised in the Suburban and later took the Iselin Handicap from Precisionist and Lady's Secret. Little Missouri won the Brooklyn. The names of the winners simply did not match the prestige of the events.

Super Diamond took the West Coast's major summer handicap, the Hollywood Gold Cup, from Alphabatim and Precisionist. Lady's Secret went wire to wire in winning the Whitney against males at Saratoga, then all eyes focussed on the Fall handicap triple crown at Belmont Park — the Marlboro

○ MILLION DOLLAR MARE: Estrapade and Fernando Toro are well clear in the Budweiser-Arlington Million.

Picture: LOU HODGES

Cup, Woodward Stakes and Jockey Club Gold Cup.

Turkoman came back to win the Marlboro, and Precisionist blew his rivals off the track in the Woodward. Then Turkoman let Horse of the Year honours get away in finishing a fast-closing head second to Creme Fraiche in the Jockey Club Gold Cup.

Developments

Among the two-year-olds, unbeaten Polish Navy, Capote, Gulch, Demons Begone and Bet Twice all moved towards a showdown in the Breeders' Cup Juvenile after good seasons to that point. And fillies such as Personal Ensign (unfortunately sidelined with injury just before the Breeders' Cup), Sacahuista, Tappiano and others also showed promise.

Lady's Secret held a hammer over the heads of her rivals in the female handicap division, and the three-year-olds who might try her at Santa Anita were at an equal disadvantage. Groovy was the sprinter to beat; Palace Music would carry America's hopes in the Breeders' Cup Mile, while Manila, the developing three-year-old, and Estrapade, winner of the rich Budweiser-Arlington Million, would do so in the Turf.

Horse of the Year honours would be decided on the track. Turkoman would win it with victory in the Classic; Precisionist could get it from the same race, and Lady's Secret would be heiress apparent if she took the Distaff and the other two flopped.

Breeders' Cup

For better or worse, races on Breeders' Cup day, this time at Santa Anita, have become the definitive events of the American season, though sometimes to the disadvantage of horses who have won earlier important races only to lose out at Breeders' Cup time, and certainly for horses who for one reason or another fail to make the big fields.

But those same Cup races can also point out true champions, and they offer simultaneously a target

○ **MUD IN YOUR EYE: Another easy win for the flying filly Lady's Secret, who lands the Whitney Handicap.**   Picture: BOB COGLIANESE

○ **GHOST FIGURE: Lady's Secret has no challengers in the Maskette Stakes at Belmont Park.**

Picture: BOB COGLIANESE

O FOUR GLORY: Manila strides away to win the Cinema Handicap at Hollywood Park.

and an obstacle for those horses coming from other parts of the world for the glory and the rich rewards. The 1986 Breeders' Cup races fitted that description in every way.

D Wayne Lukas and his partners and clients again used the stage to display and promote their equine products. Their Capote took a championship with victory in the Juvenile, beating all the other outstanding colts who could be assembled, and Lady's Secret solidified her position as one of the best of her sex ever seen on an American track.

Brave Raj dominated the Juvenile Fillies for deserving owner Dolly Green. Smile, second in the Sprint a year before, added to a marvellous season for his owner Frances Genter with a win at most generous odds, and

Skywalker came back from a serious injury in 1985 to continue the string of surprise results in the Classic. That leaves the turf races.

Last Tycoon came almost directly off the plane bringing him from France to spring a 39-1 Pari-Mutuel surprise of enormous proportions in the Mile, having established his reputation in Europe as a sprinter. But the Turf was truly the event of the day.

Dancing Brave, whom so many had talked about as champion of the world, could not cope with a taxing season and an ill-conceived invasion to a distant continent (his land of birth ironically) and had to settle for fourth place.

No-one doubts that the colt was below the form which took him to brilliant victory over one of the finest fields assembled for the Arc de Triomphe a few weeks earlier.

And in the eyes of his loyal supporters it would not have mattered which of the three had beaten him, had it been just one.

All were considered his inferior. Truth is, though, that all three were better prepared on the day. And it could be that the winner, Manila, who touched off Theatrical in the last dash, is in a class with Dancing Brave.

Manila had come from the maiden ranks earlier in the year and developed into America's best grass horse and possibly its best three-year-old or horse of any age. Literal translation of form, especially that against Damister in the Turf Classic, Manila's last race before Santa Anita, was misleading.

On the day Manila overcame his own obstacles, and was manifestly the best.□

● PARADISE LOST: A superb setting but no joy for British runners in the Breeders' Cup Turf race at Santa Anita, California.
   Picture: GEORGE SELWYN

CHAPTER 25

Breeders' Cup

by GEORGE ENNOR

O OFF THE TURN: Skywalker leads the pack as he makes the best of his way home in the Classic, richest race on Breeders' Cup Day at Santa Anita. Picture: ASSOCIATED PRESS

Breeders' Cup

by GEORGE ENNOR

WHEN I WAS at prep school, light years ago, a staple part of my diet seemed to be Frys' Five Boys chocolate. I have vivid memories of the label, which depicted five facial expressions of a typical schoolboy, beginning with misery and ending with delight as a bar of Five Boys was presented to him.

That label in reverse sums up the looks of those who carried such high hopes to California for the third running of the Breeders' Cup races last autumn. As our team gathered at Heathrow at 8.30am (large Bloody Marys for some), the only doubt was by how far Dancing Brave would win.

It is now sad history that Dancing Brave did not win at all, and that the confidence we held for him and Sonic Lady came to nothing. So it was a somewhat chastened party which set off back from Los Angeles, though to say that the defeats ruined our excursion would be a major exaggeration.

The results were a severe disappointment, but the rest of the trip had a lot to recommend it, even if it did involve getting up at 6.30am to phone copy to England because of the eight-hour time difference between California and home.

As far as I was concerned, things had got off to a somewhat tense start, as I emerged from the seemingly endless queue at the immigration counter to discover my luggage was missing.

Controlled panic set in as I reported the loss to British Airways staff. "I expect it's gone on to San Francisco," I was told. "That happens quite often; we'll have it back in a day or two." They were not quite the words I wanted to hear.

Luckily the errant case was found, having been prematurely collected by an airport employee who thought no-one wanted it, but

○ **JOB WELL DONE: Laffit Pincay raises his arm aloft to salute victory on Skywalker in the Breeders' Cup Classic.**
Picture: ASSOCIATED PRESS

by now the coach taking our party to downtown LA had departed, and not until well past halfway did anyone — apart from me — realise that I was not on board.

In fact, getting to the hotel was no problem, but by now I was having the usual difficulty of trying to adapt my body clock to the time in California. At 6pm Los Angeles time, it was 2am on my system.

With remarkable good fortune our trip to Los Angeles coincided with four days when there was no sign of the infamous local smog, and for once the San Gabriel Mountains could be seen as we drove up to the track. This was the day before the big one and all serious training was over.

At a party the previous evening I had spoken to Guy Harwood and learned that he had qualified reservations about Dancing Brave, so I was able to report that Harwood was not as happy with the horse as he would have liked.

Not, mind you, that any of us anticipated defeat, for rating Manila about the same horse as Damister, as we felt fully entitled to do, seemed to suggest the American hope would not be good enough.

Although the temperature had been unbearably high when the English horses first arrived, by the big day it had cooled down to a very pleasant 70 degrees or so, and with the first race due off at 11.15am and huge crowds expected — the gate was some 69,000 — we had to make another early start. Luckily the breakfast restaurant, where the food was good but the service proceeded at a snail-like pace, started operations at 6.30am.

There was no European interest in the opening two-year-old race, but we had arrived to be greeted with the news that Park Express would not be able to take on Lady's Secret in the Distaff. And things were not to improve for her trainer Jim Bolger, as Polonia was always struggling in the Breeders' Cup Juvenile Fillies and she trailed in a never-dangerous ninth

behind the impressive Brave Raj.

Never mind, we thought, we did not really expect too much of Polonia, we still have Sonic Lady and Dancing Brave to come.

It was almost certainly too much to expect that Green Desert and Double Schwartz would be able to handle the dirt and the home-trained speed merchants in the Sprint. They kept in touch with the leaders for about four furlongs, but were hard at work to do so and at the line filled the last two places.

There was a certain amount of grim satisfaction in the result, not so much from the deserved victory of the versatile Smile, but in the defeat of the 2-5 chance Groovy. Maybe a bit carried away, his trainer Jose Martin had dismissed Groovy's rivals with total contempt, saying that his horse was the fastest thing on four legs and nothing would get near him. In the event Groovy did not hit the gate, never got to the front and finished fourth. The jockey was blamed.

Sonic Lady's performance in the Breeders' Cup Mile was to be the first real test of our aspirations, and when she came off the home turn poised to strike, things looked good. But though she got to the front, Sonic Lady could not get away from her rivals, and in the final 100 yards she faded into seventh place behind Last Tycoon, on whom Yves Saint-Martin rode one of the finest races of his career.

As many of us looked at the Tote Board before the race we agreed that 35-1 against Last Tycoon was a remarkable price. If he stayed the trip he would have a major chance. Plenty were prepared to take that chance, but the queues were so long that hardly anyone got on. The only man I know who had real cause to celebrate was John McCririck.

We could claim a very tenuous connection with Last Tycoon as he was trained in Europe, but it was difficult to make out a case for putting him up as a winner for the English team. And it was difficult,

in the post-race Press conference, for the winner's trainer Robert Collet to understand through the interpreter why the official conducting affairs kept asking him about Lashkari and the Aqueduct elephant juice!

The style in which Lady's Secret did what was expected of her in the Breeders' Cup Distaff made it apparent that Park Express would have managed no more than a place behind her, but that would have been a handy £157,343 for second, which must have made the filly's colic and high temperature all the more frustrating.

But now we were going to show them. This was the Breeders' Cup Turf; this was Dancing Brave; those Americans would see a real racehorse.

Stories of how Harwood had come close to pulling out Dancing Brave were well known by now, but he had said that the colt had perked up considerably in the cooler weather, and though no-one in the English party thought he was at his best, we were full of hope.

As he moved up on the heels of the leaders down the back straight those hopes rose steadily higher, although, as we learned later, they were never shared by Pat Eddery. On the home turn they were lost for ever. Dancing Brave, who had cornered so well in training, hung out to his right off the bend. Eddery gave him two cracks and nothing happened. We were left to watch in stunned and gloomy silence as Manila, Damister's Belmont conqueror, got up on the line to beat the ex-Irish Theatrical by a head. It was woe, woe and thrice woe.

Bold Arrangement did nothing to lift the gloom in the Classic, the last of the Breeders' Cup races, and we were left to ponder on things that might have been. With the usual brilliance of post-race knowledge we can point to matters which should, perhaps, have been handled differently, and it is of undoubted significance that Robert Collet chose to take over Last

Tycoon at the latest possible moment.

It is sometimes so easy to forget how vast a country the United States is. To point out that Pebbles survived the transatlantic trip and won in Aqueduct in 1985 is no criterion. New York is not much more than halfway between London and California, and there is a huge difference between the temperature there and in Los Angeles in November.

It seems that those aiming at subsequent Breeders' Cup days, especially if the races stay on the West coast, may have to make much longer-range plans and either take the horses out there much earlier or follow the apparently successful Collet policy of avoiding jet lag by arriving as late as is practicable.□

○ ROUND THE BEND: Lady's Secret, who made all the running in the Distaff, leads into the Santa Anita straight. Picture: GEORGE SELWYN

O **DOWN IN THE JUNGLE: Punters have to face rumour, gossip, opinion and bravado in the racecourse betting market.**
Pictures: GEORGE HERRINGSHAW/GEORGE SELWYN

Odds and Ends

by JOHN McCRIRICK

WHERE DOES "double carpet" go alongside "up the arm" with "the thumb"? Only in the jungle that is the racecourse betting ring, unique for its intensity, action and unpredictable drama.

An incestuous stock exchange, where rumour, gossip, opinion and bravado are precursors of those mercurial twin gods, success and failure.

Less than five per cent of the £3,000m horse-race betting turnover finds its way on to the course, yet this fallible microcosm is used to decide those all-important starting prices on which the fate of millions of pounds rests.

Is it fair? Does the ring, with all its quirks and possibilities of manipulation, accurately reflect the huge sums wagered in Britain's 10,000-plus betting shops? It isn't, and it doesn't. Nor would any other method, short of a Tote monopoly, with every bet going into a centralised pool.

The sole justification for upholding the system over all others is that it is a free market. Anyone can participate.

So don't complain when Ladbrokes, the "magic sign", or other betting-shop chains get their teeth into a beast you have backed

and shorten its price. That is what can happen in a free market. Whether you of approve how an individual or firm conducts its business is immaterial.

In a discussion paper issued more than three years ago, Tom Kelly, director general of the Betting Office Licensees Association, which represents mainly the Big Four bookmaking companies and their near-4,000 shops, handling 60 per cent of turnover, laid out a scheme whereby starting prices could be computed from a handful of shops. A method similar to calculating the Top Twenty records, with sample offices being used, was suggested.

Off-course bookmakers would love the implementation of computerised SPs, but the public outcry at the time ensured the idea was stillborn.

But the nightmare could happen. Many fear that this year, with bookmakers having a major stake in the transmission of live racing by satellite television into betting shops for the first time, and without the middle men of Exchange Telegraph to hold the line independently, the end of racecourse SP is only a matter of time. It is a facile view, though

popular. Having been the only journalist to forecast Extel's doom in the battle for satellite rights, I go for the double. I maintain that the present system will remain sacrosanct, as promised by the Big Four and others.

They are men of their word, and when SPs are still being garnered from racecourses into the next century, long after we have passed on, perhaps belated apologies will be forthcoming!

So let's look at how the market operates and examine why bookmakers who send money to the course to influence (a code word for shrivel up) prices have no right to complain when an SP turns out to be, in their subjective post-race view, "too big".

Shortening up horses — often others lengthen as a result — and the "knock-out", when the "bogey" (biggest loser) is pushed out by one or two layers already "on" at SP and then obliges, are part of the jungle skirmishing.

So what kind of characters make up today's ever-fluid betting market?

Wealthy layers stand up alongside those barely able to scrape together the day's exes — it can cost around £200 for a firm to set up and that takes some getting back before any thoughts of profit. The cautious and the foolhardy; the opinionated and the timid; those for whom every race seems to be a "disaster", and others with a seemingly uncanny knack of getting it right.

Competitive markets, with plenty of money circulating, are rare, so weak markets make for a major single problem.

At the Cheltenham Festival in March and Royal Ascot in June, bookmaking — literally "making a book" — is possible. Bets come in for almost every horse on the card, and the "play-the-game" bookie can practise his ancient craft.

"Play the game" ideally means having the favourite a loser, the second best a small loser, the third best a commensurately small winner, and the rest securing bigger sums.

Very occasionally, especially if the layer "cops a thick-un" (lays a big bet) about the "splonk" (favourite) early on, at say "wrist" (5-4) and it drifts out to "bottle" (2-1), he could be in dreamland. Either he could "hedge" (lay off) part of the bet at the new price, or he could end up with every horse in the race a winner.

More often, though, as they will pitifully explain, when the "jolly" (another slang term for the favourite) slides, the thick-un comes in for a "Burlington Bertie" (100-30) chance who suddenly contracts to "shoulder" (7-4). So, without a farthing for the original favourite, the book is in deep trouble.

Does the bookmaker hedge at the shorter price, take a chance that it will be beaten, or fire away with the rest at over the odds, often to try to get some balance in the book?

At an average meeting, notably midweek, there is not enough money around to "play the game", and £1,000 or so sent down from an office for a horse can radically alter its price. Here the punters' pal is the inveterate favourite layer.

When it boils down to a contest between the layer keen on "getting" (taking money on) a horse, and the office agents trying to "shut him up" (ensure the price is taken and the books are 'full up' or overloaded), the result is usually one way. Off-course conglomerates, being multi-national corporations, have the resources.

By the way, I am not being sexist when referring to racecourse bookmakers as male. Looking at some of them, you might doubt it — sorry fellas! — but female bookies, with their own pitches, are an extremely rare species. There is no denying that the almost exclusive male domination needs to be broken. So, girls, how about it?

But, back to our free-market thinking, compulsion can have no place. Very often the four-figure sums bandied about are not from punters, but bookmaker to bookmaker. Many of them are little different to backers, betting on horses, using their own judgement rather than attempting to make a book. It truly does take all sorts to make up that free market.

But for the average layer it is important to take bets at the shortest possible price, where he can get the value. An easy example, a three-horse race, explains the thinking.

If the prices offered are evens, 2-1 and 5-1, that means, forgetting the four per cent on-course tax, a punter could support each of the trio to return £100 without losing. The stakes are an even £50, £33.33 at 2-1 and £16.67 at 5-1.

To avoid being the stakeholder like that, bookies try to give themselves a percentage profit margin such as that offered by 10-11, 7-4 and 9-2, which equals 6.8 per cent in favour of the books.

At times, far too often, the margin is grotesquely unfair to punters. That is the time to keep out. But if, by shopping around, a punter can get 6-5, 9-4 and 11-2 (91.7 per cent), that is the moment to

start investing. It does not happen often!

More likely our evens chance was backed down from 6-4, while hardly anything came in for the other original "ear'ole" (6-4) horse, with support perhaps for the outsider of three, that old system so commented upon when it comes up.

So though the figures might read at our original evens, 2-1 and 5-1, in fact the prices laid have been 6-4 downwards, 2-1 (at last punters stepped in) and 6-1.

Value, as to the merits of horses and prices, means so much. Almost invariably in betting shops the figures favour the books, but on racecourses this is not always the case.

Crucial to layers is the "tissue", a betting forecast compiled privately in the morning. This allows for the likely popularity of various runners, early moves in the London offices, and the intuition of the shrewd compilers.

One main purpose of the tissue is to prevent the purchaser, the vulnerable chap on the stool beside his "joint" (board), from "falling". No, not off his stool or more likely beer crate, but laying a far bigger price than necessary.

Pitted against him are the "faces", those who reckon they are "in the know". Scouting around, waiting to pounce on any perceived "rick" (mistake), these characters, watched closely by workmen from several firms, step in early and their activity can set the market alight.

So can gossip, rumour, slander, innuendo — all freely available in the racecourse hothouse.

If you were told, conspiratorially, more than once that "the jolly's not off, he's done a leg, they don't really want to run him but the owner insists", would you go ahead and have your maximum on him?

Maybe yes; maybe no. Well, get out of that ill-informed, claustrophobic betting shop and join the free market. You'll soon find the answer!□

● **CENTRE OF ATTRACTION:**
The Park Paddocks sale ring at
Newmarket, where Tattersalls
stage many of the world's
finest bloodstock auctions.
     Picture: GERRY CRANHAM

CHAPTER 27

Sales

by TONY MORRIS

○ STANDING PROUD: The colt by Northern Dancer out of South Ocean made top price of $3.6m at the Keeneland July Select Sales to Darley Stud Management.
Picture: BILL STRAUS

Sales

by TONY MORRIS

NEARLY ALL the most conspicuous features on the 1986 domestic yearling sales scene were those generally associated with strong, healthy trade. For a start, there were plenty of buyers.

Certainly they were harder to please than in some years, but they could hardly be blamed for wanting correct conformation; in any case, breeders had long since recognized that demand and had been trying to meet it.

There was also plenty of money. It was not tossed into the market like so much confetti, as it had been when the irrational bidding duel featured so prominently in

1983 and 1984; but everybody knew that those days had gone, if not for good, at least for the time being.

In 1986 buyers behaved much as in 1985. While they could not be induced to go mad, they could always be depended upon to pay realistic sums for yearlings realistic in terms of earnings potential, eventual re-sale prospects and/or ultimate value for breeding purposes.

But the abundance of buyers and money could not obscure one basic fact which cast a pall over the proceedings throughout the season. Producers had spent too much on their products.

More than half the yearlings sent to market by their breeders failed to return the outlay on them. More than half those put back in the market by investors who had bought them as foals also realized losses.

Here was the absurd anomaly of 1986. The horses fetched good prices, yet those who sold them were, more often than not, out of pocket.

It was by no means the first time that the industry had failed to get its sums right, but it was the first time in a dozen years that the miscalculations had caused such dire distress. Yet the worst of this latest disaster for breeders could so easily have been averted.

When the top came off the yearling market in 1985, it was obviously no aberration. The time had arrived for a downward adjustment of stud fees in line with the established lower value of the product. But that did not happen. The stallion studs held fees for 1986 at 1985 levels, and in all areas of the market breeders found themselves forced to invest amounts that were illogical in terms of the value of the last yearling crop and could not square with the likely value of the next.

When, as was wholly predictable, the '86 yearling market broadly accentuated the trends set in '85, breeders found themselves in a grim situation. The loss on this year's account was bad enough, but their investments were already

made in the yearlings of 1987 and 1988 - both crops assuredly conceived at prices which made them odds against to recover their production costs.

Remarkably, stallion masters seemed reluctant to learn the lesson of the season's yearling trade when it came to setting the fees for 1987. A number of horses, particularly some of those at the top of the market who had previously been wildly over-priced, did have their fees reduced. But many did not come down far enough and many more were left, nominally at least, at patently uncommercial prices.

The omens for domestic yearling trade in 1986 were far from propitious, as values had dropped appreciably at all the major North American auctions, even for the top-quality product. Yet here there

was never a hint of panic. The season approached with breeders resigned to the prospects of a buyers' market and poor returns, but none the less confident that the market slump would not be one of anything like North American proportions.

Confirmation of that view came immediately, when Doncaster's St Leger Sale was even able to show gains in one or two respects.

The average was up by almost eight per cent at 7,751gns; the median was the second best-ever at 5,600gns, and as 84.1 per cent of the lots offered changed hands, both sides of the market clearly displayed a positive attitude towards trading.

But there were other ways of assessing the Doncaster performance. It obviously was not very satisfactory that the most

○ WORLD'S STAGE: Keeneland Sales in July and all eyes are on the best international bloodstock.

Picture: BILL STRAUS

expensively produced crop ever sold there should realize only the fourth-highest average on record. And it was reasonable to suppose that cosmetic changes to the catalogue, notably the abolition of the select session and an overall reduction in size, were made specifically to boost the average.

Top price of the sale was only 45,000gns, for a bay son of Rusticaro out of Coumfea, bought by Andy Smith to race from John Sutcliffe's stable. Yet as long ago as 1981 we had a six-figure lot in the St Leger catalogue, and the individual record of 140,000gns has stood since 1983.

Another sale with a long-standing individual record is Ballsbridge, and this year's top bid of IR32,000gns there went little more than halfway towards it.

Tattersalls (Ireland) were able to report an upturn in the average, by seven per cent, and there was general satisfaction over the first seven-figure turnover, which increased by some 33 per cent. However, there was a degree of inevitability about the improvement in the aggregate, which resulted from an almost exactly identical growth in numbers offered. The advance in the average was insufficient to lift it above the level reached way back in 1979.

The sale has owned a credibility problem, in terms of the quality of its catalogue, for too long; perhaps we must wait for a change in that situation until 1988, when Tattersalls launch a direct challenge to Goffs in the Irish market by moving to new premises at Fairyhouse.

Tattersalls were able to look back on both their 1986 major English yearling sales with some satisfaction. They pruned the prestige Highflyer catalogue with a view to protecting the average, and produced the desired result - an insignificant drop of two per cent.

In effect, the Highflyer trading was much the same as in 1985, downturns in the select session average (by seven per cent) and in

the overall median (from 48,000gns to 41,000gns) being all but offset by stronger demand through the three non-select days. Almost 87 per cent of the lots offered changed hands, a significantly higher ratio than in the previous year.

Inevitably, the relative success of the sale owed much to the Maktoum family, whose expenditure amounted to more than 33 per cent of the week's takings (26,694,600gns). Their acquisitions included 26 of the 87 sold in the select session and were headed, uniquely in Highflyer history, by a colt who did not even turn up at Park Paddocks. That was a Nureyev colt out of the Athasi Stakes heroine Etoile de Paris, who developed lameness on a splint a week before the sale and could not be sent from Yeomanstown Lodge Stud in Ireland.

However, he did come under the scrutiny of Sheikh Mohammed's scouts at his home base, and when they were convinced of the temporary nature of the colt's problem, he was acquired privately for 600,000gns. Under Tattersalls' conditions of sale, commission was payable to them, so he was duly recorded as the top-priced lot of the week.

The highest-priced transaction conducted in the ring was one of 560,000gns, for a bay filly by Mill Reef out of Elegant Tern. This was another notable event, as it marked a return to sales prominence of Lady Beaverbrook, who in the late sixties and early seventies had been the most powerful force in the marketplace. Her victory over the Susan Piggott Agency was greeted with a spontaneous burst of applause - a mark of the affection in which she is held, and of the industry's gratitude for her staunch support over many years.

Between the two Newmarket auctions, Goffs held a "curate's egg" of a sale at Kill, where the last three days went some way towards retrieving a situation that appeared lost on the opening

Invitational night. In the words of Goffs' Managing Director Jonathan Irwin, the "select" portion of the catalogue was "a bloodbath". The selection did not appeal to buyers generally; the lack of even one star colt was a tremendous handicap; and one or two of the most apparently notable "transactions" stretched credulity. It came as no surprise to learn that there would be no Select Sale in 1987.

The Kill market was always going to be down after that disastrous beginning, but trade rallied exceptionally well over the following two days of the Premier Sale, in which the average rose by 11.5 per cent. That meant the overall average slipped back only as far as IR25,172gns, less than in each of the three previous years (and well under 1984's record IR37,445gns), but not catastrophically so.

In some respects Tattersalls' October Open Sales, last in the series of major yearling auctions, must be counted the best. The average was down, but by a mere 1.6 per cent, and that in the largest-ever October catalogue. Demand was strong throughout the week, with an amazing 86.2 per cent of the 952 yearlings offered changing hands - the highest sold/offered ratio in October since 1963.

Inevitably, there was a shortage of high-class individuals, but we did get a record-priced lot in the 220,000gns Mill Reef colt out of Calandra, and there was satisfaction to be gained in the rise of the median from 9,000gns to 10,000gns.

The October Open is the sale which involves the broadest cross-section of the industry, on both sides of the market, and in a sense it typified the state of business throughout 1986. Keen demand from buyers and a strong desire to trade from buyers and sellers alike — they were the most obvious characteristics of the trade. And had it not been for those excessive production costs, there would have been cause for celebration all round. □

**O JOEL JEWEL: Fairy Footsteps makes top price of 720,000gns in the dispersal of Jim Joel's broodmares at Tattersalls'
December Sales, Newmarket.**
Picture: JOHN CROFTS

O SHOW STOPPER: David Pym conducts the business from the auctioneer's rostrum at Tattersalls in Newmarket Pictures: ALAN JOHNSON

● TRAGIC HEROINE: The Cheltenham crowd acclaim Dawn Run's Gold Cup triumph, but two months later she died in action.
Picture: SPORTING PICTURES (UK)

CHAPTER 28

Dawn Run

by JOHN OAKSEY

○ **GOING DOWN: Dawn Run and Jonjo O'Neill take a tumble in the Whitbread Gold Label Chase at Liverpool.**
Picture: ALAN JOHNSON

Dawn Run

by JOHN OAKSEY

THEY DON'T COUNT decibels at Cheltenham and there is no reliable way of comparing the enthusiasm of different groups of human beings. But in the 30 years I have been watching racing, no combination of horse and rider has had a more dramatic effect on a racecourse than Dawn Run and Jonjo O'Neill at Cheltenham in the 1986 Gold Cup.

What's more, this was the second time they had taken Cheltenham by storm. Maybe Dawn Run's welcome after winning the Champion Hurdle two years earlier depended more solidly on the "Irish roar", but both halves of her unique double resulted in unforgettable scenes.

Of course, not all the cheers were for Dawn Run alone. It helped that she happened to be ridden by the most universally loved and respected Irish jump jockey there has been, and that she was in the care of a popular and skilful trainer (Paddy Mullins) and owned by a woman (Charmian Hill) almost as remarkable and every bit as stubborn as the mare herself.

The 1986 Gold Cup seemed to be the perfect climax to a fairytale, made all the more magical by its extraordinary cast. How could we guess that it was to be the penultimate act of a tragedy, that less than three months later the star herself would be dead and her principle male supporter fighting the threat of cancer?

One of the many reasons why we loved Dawn Run was her unpredictable tendency to take unnecessary chances. She never shared Arkle's infallibilty, any more than she showed his unique margin of superiority. Even over hurdles she made you gulp, and blunders caused her only "failures" over fences.

It seems incredible that Dawn Run was only eight years old and running only her fifth steeplechase when she and Jonjo made history at Cheltenham. Was it really just three years since she served notice of her future intentions at Liverpool, trotting up in a handicap one day and coming back to run the Champion Hurdler Gaye Brief to a dwindling, hard-fought length the next?

That was in April 1983, nine months after the stewards of the Irish Turf Club had the temerity to tell Mrs Hill that her permit to ride as an amateur was not being renewed. Although I don't think they said so, their decision was doubtless not unconnected with the fact that three years earlier, when she was just over 60, Mrs Hill was carried off Thurles racecourse with a broken neck, several broken ribs and severely damaged kidneys.

It was, coincidentally, at much the same time that Jonjo O'Neill smashed his leg in the fall which so nearly ended his riding career. Mrs Hill had already won a steeplechase on the horse responsible, Yes Man, to become the first woman in Irish racing history to ride a winner on the Flat, over hurdles and over fences. She had also been the first to ride against men in Ireland, and her eight-year career under Rules followed 14 riding sucessfully in Ladies point-to-points!

Six months and several hospitals after that dreadful fall, Mrs Hill insisted on riding again, weighing six stone instead of her usual eight. She won a bumpers race within a year!

In November 1981 she and her son Oliver bought a three-year-old Deep Run filly for 5,800gns. Mrs Hill's daughter was preparing for a marathon at the time, and it was from her early morning training that Dawn Run got her name.

Although warned that the filly was only barely broken, Mrs Hill typically got on her back after only a week of lungeing!

I remember meeting Mrs Hill in London in October last year and rather foolishly asked if she was still riding. For answer she pointed

O ALL SMILES: Owner Charmian Hill after Cheltenham victory.
Picture: PRESS ASSOCIATION

○ GOING FOR GOLD: Wayward Lad leads over the last fence in the Cheltenham Gold Cup from Forgive'N Forget (left), with Dawn Run poised to challenge.
Picture: SPORTING PICTURES (UK)

to a four-inch scar running perpendicularly down her 67-year-old forehead. "Backing a three-year-old last week," she explained. "Stupid thing threw its head up and hit me in the face."

There was no behaviour of that sort from Dawn Run. "I just sat on her back and rode away," she said. "If she saw anything she didn't like, she would just stand still until I said 'Go on'. She was lovely to ride."

The morning she received the Irish Turf Club letter, Mrs Hill, whose permit still had eight days to run, was getting ready to ride Dawn Run in her third race, a two-mile bumper at Tralee. The Castlemaine INH Flat Race was the last on an evening card, and no

doubt inspired by her owner-rider's indignation flowing down the reins, Dawn Run led very nearly throughout. It was the first of 21 victories, three on the Flat, 13 over hurdles and five over fences. She ran 35 times, fell twice, unseated her rider once, and only three times finished out of the first three.

To the end of Dawn Run's life, Mrs Hill rode her regularly at Mullins' Kilkenny farm. The great mare sometimes looked to uninformed observers to be going plenty fast enough, but her trainer's reaction was always philosophical. "Well, they both enjoy themselves, you see," he would say quietly.

Nevertheless, despite that timely

victory at Tralee, the Turf Board Stewards stuck to their guns. So Dawn Run had the first of several jockey changes and Tom Mullins, youngest of Paddys four sons, rode her for the next two races. She won both, the second against some quite good Flat horses. So Tom has the happy and unique distinction of never having been beaten on Dawn Run.

Every member of the Mullins family has ridden at least one winner — Paddy, his wife Maureen, their daughter Sandra and all four sons. But only Tony is light enough to be a professional and although another stable jockey Peter Kavanagh rode Dawn Run in her first hurdle race, Tony took over in the next five, winning three, including the valuable Findus Beefburger Hurdle at Leopardstown.

That was easily the best race the mare had contested so far and it was also the first of seven times she met the admirable Buck House, winner in 1986 of the Queen Mother Champion Chase. Poor Buck House never managed to beat Dawn Run, not even in their final controversial two-mile match at Punchestown, the last race his old friend and rival was to win.

Of course I don't know that they were friends. We can't hear horses talk and don't really know how they communicate. But in human terms, it would be safe to say that between these two there must at least have been enormous mutual respect.

Buck House's luck was to run out in an even sadder though less dramatic way than Dawn Run's. A fatal attack of colic on his summer holiday struck him, and she did not long survive him.

It was the mare's first visit to Cheltenham, for the Sun Alliance, which began the controversy, destined to last until her death, about who should ride her in the most important races outside Ireland. Ron Barry, who always thought he would have won if he had known Dawn Run a little better, was, quite reasonably, preferred to the inexperienced Tony Mullins at Cheltenham, but Tony was back for those two significant races at Liverpool and he rode the mare when she rounded off a triumphant first season by winning the BMW Champion Novice Hurdle at Punchestown. It was just 11 months since Mrs Hill had ridden her for the first time at Clonmel, and she won eight races and £35,942.

Now, with the Champion Hurdle on the horizon, the jockey argument became even more heated. After a warm-up on the Flat, Mullins won on Dawn Run at Down Royal but again she jumped the last fence badly and Mrs Hill made up her mind.

O TONY MULLINS: Not always in favour.　　　　Picture: SPORTSFILE

Jonjo O'Neill was engaged to ride at Ascot and so began the triumphant five-race partnership which gave them the Irish and English Champion Hurdles and reached that unforgettable climax with Mrs Hill carried shoulder high around the Cheltenham winner's enclosure.

Happy as Irishmen were that day, some still thought Dawn Run went better when "given her own way" on a loose rein by Tony Mullins, and with Jonjo injured, that theory seemed to be reinforced when the mare ran away with the Sandeman Hurdle on Grand National day. Buck House, who had looked such a danger two from home at Cheltenham, was left trailing this time, and so was the Champion Hurdle second, Cima.

So Tony kept the job that summer when Dawn Run went to France for the Grande Course de Haies (French Champion Hurdle) at Auteuil, a race no English or Irish horse had won. Despite hard ground and a colourful rumour that the devious French intended to "murder" her on one of the early bends, she was magnificent, never letting anything near enough to feel her slipstream, let alone do her any harm.

The next argument was whether she would start steeplechasing or stick to hurdles. Mrs Hill won that

too, and after a well-deserved holiday, Dawn Run began her new career in the Nobber Chase at Navan. It was what the Irish call a "grand soft day", and a damp but happy crowd were even happier when their herione completed a dazzling clear round. She stood back and flew some of the fences but reassuringly "fiddled" a couple too, as though she had been chasing all her life.

Inevitably Buck House was there, but hard though he tried to bustle her into a mistake it never looked like working.

"Now bring us back the Gold Cup," they shouted. But a strained ligament kept Dawn Run off the course for the rest of the season. In any case she would have stayed in novice chases.

A summer's rest put the leg right and Dawn Run won her next two steeplechases impressively, beating more-experienced horses in the process. Tony Mullins, at that stage unbeaten on the mare in three attempts over fences, seemed to have won back the ride for good. But Dawn Run's last season was marred by three serious jumping miscalculations.

The third, at Auteuil, broke her neck and caused her death, and the first, at Cheltenham irreparably damaged Tony's claim to a place on her back. The second, incidentally, showed that even Jonjo O'Neill's skill was not proof against her wayward carelessness, but that, the first fall of her career, came at Liverpool and after the Gold Cup.

None of these blunders was caused by pressure or fatigue. At Cheltenham, asked to stand back a long way even by her standards, Dawn Run simply took one stride too many, and at Liverpool she ignored the first fence completely.

One of the things which makes her Gold Cup win such a miracle is that it came in the middle of this disastrous series. That day, under extreme pressure for most of the last half mile of a race run in a record time which exhausted all the best male chasers, Dawn Run

○ **JUST CHAMPION: The mare who made history.** Picture: STEWART KENDALL

made only insignificant mistakes. The truth is that she thrived on pressure; it always brought out the best in her.

But after Dawn Run had unseated Tony Mullins at Cheltenham, circumstances, including the weather, conspired to put most of the pressure on her connections. It was above all an impossibly difficult position for Tony's father Paddy, who loathes publicity at the best of times and now, training a virtual novice for the Gold Cup in foul weather (there was no racing in England for most of February and precious little in Ireland), the last thing he needed was the Press hanging round asking awkward questions.

Nor, even after he had been asked to ride Dawn Run in her hoped-for warm-up race at Punchestown, was the situation all that pleasant for Jonjo O'Neill. For example, his first attempt at getting Dawn Run over a steeplechase fence was an embarrassing disaster. No-one will know exactly why Jonjo was asked to school Dawn Run on her own at Gowran Park, but the mare herself, rested since the Cheltenham debacle, clearly did not think much of it.

"She very nearly stopped with me and scarcely jumped one fence properly," Jonjo recalls. He thinks it is a blessing now that the Punchestown race was called off, but although Dawn Run jumped better, with company, in their second racecourse school together, it was hardly the perfect preparation for a battle against seasoned jumpers such as Run and Skip, Forgive'N Forget and Wayward Lad.

Wise-after-the-event critics of the decision to send Dawn Run to France should remember how much greater a risk, on the face of it, running in the Gold Cup involved. If you don't start, you can't win, and at Cheltenham daring was magnificently rewarded.

I shall always believe that tackling the last two fences in the Gold Cup were the bravest thing Dawn Run ever did. Jonjo says that she was always off the bridle after dropping her hind legs in the water. "She had to be great at the second-last," he says, "and then Forgive 'N' Forget and Wayward Lad came past us as though we were standing still. I couldn't believe my eyes."

But Jonjo knows the Cheltenham hill and he knew what a gallop it had been. "Watching her ears, one forward, one back, coming down the hill, I thought, 'come on old girl, you've a bit more in the tank than you're letting on.' She did the last on her own, I didn't dare ask her, but Wayward Lad landed running and got away."

If the last two fences were Dawn Run's finest hour, the run-in was assuredly Jonjo O'Neill's. The ride he gave her was a magical mixture of mind-reading, sympathy and determination. He knew from experience that Dawn Run liked time to get going. "Don't forget she really was a big mare," he says. "If you asked her too quickly, she'd tell you to get stuffed." But just think of the nerve it needed to sit still at that moment.

One danger, until then apparently the biggest, disappeared when Forgive'N Forget hit the last, and then, after going clear, Wayward Lad began to hang left. "I let her come across behind him," Jonjo says, "and when she saw he was weakening, that was it."

You can call it fanciful to suppose that horses know, or care, how their opponents are feeling. But Jonjo believes that Dawn Run knew at Cheltenham, and so do I.

"She had so much character that you could never be sure what she would do next," he says. "But when she made up her mind, either way, all you could do was watch. You might help a bit if she let you, but it was always her decision".

To say that Jonjo "helped a bit" is the understatement of the age, but between them they did it and no-one lucky enough to witness the 1986 Gold Cup will forget the sight of Jonjo riding back, arm aloft in delighted triumph.

Characteristically though, he took special pains to share the credit with Tony Mullins; Dawn Run's career had indeed been a shared achievement. Owner, trainer and jockeys all played a part, but in the end, as Jonjo says, it was "the mare's decision".

No-one can be certain how long she would have cared to defend her crown and now, alas, we shall never know. All you can say for sure is that Dawn Run gave the human race far more, in terms of pleasure and excitement, than we could ever give her in return.

It must be a million to one against a mare emulating her unique Gold Cup-Champion Hurdle double, and only two horses have even come near it. We can thank our stars that we were around to see her, and pray that Jonjo, her greatest accomplice, not only wins his personal battle but one day finds something nearly as good as Dawn Run to train. □

O WE'VE DONE IT: Jonjo O'Neill salutes Gold Cup victory.

Picture: ALAN JOHNSON

● STREAMING OVER: The field for the 1986 Seagram Grand National takes the third fence, with the winner West Tip in the air.
Picture: GEORGE SELWYN

● STREAMING OVER: The field for the 1986 Seagram Grand National takes the third fence, with the winner West Tip in the air.
Picture: GEORGE SELWYN

CHAPTER 29

National Hunt

by NEIL MORRICE

O NO GOING BACK: Mark Dwyer looks for dangers but Galway Blaze has the Hennessy Cognac Gold Cup sewn up at the last fence.
Picture: ALAN JOHNSON

National Hunt

by NEIL MORRICE

LIKE A HITCHCOCK MOVIE, the 1985-86 National Hunt season maintained its suspense until the final curtain. It ebbed and flowed with triumph and tragedy from the beginning of August until the end of May.

We hailed Dawn Run as the first horse to pull off the Champion Hurdle-Cheltenham Gold Cup double, only to hear the news in midsummer that she had been killed in the cauldron heat of Auteuil.

Jockey Richard Linley hardly had time to let Half Free's second Mackeson Gold Cup success sink in before his wife Beverley was killed and he himself badly injured in a road accident on the way home from Wincanton races.

The shortcomings of the Market Rasen Stewards were exposed one cold Friday in November eight days later when Galway Blaze, who trailed at the Lincolnshire track, treated his rivals in the Hennessy Cognac Gold Cup almost with disdain.

Jimmy FitzGerald's gelding finished a remote third behind Planetman and The Last Prince on his seasonal reappearance at Market Rasen. Beaten a total of 24 lengths, he earned the comment in racing's official form book: "Bit backward: held up: steadied and lost touch 13th: headway from three out: never nearer."

At Newbury he left the form well behind and romped to the easiest Hennessy success since the great Arkle 20 years earlier. Mark Dwyer produced him full of running to take over at the second-last fence, and they raced clear of Run and Skip to win by 12 lengths.

There was an argument for saying the damage was done not at Newbury, but at Market Rasen, where it seemed that a case of schooling in public was allowed to pass without comment, only to be made to look worse by the manner of the Hennessy triumph.

Burrough Hill Lad, the Gold Cup winner of 1984, made his comeback in Chepstow's Rehearsal Chase at the end of November. He won the race, but that is all. He emerged from gathering mist in front at the final fence, but had to be ridden right out to hold West Tip, whose own slice of glory comes later.

Tragedy was again lurking around the corner. Only a week later, Oliver Sherwood lost The Breener, an oustanding prospect and normally a safe jumper, in a fall at Cheltenham. The race went to Von Trappe, who failed to complete in three of his seven chases.

David Elsworth's training skills were amply demonstrated for the second year running by the exploits of Combs Ditch, who was

O WAITING GAME: Winner Combs Ditch trails Door Latch and Forgive'N Forget (right) in Haydock's Peter Marsh Chase. Picture: ALAN JOHNSON

O KEMPTON KING 1985: Wayward Lad comes back to form to beat Combs Ditch (left) for his third King George VI Chase success. Picture: ALAN JOHNSON

○ **SKIN DEEP: Not a good jump but Very Promising has the measure of the previous year's winner Half Free in the 1986 Mackeson Gold Cup at Cheltenham.**
Picture: GERRY CRANHAM

produced in tip-top condition to win Cheltenham's Still Fork Trucks Gold Cup on his first outing of the season. Twelve months earlier, Combs Ditch had defied an absence from the racecourse of 20 months to win a handicap hurdle at the Cotswold track.

Combs Ditch went to Kempton Park on Boxing Day as one of the favourites for the King George VI Chase, but it was the North's Wayward Lad who had the last laugh. Starting at what quickly became apparent was a generous 12-1, after a surprise defeat by Earls Brig at Haydock Park, Wayward Lad made history by becoming the first horse to win the

King George three times. In a driving finish, he held the customary late challenge of Combs Ditch by a neck, with Burrough Hill Lad a further 16 lengths adrift in fourth.

Not for the first time, Burrough Hill Lad's jockey Phil Tuck was replaced at the owner's insistence, and Peter Scudamore, who had not ridden Burrough Hill Lad over fences, took over to win Sandown Park's Gainsborough Chase five weeks later.

Before leaving the Christmas period behind, a word about rising star Richard Dunwoody. The Ulsterman stole the show on the second day of the Kempton meeting, completing a four-timer

on Roadster, Von Trappe, Tugboat and Sylvan Joker and finishing second and third on his two other rides.

David Nicholson, who started the season with a flourish, turned to his stable star Very Promising to lift him from a spell in the doldrums by winning Ascot's Embassy Premier Chase Final in January. But the eight-year-old had to be given a very hard race by Scudamore to resist Mr Moonraker's late rally by a short head.

A 30-length annihilation of 17 selling chasers by Silver Ace at Wincanton on 24 January was the beginning of a success story which typifies the skills of West country trainer Martin Pipe. His Midas touch enabled Silver Ace to complete a nap-hand at Market Rasen, Plumpton, Sandown and Devon and Exeter, the last-named in a valuable handicap.

On each occasion Silver Ace made the running, and apart from squeezing home at Sandown, he came home unchallenged. He was in front and moving like a winner when falling on his final outing at Wincanton.

Silver Ace was not the only rags to riches story to emerge from the Pipe stable (Redgrave Artist won five on the trot after being bought out of a Worcester seller for a mere 1,000gns), but the trainer's outstanding ability to make something out of nothing was never better illustrated than through the seven-year-old.

February brought the delayed returns at Sandown of Champion hurdler See You Then and Burrough Hill Lad.

'See You When?' had been the slogan bandied about Lambourn before Nick Henderson produced his champion looking big and well for the Oteley Hurdle. The six-year-old was ominously easy in the market, drifting from 6-4 to 3-1, but he made mincemeat of his eight rivals, needing only to be pushed out after the final flight to beat Sabin du Loir by two and a half lengths.

Burrough Hill Lad's army of followers were treated to a similarly fluent display when the ten-year-old clicked for Scudamore and they romped home ten lengths clear of Rainbow Warrior in the Gainsborough Chase.

The following week was hardly out when the freeze set in. A total of 59 meetings were lost in the next month, and when racing resumed at Catterick Bridge on 5 March, the Cheltenham Festival was less than a fortnight away, and trainers were fighting against the odds to get their stars fit for the big occasion.

Sandown, so often the scene of memorable finishes and fine achievements, gave us something to savour three days before the

○ **OVER AND OUT: The field jumps Becher's on the first circuit in the Seagram Grand National.**

Picture: GERRY CRANHAM

Festival, and William Hill Imperial Cup day will go down as one the Queen Mother will never forget. Jumping's most popular owner was on hand to see her horses Special Cargo, Insular and The Argonaut complete a memorable treble.

Veteran Special Cargo set the ball rolling by getting up to beat Prydel a neck in the Horse & Hound Military Gold Cup, after a leather had broken four fences from home. More drama was to come in the Imperial Cup, where Insular flattened the last two obstacles before resisting the renewed challenge of Hypnosis by threequarters of a length. And novice chaser The Argonaut set the seal on a glorious afternoon by winning the Dick McCreery Cup.

Despite the fears expressed during the freeze-up, Cheltenham dawned as bright as ever, and on Tote Gold Cup day we were treated to one of the greatest steeplechases ever witnessed at the Prestbury Park course.

Dawn Run and Jonjo O'Neill, winners of the Champion Hurdle two years earlier, pulled the race that mattered out of the fire when all had seemed lost before the last fence. Rallying the great mare at the obstacle, O'Neill inspired a terrific leap which put her in with a chance of catching Wayward Lad and Forgive'N Forget.

Dawn Run refused to let the opportunity slip away, and she wore down Wayward Lad 50 yards from the post to win an unforgettable race by a length.

The cheers which echoed across the Cotswolds had not been heard since the halcyon days of Arkle, and the scenes of delight and emotion in the unsaddling enclosure will long be remembered by those who were privileged to be there.

On the first day of the Festival See You Then won the Champion Hurdle for the second year running, when beating former champion Gaye Brief by seven lengths. Nick Henderson deservedly received the plaudits

for this success, as See You Then is not an easy horse to keep sound and does not stand much racing.

River Ceiriog initiated a double for the Lambourn trainer when running away with the Waterford Crystal Supreme Novices' Hurdle, indicating he will be a smart understudy should anything happen to See You Then before his hat-trick bid in March.

Oregon Trail, splendidly ridden by Ronnie Beggan, crowned a memorable first season for trainer Simon Christian by wearing down

Charcoal Wally up the hill to win the Arkle Challenge Trophy.

Justice was done in the Waterford Crystal Stayers' Hurdle. Crimson Embers should have been awarded the race 12 months previously but the Stewards chose a Nelson's-eye approach to the run-in wanderings of his stablemate Rose Ravine. This time Crimson Embers ranout a 15-length winner from Irish raider Ravaro.

Crimson Embers' trainer Fulke Walwyn had further cause to celebrate 24 hours later when Ten

⬤ TRIPLE THANKS: The Queen Mother greets Special Cargo, one of three winners for her at Sandown on 12 April. Picture: PRESS ASSOCIATION

Plus confirmed his status as the top young hurdler in the country in the Sun Alliance Novices' Hurdle. The six-year-old extended his unbeaten sequence to four in the hands of Kevin Mooney, who promptly declared that Ten Plus would win a future Gold Cup.

The Irish enjoyed their best day of the meeting by plundering the Queen Mother Champion Chase with Buck House and the National Hunt Chase with Omerta.

Buck House poached a lead which Very Promising failed by three lengths to peg back, while Omerta justified strong support under top Irish amateur Lorcan Wyer and galloped home unchallenged in his stamina test. Wyer was later to join Peter Easterby as a professional.

The Terry Ramsden-owned, Mick Ryan-trained Motivator landed the gamble of the week in the Coral Golden Hurdle Final, beating Emo Forever six lengths.

Cross Master put Midlands trainer Tom Bill firmly on the map with a thrilling head victory form Strands of Gold in the Sun Alliance Chase. In an incident packed race, in which only ten of the 30 runners got round, Cross Master held on under strong driving from the second-last fence.

David Nicholson, whose stable had continued to be beset by a virus, ended his Festival blank in style through a last-day double with Solar Cloud and Charter Party. Solar Cloud went clear before the penultimate flight in the Daily Express Triumph Hurdle and held on under a power-packed Scudamore ride from the fast-finishing Brunico. Charter Party followed up with a three-length defeat of Catch Phrase in the Ritz Club National Hunt Handicap Chase.

This event showed how cruel the racing game can be, as it was here that Stuart Shilston, who had been the toast of Lambourn after Crimson Embers' success two days earlier, took a crashing fall from Contradeal and had to miss the remaining ten weeks of the season.

O ALL POWERFUL: See You Then surges through to win the Champion Hurdle at Cheltenham.　　　　　Picture: MARK LEECH

● **NATIONAL SPIRIT:** Young Driver leads over the last fence in the Seagram Grand National, but West Tip (right) was waiting to pounce.
Picture: GERRY CRANHAM

O STAR TURN: River Ceiriog runs away with the Waterford Crystal Supreme Novices' Hurdle. Picture: ALAN JOHNSON

And so on to Liverpool, where Richard Dunwoody, who for two seasons had been on many people's lips as the natural successor to John Francome, stole the show.

On West Tip, who had been travelling so smoothly in the previous year's Seagram Grand National before he fell at Becher's on the second circuit, he gave a perfect performance over the Aintree fences.

The Ulsterman and the nine-year-old West Tip never made the semblance of a mistake, and Dunwoody waited until after the elbow to pounce on Young Driver, delivering his decisive challenge with the cool confidence of a man holding a royal flush at poker.

Two days earlier Dunwoody had also stolen the headlines with another fine ride on former eventer Glenrue in the Whitbread Trophy. They led for most of the two and threequarter mile trip to score by a rapidly-diminishing neck from Bright Oassis.

Liverpool's second day brought the British debut of a possible new

O NEW PRETENDER: Dark Raven shows his class by beating Raretylo (left) in the Glenlivet Hurdle. Picture: ALAN JOHNSON

pretender to See You Then's Champion Hurdle crown in the unbeaten Dark Raven, from the powerful Dermot Weld stable. He toyed with his 15 opponents in the Glenlivet Hurdle, running out a four-length winner from fellow countryman Raretylo.

The Sandeman Aintree Hurdle, traditionally a curtain-raiser on Seagram-sponsored National day, produced surprise defeat for See You Then at the hands of Aonoch, who had tailed off more than 15 lengths behind him at Cheltenham.

Fred Winter, who relinquished his trainer's title no distance at all to Lambourn neighbour Nick Henderson, enjoyed the last laugh in Sandown's Whitbread Gold Cup. The six-times champion trainer sent out Plundering to beat the mare Buckbe in a memorable finish.

It was a bad season for injuries, and one which claimed the life of amateur Michael Blackmore at Market Rasen. Riding the five-year-old Silent Shadow in an amateur hurdle, Blackmore came down at the third flight and was trampled on by the oncoming pack. He later died of chest injuries.

A race, the Michael Blackmore Amateur Riders Handicap Chase over two and a half miles, was run for the first time at Warwick on 27 December to commemorate the Hertfordshire rider who loved the sport so much, but lost his life to it. There were 114 reported injuries through the season, and more than 40 jockeys (Flat and jumps) were on the sidelines at the same time toward its end.

The current season's first big sponsored chase, Cheltenham's Mackeson Gold Cup, provided its usual drama.

Subsequent Hennessy winner Broadheath was brought down midway through the race, leaving Half Free to battle up the hill with Very Promising in pursuit of an unprecedented third consecutive Mackeson. While Half Free gave his all, the concession of weight to Very Promising proved too much and he had to give best in a memorable finish.

If Michael Blackmore's death wasn't enough tragedy for one year, that of Jayne Thompson after a fall at Catterick Bridge, the first girl jockey to be killed as a result of an accident on the racecourse, illustrated the price we ask of others for our enjoyment.

Newbury's Hennessy Cognac Gold Cup gave West Country racegoers the opportunity to revel in glory when the David Barons-trained Broadheath held Les Kennard's Two Coppers in a slogging match over the final four fences. After successive wins by the top-class chasers Bright Highway, Diamond Edge, Bregawn, Brown Chamberlin and Burrough Hill Lad, it was the kind of result which said everything about the attraction of National Hunt racing. □

O GRABBING GLORY: Plundering takes the last ahead of Buckbe in the Whitbread Gold Cup. Picture: ALAN JOHNSON

O LOOK NO HAT: And nearly no win as Broadheath blunders at the third-last in the 1986 Hennessy Cognac Gold Cup. Picture: GEORGE SELWYN

● TAKE YOUR PICK: The
Daily Express Triumph Hurdle,
always strongly contested and
one of Cheltenham's biggest
betting races.
     Picture: GERRY CRANHAM

CHAPTER 30

Triumph Hurdle

by PETER O'SULLEVAN

○ **KNOCKOUT BLOW: First Bout takes the four-year-old hurdling title in the 1985 Triumph.** Picture: GERRY CRANHAM

Triumph Hurdle

by PETER O'SULLEVAN

HURST PARK had one of the best Silver Rings in the country. From that vantage point I saw the French-trained Grey Talk tackle the inaugural Triumph Hurdle on 11 March 1939.

The race was the brainchild of outstanding administrator Major (later Sir) John Crocker Bulteel, who had come down from Liverpool to take over as Clerk of the Course two years earlier. It was a four-year-old championship with a prize worth aiming for.

At £830 to the winner it topped the Champion Hurdle by over £100 and was less than £300 short of the Cheltenham Gold Cup.

Penalised for success on home ground, Grey Talk, a son of Gris Perle, had to concede 12lb to Quartier-Maitre, the most fancied local, with whom he shared 5-2 favouritism.

By the time the 15-runner field turned into the straight with less than half a mile to run, it was clear that neither M. James Hennessy nor his stable trainer George Batchelor had travelled in vain. And Grey Talk was chased home at eight lengths distance by Fred Rickaby on Carton, with the following year's Lincoln winner Quartier-Maitre back in third.

Hurst Park closed during the second World War but re-opened on a sunny Easter Saturday 1946, when the gates had to be shut long before an estimated 100,000 crowd could be accommodated in the enclosures. The 30,000 race cards had been sold half an hour before the first.

Crocker Bulteel revived the Triumph in 1950 and the French were back in force. Like his predecessor Grey Talk, Maisons-Laffitte-trained Abrupto had to concede weight because of his successes at Enghien, where the hurdles were easier than at Auteuil.

Some thought the unfamiliar Hurst Park obstacles would floor Abrupto. They nearly did once or twice, but he survived errors to win readily in the end. So did compatriots Blue Song (1951) Hoggar ('52) and Clair Soleil ('53).

The last-named had been bought shortly before the race by Gerry Judd, a patron of Ryan Price, but was still officially in the hands of Francois Mathet.

Would it ever end? Epsom trainer Tommy Carey was sure that his Prince Charlemagne, the previous year's Derby failure, had the necessary qualities not only to stem the export tide but also to enable him to launch an old-fashioned gamble.

He suggested to 18-year-old Lester Piggott that he should ride the horse in a "school" over hurdles at Kempton Park. "I don't know what we went with," Lester later related. "But when we pulled up Tommy just said, 'You'll win the Triumph'".

In the event blinkered Prince Charlemagne, running over hurdles for the first time in public and backed down to 11-4 favourite, bolted in by six lengths, despite comprehensively uprooting the last flight.

In the interim Sir John Crocker Bulteel initiated another event which was to assume enormous significance, this time in the Flat-racing calendar and one in which Lester Piggott was to play a prominent role for more than a quarter of a century - the King George VI and Queen Elizabeth Stakes.

With closure sadly imminent, the Triumph was run at Hurst Park for the last time in 1962. It left many a punter, especially among the Ryan Price entourage, reflecting that the builders could have performed a useful service by moving into the lovely Molesey riverside site a year earlier.

Ryan, who had won the 1961 renewal for Miss Enid Chanelle with Cantab, was even more confident of collecting for the same owner with the high-class Catapult II, whom he had bought for £6,000 in France. Catapult, fourth in the prestigious Prix de la Salamandre as a two-year-old, had schooled

brilliantly. Although unraced over hurdles in England he was sent off 7-4 favourite, despite the presence of the highly-rated Tudor Treasure.

Around this time one of the best-liked Paris-based horse dealers was an elderly Englishman named Sid Walker, whom, I suspect, Ryan Price supported as much out of the goodness of his heart as for his talent-spotting ability.

One of Sid's Chantilly clients, the American owner Ralph Beaver Strassburger, felt he owed Ryan compensation for a previously unsuccessful deal. So with the next purchase he threw in, gratis, a little rig with no form named Beaver II.

Beaver proved a skilful ejector of lads at Findon but showed little other aptitude. Having sold a half-share in him very cheaply to an enthusiastic new owner, Ryan had no intention of running him in the Triumph, although the little horse had suddenly progressed well. But his partner pleaded successfully.

O SHINING BRIGHT: Solar Cloud shows the style which brought him victory in the Daily Express Triumph Hurdle in 1986.
                                                                          Picture: ALAN JOHNSON

CAVALRY CHARGE: Pagan Sun leads the 1985 Triumph Hurdle field, from (left to right) Try To Stop Me, Life Guard, Brimstone Lady, Humberside Lady, Pukka Major and Irish Harvest.   Picture: GERRY CRANHAM

Fred Winter naturally selected Catapult, leaving Josh Gifford to partner the surely underpriced 100-6 outsider Beaver.

Catapult was a free-running horse at the best of times, more so when Willie Robinson and Tudor Treasure took him on from the outset. Tudor Treasure was the first to crack but two out Catapult was legless. Some way in arrears the mini-Beaver was turning hand springs. He sailed by without breaking sweat.

When the winning duo returned to the unsaddling enclosure they could have been excused for thinking they had interrupted a memorial service."You can't kill a Beaver with a Catapult!" read Sid Walker's exultant telegram to the shellshocked Captain.

The Triumph might have died along with Hurst Park, except for the intervention of Beaverbrook Newspapers, and Sir Max Aitken in particular. Recognising the value of racing in the context of newspapers, and feeling sympathy towards all those people in the sport/industry whose livelihood had been affected by lengthy closure due to an epidemic of foot and mouth disease, Max proposed a full day's sponsorship at Cheltenham's April meeting in 1963.

The day was such a success that it was repeated the following year, when the great Fred Winter had his last ride over hurdles in the Clive Graham Handicap, wearing this writer's undistinguished black and yellow colours and finishing second on Friendly Again.

Firmly supported by Vi Aitken, Clive and I discussed with Max the potential of sustaining sponsorship and concentrating on a single event. Why not resurrect the Triumph? The revival run on firm ground in April 1965 attracted seven runners. Lord Howard de Walden's Bronzino was 8-11, though concede up to 15lb to his rivals. He ran third in the smallest field to assemble for the race at Cheltenham.

After Persian War's victory in 1967, the Daily Express Triumph Hurdle moved to the Festival fixture. The turn-out doubled, but the fear that removal of penalties would result in an outstanding young horse getting a virtual walkover still lingered.

It lingered until 1973, when weight differentials were finally dispensed with and the Triumph became a true championship.

Back into the limelight stepped the gallant Captain Price, with a characteristically forthright view that the two runners from Findon, Moonlight Bay and Padlocked, "would definitely finish first and second".

In an 18-horse race bookmakers went 10-1 bar the Price pair. Their assessment proved well justified. Padlocked (Paul Kelleway), the 11-4

O HEART STOPPER: Attivo survives a last-flight mistake to beat Banlieu in the 1974 Triumph Hurdle.
Picture: GERRY CRANHAM

O CLOUD NINE: David Nicholson trains his first Cheltenham Festival winner with Solar Cloud in the 1986 Triumph Cloud.

Picture: TREVOR JONES

❍ SEE YOU WHEN?: Northern Game (right) is only third over the last flight, but he catches See You Then (left) and Manpower to take the 1984 Triumph Hurdle.
Picture: GERRY CRANHAM

second favourite, led to the second-last, but Moonlight Bay (85-40) and his stylish rider Johnny Haine were always travelling easily and leading over the last, they ran on well to beat Padlocked two and a half lengths into second place.

There are now few, if any, more competitive races at the greatest jumping Festival in the world than the Triumph, and none which inspires more extravagant betting, both ante-post and on the day.

Remarkably the shortest-priced winning favourite in the history of the race was a little old one-time failed selling plater on the Flat called Attivo, who started at 4-5.

Winner of his introductory race over hurdles by an official distance at Cheltenham on New Year's Day 1974, "Percy", as he was known in Cyril Mitchell's yard, next took his turned-out Charlie Chaplin feet to Newbury, where strong market opposition reflected a widespread view that 1 January had been a fluke.

Happily nothing occurred to justify the theory in the Stroud Green Hurdle, which he won by 20 lengths. Cyril favoured a cruise round Kempton next to collect the not inconsiderable Yellow Pages prize. But the owner had always preferred the idea of going to the Festival "fresh". So it was agreed to wait until the day.

The next worry was the ballot. At that time, in order to comply with the safety factor the field was reduced, if necessary, by random selection. It meant that proven young hurdlers were as vulnerable as newcomers.

Then there was the weather. On the day before the meeting was due to open the Cotswold arena was shrouded by a two-inch snowfall. As it began to melt, course chairman Sir Randle Feilden issued a provisional, revised running order (the Champion, Gold Cup and Daily Express Triumph would be re-opened and run in April) and confessed, "It's flooding I am most afraid of now."

The weather made travelling an extra hazard. Attivo hated sleeping in a strange bed. Dare we risk going from Epsom to Cheltenham on the morning of the race? Cyril thought not. "We'll have to send him overnight and just hope to God he sleeps better than his owner," he reasoned.

There were eight flights of hurdles and 20 rivals, many of them clear winners last time out. But only one was unbeaten, so far.

Young Robert Hughes, Attivo's regular partner, was unable to claim the 5lb allowance to which he was ordinarily entitled because of the value of the race, £8,980.50. It was not until approaching the last flight well clear that he overlooked his only instruction, "always keep a finger in the neck strap". Attivo, perhaps distracted by the cries of the crowd, belted the hurdle. Robert catapulted skywards. One commentator's heart missed a beat or two.

When Robert came down, Attivo was there, and the reunited pair had four lengths to spare over Ron Barry and Banlieu at the line. That was a Triumph I will never forget.□

● **ONE TO WATCH: Barney Burnett** emerged as an Irish star of the future.
Picture: CAROLINE NORRIS

CHAPTER 31

Irish National Hunt

by TONY O'HEHIR

O BITTER BLOW: Buck House, seen on his way to victory at Gowran Park, was the tragic victim of a colic attack.

Picture: TIM HANNAN

Irish National Hunt

by TONY O'HEHIR

IN A YEAR when increased sponsorship and a IR£250,000 Government grant boosted prize money for jumping in Ireland, it took a rare mistake by one trainer and an inspired idea from another to set in motion the event of the year.

Racing's super match between Dawn Run and Buck House at Punchestown in April was never meant to happen. Instead they were supposed to meet at Gowran Park in May in the Coolmore-Purcell Exports Champion Chase, a race devised to attract both horses.

But Dawn Run's trainer Paddy Mullins missed the entry date and an eagerly-awaited clash between the Gold Cup heroine and the Two-Mile Champion was lost. Or was it?

Enter Vincent O'Brien, on the day his Tate Gallery flopped in the Gladness Stakes at The Curragh in April. O'Brien, his son-in-law and Coolmore boss John Magnier and Seamus Purcell asked the Turf Club's Cahir O'Sullivan if anything could be done to get Dawn Run into the Gowran race. O'Sullivan told them the Rules could not be bent, and it was then that O'Brien floated the idea of a match.

Punchestown's festival meeting was an obvious venue and a winner-take-all IR£25,000 clash was arranged for 23 April. An opportunity had finally arrived for Turf Club boss O'Sullivan to perform the function associated with his antiquated title as Keeper of the Match Book.

The Racing Board's decision to contribute IR£10,000 to the event angered many trainers, but even those most opposed to the idea had to admit it was a resounding success.

In Ireland the jumping game dwarfs the Flat in terms of public popularity, and they thronged Punchestown in their thousands. The attendance was a course record and the event lived up to expectations.

Level weights favoured Dawn Run but the Buck House camp thought the trip might not. After the pair had battled for the lead from three fences out, Dawn Run forged clear to win by two and a half lengths.

Tommy Carmody had tried everything he could on Buck House but the mare would not be denied. Her win was just reward for Tony Mullins, who contributed so much to her career.

Sadly both horses never raced again in Ireland. Dawn Run was killed in action in France, and Buck House died after an attack of colic on his owner's farm.

These two great chasers were responsible for half Ireland's score at the National Hunt Festival in March. Cheltenham might not be part of the brief for these purposes, but since it has been described as Ireland's most popular race meeting, the fixture cannot be ignored.

Attitude Adjuster won the Christies Foxhunters Chase under 11-times Irish champion amateur Ted Walsh, who immediately announced he would not ride over jumps again. And Homer Scott, whose stable has consistently been

O TALLY HO: An Irish victory for Attitude Adjuster (left), who leads third-placed Mister Donovan in the Christies Foxhunters Chase at Cheltenham. Picture: ALAN JOHNSON

a thorn in the side of the bookmakers over the last two years, had his first Festival win, with Omerta in the National Hunt Chase.

Omerta returned from Cheltenham a strong fancy for the Jameson Irish National at Fairyhouse on Easter Monday, but he found the older, more-experienced Insure ten lengths too good for him in the soft ground. Run and Skip, Righthand Man and Maori Venture came from England but all three were pulled up as only five of the 15 starters completed the course.

Insure's win was a career highlight for owner-trainer Pat Hughes, brother-in-law of Eddie

Harty, and for jockey Mickey Flynn, 21. Hughes' patience and skill is best exemplified by his handling of Barrow Line, who won four hurdle races before switching successfully to novice chases.

Barrow Line went to Hughes as a three-year-old but did not race until late-1985, when he was eight. He had broken down three times but Hughes believed that this brother to Bobsline was something special and his persistence was rewarded.

For once, Ireland's best novice hurdler did not go to Cheltenham. Instead, Barney Burnett, named after an American friend of owner Paddy Donovan, visited Fairyhouse and Punchestown. He won both

○ **CLOSING DOWN: Bonalma on his way to winning the last running of the Irish Sweeps Hurdle.**

Picture: CAROLINE NORRIS

races by ten lengths and was particularly impressive in Punchestown's BMW Champion Novice Hurdle. Unfortunately Ruby Walsh's gelding aggravated a back muscle injury in November and his reappearance was delayed.

In the first half of the year Herbert United and Bonalma won Ireland's two richest hurdle prizes.

At Leopardstown in January Bonalma took the last running of the Sweeps Hurdle, giving trainer Arthur Moore his fourth win in the race and jockey Tom Taaffe his third.

A month later controversy surrounded Herbert United's win in the Wessel Cable Champion Hurdle, where Dessie McDonogh's

○ **TOMMY CARMODY: On the move.** Picture: CAROLINE NORRIS

seven-year-old was beaten a length and a half by Kesslin only to be awarded the race after a Stewards' inquiry. Herbert United was slightly bumped by Kesslin at the last flight but few believed it made any difference to the result.

That same afternoon a family tradition continued when Hard Case, trained by Jim Dreaper for his mother Lady Thomson, won the Harold Clarke Leopardstown Chase. Hard Case was ridden by Ken Morgan, whose younger brother Tom, 23, emerged as the jockey of the year and a match for Ireland's big two — Tommy Carmody and Frank Berry.

Carmody split from trainer Mouse Morris in the autumn to

ride for John Mulhern's main patron Miss Deborah Threadwell. He was replaced by Niall Madden. Another good job was filled by John Shortt, who joined Homer Scott when Lorcan Wyer went to Peter Easterby.

In December at Fairyhouse Shortt won the Holsten Handicap Hurdle for Scott on The Illiad, who landed the biggest gamble seen on an Irish racecourse in years.

Ireland's Festival meetings, a unique mixture of Flat and jumps, require stamina of the human rather than the equine variety. What happens on the racecourse is only part of the action, and Galway's six-day bash at the end of July is the one which attracts the largest crowds.

⭘ BARROW LINE: A credit to Pat Hughes. Picture: CAROLINE NORRIS

⭘ KEN MORGAN: Maintained a family tradition. Picture: ALAN JOHNSON

Main event of the week is the Galway Plate, a handicap chase over two miles five furlongs, won in 1986 by Boro Quarter, sporting the famous red and black colours of Dawn Run's owner Charmian Hill.

The weather was dreadful and the ground heavy as Mrs Hill's home-bred mare battled her way up the three-furlong climb from the last fence to win by four lengths. Victory gave the handicap king Paddy Mullins his first Plate success, and it was the biggest pay day in the career of jockey Peter Kavanagh. In addition to his percentage of the IR£27,786 prize, Kavanagh won IR£250 as the groom responsible for the last horse to finish, Boro Quarter's stablemate Stern Saturn.

Unlike their Flat counterparts, English jumpers failed to make much impression. An exception was Rushmoor, who made all the running under Peter Scudamore to win the Galway Hurdle for Ray Peacock.

At Listowel in September Flute Player jumped brilliantly for a virtual novice to win the Kerry National. Flute Player's owner Denis Murphy is a Kerryman and he instructed trainer Vivian Kennedy to concentrate his campaign on the County's meetings. Since he had previously

been successful at Killarney and Tralee, victory at Listowel meant he had won at all three.

Flute Player returned to Killarney in October for a match race with The Right Touch, as part of that racecourse's 50th anniversary celebrations. The race highlighted the great rivalry between Dublin and Kerry, particularly evident in Gaelic football. Flute Player carried the green and gold of Kerry and his rival Dublin's two-tone blue. True to football form, Kerry won and Dublin went home lame.

Other memorable performances during the year included Galmoy's 12-length romp under 12st in a three-mile handicap hurdle at Punchestown in April. And at the same meeting Pat Hogan's gutsy four-year-old Team Challenge ran three times in four days, covered ten and a quarter miles over the banks, won once and was beaten only a neck at the third attempt.

On a sad note, a man who for 15 years dominated on-course betting at Irish meetings, passed away in April. Sean Graham's death at 49 was a big loss to racing and racegoers, which he served so well both as a bookmaker and a sponsor.

Ireland could ill afford to lose him, Dawn Run and Buck House in one year.□

○ WATCH OUT: A Prayer For Wings looks the type to win the European Free Handicap.   Picture: DAVID HASTINGS

20 To Follow

by RACING POST TEAM

A PRAYER FOR WINGS
3 ro.c. Godswalk - Late Swallow (My Swallow)

In early October a competitive field for a Newmarket nursery, featuring nine other previous winners, was routed by A Prayer For Wings. The winner of his only previous race at Nottingham, he was always going well and quickened impressively below the distance to come home two lengths clear of favourite Girotondo.

The manner of A Prayer For Wings' victory suggests there is even better to come, a sentiment shared by trainer John Sutcliffe. The previous running of the same Newmarket nursery fell to Sperry, who then came up against Green Desert in the European Free Handicap. A Prayer For Wings could well go one better.
J. Sutcliffe, Epsom

ARDEN
3 b.c. Ardross - Kereolle (Riverman)

Arden became his sire's only winning two-year-old when he scored a comfortable success over the extended mile at Beverley in September. He was stepped up in grade at Newbury the following month for his third and final race and, with Willie Ryan making plenty of use of him, he finished a clear second behind Dollar Seeker.

Ardross, who showed top form at a mile and a half to extreme distances, did not reach his full powers until the age of four, and time and distance should reveal considerable improvement in his son. Arden acts on any going.
H. Cecil, Newmarket

CELESTIAL STORM (USA)
4 b.c. Roberto - Tobira Celeste (Ribot)

Celestial Storm, unraced at two, made tremendous strides in the second half of 1986, following an easy win in the March Stakes at Goodwood with seconds to Moon Madness in the St Leger and Triptych in the Champion Stakes. Whereas he was getting nowhere in the last furlong of the St Leger, he was flying at the end of the Champion Stakes, and it is reasonable to conclude that an intermediate distance of around a mile and a half may prove his optimum, although he is capable of winning good races over a wide range of distances.

A race such as the Brigadier Gerard Stakes, where Cumani began Commanche Run's four-year-old career, or the John Porter Stakes should be well within his early grasp, and Celestial Storm may have enough improvement in him to go to the very top.

L. Cumani, Newmarket

CLASSIC TALE

3 ch.c. Blushing Groom - Cambretta (Roberto)

Classic Tale looked an exciting prospect when beating Beeshi by seven lengths in a valuable maiden at Ascot in July, quickening away impressively in the last furlong and a half for an easy win. On the strength of that he was short-priced favourite to beat the much-vaunted Bellotto in the Acomb Stakes at York the following month, but was beaten some way out and allowed to come home in his own time, finishing fifth.

Something was clearly amiss at York and Classic Tale should develop into a high-class performer. A rangy, good-looking colt, he has enough stamina in his pedigree to suggest he will stay at least a mile and a quarter. He could prove more than a mere third string to the same stable's Ajdal and Zajal.

M. Stoute, Newmarket

DOLLAR SEEKER (USA)

3 b.c. Buckfinder - Syrian Song (Damascus)

Dollar Seeker improved with every outing as a juvenile and won the last two of his six races, at Newcastle and Newbury, putting up a good effort when beating Arden in the 23-runner Dick Dawson Stakes on the latter course.

"Make no mistake this is a nice horse," Mick Ryan told us, "but he was a slow learner and thought it was all a big game for his first three races. We'll see how he matures through the winter, but he'll probably be clobbered in handicaps so I'll look at the Classic trials. I think he's got all the ingredients: he settles well, has a good turn of foot and will have no trouble getting middle distances. He handles any going but went really well on the soft at Newbury."

M. Ryan, Newmarket

EL CUITE (USA)

4 b.c. Vaguely Noble - Assez Cuite (Graustark)

El Cuite is a lightly-raced four-year-old who has yet to be beaten. A winner at Newbury at two, he returned there to beat Hauwmal impressively in a good handicap in August and went on to pick up two Group One events abroad, the Gran Premio d'Italia at Milan and Prix Royal-Oak (French St Leger) at Longchamp.

In France, over nearly two miles, he scored a narrow win from Alesso, Valuable Witness and Faburola, and although the race was slowly run, he gave every indication he will stay well. He should have more improvement in

20 To Follow

RACING POST experts have compiled a list of 20 horses to follow on the Flat in 1987. Some of the names are familiar, some are not. They have been researched with one aim in mind — to look for improvement, and profit, in the season ahead.

A PRAYER FOR WINGS	— 3yo —	J Sutcliffe
ARDEN	— 3yo —	H Cecil
CELESTIAL STORM	— 4yo —	L Cumani
CLASSIC TALE	— 3yo —	M Stoute
DOLLAR SEEKER	— 3yo —	M Ryan
EL CUITE	— 4yo —	H Cecil
FOREST FLOWER	— 3yo —	I Balding
GOLD PROSPECT	— 5yo —	G Balding
HYDRAULIC POWER	— 3yo —	L Piggott
JUST DAVID	— 4yo —	A Stewart
KING OF MERCIA	— 3yo —	L Cumani
MAMOUNA	— 3yo —	M Stoute
MANTON DAN	— 4yo —	N Vigors
MISCHIEVOUS MISS	— 3yo —	Miss S Hall
ONE TO MARK	— 4yo —	Sir M Prescott
PERCY'S LASS	— 3yo —	G Wragg
SCARLET BLADE	— 3yo —	H Cecil
SKOLERN	— 3yo —	M W Easterby
WOOD CHANTER	— 3yo —	J Dunlop
ZERO WATT	— 3yo —	G Harwood

him and if he does not quite make the top grade over a mile and a half, he could turn out to be a formidable Cup horse. He has yet to race on really firm ground but acts on any other.

H. Cecil, Newmarket

FOREST FLOWER (USA)

3 ch.f. Green Forest - Leap Lively (Nijinsky)

Forest Flower is not the most obvious type to train on, as she showed exceptional speed at two, had to endure some hard races and is on the small side. However, on the plus side is her great courage and toughness; she had a very hard race in defeat against Minstrella in Ireland but returned with the same enthusiasm to score at Newbury and Newmarket (she was controversially disqualified after her decisive second defeat of her old foe Minstrella in the Cheveley Park). Both the sire and dam of Forest Flower did well at three. She will be hard to beat in the 1,000 Guineas and may stay beyond one mile.

I. Balding, Kingsclere

GOLD PROSPECT

5 b.g. Wolverlife - Golden Darling (Darling Boy)

Gold Prospect is admirably consistent, finishing out of the frame only three times in 13 races last year, and there is good reason to believe he can keep a step ahead of the Handicapper in the coming season. He was unraced at two and had only two outings at three, so for a horse of his age there is relatively little mileage on the clock.

He overcame an apparent aversion to firm ground in 1986, but the chances are he will always appreciate give under foot. He had the speed to win over six furlongs first time out (he seems to go well when fresh), but wound up by outpacing a big field of milers at Newbury and his future is almost certainly over the longer trip. A big handicap win is within his grasp.

G. Balding, Weyhill

HYDRAULIC POWER

3 ch.c. Northfields - Princess Biddy (Sun Prince)

Yarmouth, schooling ground for many of Newmarket's precocious youngsters, was awash with rumours about Hydraulic Power on his debut, but the attractive colt was all at sea. It was a different story on his return four weeks later when he justified his reputation, cruising home from subsequent Somerville Tattersalls Stakes winner Imperial Frontier over six furlongs in a good time.

Michael Albina, who has handed him over to Lester Piggott, spoke of him in the same breath as his best horse Silver Hawk (placed in the 1982 Epsom and Irish Derbys). He expects him to get a mile plus and develop into a Classic contender.

L. Piggott, Newmarket

JUST DAVID

4 b.c. Blakeney - Reltop (High Top)

Unraced at two, and first or second in four of his five outings last season, this lightly-raced, strapping son of Blakeney is just the type to progress with age.

Just David started in minor company at Bath and Catterick Bridge, far from ideal tracks for one of his size. He improved to touch off Cox Green in a Goodwood handicap prior to running respectably under a penalty in the Tote-Ebor. Stepped up another half-mile to two and a quarter miles, he was pipped on the post by Ightham at Yarmouth but confirmed that staying is his game. According to his trainer, he has yet to race on the easy surface he requires, and there should be plenty of improvement to come. Just David can make up into a live contender for the top stayers' handicaps.

A. Stewart, Newmarket

KING OF MERCIA

3 b.c. Great Nephew - Saint Osyth (Blakeney)

King of Mercia showed more than average promise in his only race as a juvenile and seems capable of developing into a useful staying handicapper. A 33-1 chance with plenty of scope about him, Luca Cumani's colt was a fast-finishing third of 19 to Dry Dock and Altountash in a Newmarket maiden race over a mile, beaten just over a length.

The form appeared not to work out particularly well, but with normal improvement King of Mercia would be sure to win an average maiden. He can go on from there and, even if he does not turn out one of Cumani's very best, should win a decent handicap or two.

L. Cumani, Newmarket

MAMOUNA (USA)

3 ch.f. Vaguely Noble - Mabira (Habitat)

Mamouna turned in an excellent effort on her only outing as a juvenile when as a 33-1 chance she made her shorter-priced stable-companion Milligram struggle in a valuable maiden at Newbury in September. Both the winner and the third, Gold Fee, went on to show smart form, and Mamouna looks certain to improve. She will stay at least a mile and a quarter and should develop into a high-class performer.

M. Stoute, Newmarket

MANTON DAN

4 b.c. Tower Walk - Balgreggan (Hallez)

Manton Dan is a useful sprinter who could make the jump from handicap to Listed and Pattern company. He ran eight times at three, putting up his best effort when landing his third win of the season in the valuable Hong Kong Marlboro Cup Handicap over six furlongs at York, beating Our Jock.

Nick Vigors has excuses for both Manton Dan's subsequent defeats and has an interesting observation to make about him: "Although he's won three races over six furlongs, I honestly think his style of racing is best suited to five furlongs; he has got a tremendous amount of speed. And I've always thought he'd make a better four-year-old."

N. Vigors, Lambourn

MISCHIEVOUS MISS
3 b.f. Niniski - Willow Walk (Farm Walk)

Mischievous Miss made a promising debut over six furlongs at York in September, despite showing signs of greenness. She made progress from the rear at halfway and ran on really well to finish three lengths third to Lucky Stone.

She looked a little unlucky when fifth to Sunerta over seven furlongs at Ayr a fortnight later, and ran far better than her finishing position suggests when sixth to Ala Hounak over a mile and a quarter at Doncaster on her only other start, where she was held up and given plenty to do after a sluggish start. Mischievous Miss is qualified for handicaps and should develop into a useful middle-distance stayer.
Miss S. Hall, Middleham

ONE TO MARK
4 b. or br.g. He Loves Me - Markon (On Your Mark)

The lightly-raced One To Mark lost his maiden tag in a small Edinburgh conditions race before disappointing at Newmarket, where there were valid excuses; he was ridden by an unfamiliar jockey and, more importantly, was found to have chipped a bone in a knee.

One To Mark has been successfully operated on and his trainer Sir Mark Prescott, masterful in his placement of horses, believes he could be another Forward Rally.

Forward Rally underwent a similar operation before winning three races in 1986, including the Zetland Gold Cup at Redcar. One To Mark, who will be similarly campaigned, should improve and prove equally profitable to follow.
Sir Mark Prescott, Newmarket

PERCY'S LASS
3 b. or br.f. Blakeney - Laughing Girl (Sassafras)

Percy's Lass, unbeaten in three starts over trips which, on breeding, ought to be all too short for her, looks a likely money-spinner at middle distances.

After wins over six furlongs at Lingfield Park and Salisbury, she showed her class in the seven-furlong Holsten Pils Nursery at Ascot in October. Conceding 7lb or more all round, she quickened superbly after leading a furlong out and hacked up by five lengths from Diamond Flight.

The form looks solid, and the winner's performance ranks not far below those of the Pattern fillies. The Handicapper has been unusually lenient with Percy's Lass, but she has the potential to make her mark in better company.
G. Wragg, Newmarket

SCARLET BLADE
3 ch.c. Kris - Red Velvet (Red God)

Scarlet Blade, winner of his only race at two, has all the potential to develop into a Classic colt. Henry Cecil's son of Kris hinted at his ability in some highly encouraging gallops before making his debut in Newmarket's Houghton Stakes, where he was the most fancied of three runners from the stable. Scarlet Blade was in front fully half a mile from home and in a desperately tight finish showed tremendous determination narrowly to hold off favourite Bashayer and stablemate Flood Mark.

Scarlet Blade was backward and not fully wound up in the Houghton and there is plenty of scope for improvement. Sheikh Mohammed's colt is likely to start his three-year-old campaign in one of the Guineas trials and should develop into a leading miler.
H. Cecil, Newmarket

SKOLERN
3 b.c. Lochnager - Piethorne (Fine Blade)

On the face of it a fourth and three unplaced efforts do little to inspire confidence in Skolern, but delving below the surface, there is a well-handicapped three-year-old bursting to get out.

Skolern was noted when a fast-finishing fourth on his debut in a six-furlong conditions race at Catterick Bridge. Similarly eye-catching performances followed over five furlongs at Ripon and six at Haydock Park.

By a sprint sire and out of a middle-distance mare, he may prove best around a mile, a trip over which he was given one run at the end of the season.
M.W. Easterby, Sheriff Hutton

WOOD CHANTER
3 gr.c. Vitiges - Castle Moon (Kalamoun)

Wood Chanter comes from an excellent winning family, the most famous member of which is his brother, St Leger hero Moon Madness. The latter raced only once at two and John Dunlop has followed the same policy with Wood Chanter, who after having to switch, caught the eye with a strong finish into fourth place behind Roman Gunner in a Newmarket maiden in August. There was no interest in him in the market and his connections will view him much more as a second-season prospect. He will probably need at least a mile and a quarter to be effective.
J. Dunlop, Arundel

ZERO WATT (USA)
3 b.c. Little Current - Ruby Tuesday (T.V. Lark)

Zero Watt drifted badly in the betting on his debut at Newbury in September but he turned in a performance full of promise. Slowly away and then denied a clear run, he ate up the ground in the closing stages but failed by threequarters of a length to catch Thameen.

Twelve months earlier Shahrastani had been an unlucky loser of the same event and it would be no surprise if Zero Watt also did well in top company at three. He is a half-brother to the very useful sprinter Green Ruby, but as a son of the Preakness and Belmont Stakes winner Little Current, he should be suited by middle distances.
G. Harwood, Pulborough □

○ CHAMPION STYLE: Gary Carter took the apprentices' title outright after sharing it in 1985.   Picture: TONY EDENDEN

Apprentices

by MARK COTON

IN A YEAR when Pat Eddery took over the Piggott mantle and the big names again dominated the jockeys' championship, apprentices rarely hit the headlines, prompting the question: Where are the champion jockeys of the future?

Gary Carter again rode with style and confidence and won the apprentice title outright, having shared it with Willie Ryan in 1985. But his total of 34 winners was the lowest for a champion for 23 years and indicates the struggle our young riders are having.

The economic climate has put the squeeze on opportunities. Vast rewards open to the top horses mean that the leading owners are demanding and getting the best riders. It is a sad fact that none of the leading 12 stables, who won 836 races worth over £5.7m between them, retained a leading apprentice in 1986.

And the harsh realities of racing at the lower levels, where one winner can make or break a season, mean that many trainers are not prepared to take the risk of blooding an inexperienced rider.

Gary Carter confirmed how tough it is. "It's now incredibly competitive with so many stables retaining their own jockeys," he says. "A young rider has to be something special to make the grade. A few years ago the top apprentice might ride 80 winners a season, but there are far fewer opportunities now".

Carter, at least, seems well set. He has negotiated a difficult hurdle, having ridden a steady flow of winners since losing his claim on Kufuma in early-September, and will ride for Geoff Huffer, Philip Mitchell and Gavin Pritchard-Gordon in 1987.

Winning a Group Race in Germany on Sylvan Express, and

O NAMES TO NOTE: Tony Culhane (left), who shone on Absheer (No 9) at Ascot, and Dale Gibson, seen winning on Hamper (right) at York.
Pictures: ALAN JOHNSON/ALEC RUSSELL

participating in the five-venue European apprentice championship backed by Long John Scotch Whisky were two of the highlights of last season for Carter, and he acknowledges how important they were in broadening his experience — for one thing, the European adventure taught him how to cope with the bad luck of the draw!

One trainer with more experience than most in developing apprentices is Reg Hollinshead, who has had Walter Swinburn, Tony Ives and Paul Eddery, among others, in his care.

He agrees that things are much tougher for young riders and regrets that the Polycell-Willie Carson Apprentice Challenge was not renewed last season. But he could have another future star on his hands in Manchester-born Tony Culhane, 17, who rode nine winners last season.

Culhane impressed hard-bitten regulars when riding a particularly cool race to win on Absheer at Ascot in October, keeping his mount perfectly balanced in a last-furlong battle with the equally-promising Mark Giles from the Michael Stoute stable, on Verdant Boy. Culhane will ride regularly

for Hollinshead in 1987 and is a name to bear in mind.

The Rugeley trainer also has a good word for Peter Hill, who has plenty of experience but still claims the 7lb allowance. "He can do 7st and is especially good value for his claim. He was riding work for Barry Hills towards the end of last season and rode a winner for the stable. His career should take off soon," was Hollinshead's verdict.

That expression should also apply to Dale Gibson, who is based with Willie Hastings-Bass at Newmarket. This yard seems to appreciate the value of apprentice races and Captain's Neice was placed to run up a sequence of three victories in this grade under Gibson's tidy, effective handling.

It was good to see the girls holding their own, with three names among the leading 12 apprentices. Nigel and Kim Tinkler are building an impressive husband and wife partnership at Malton, while Julie Bowker had a rewarding association with the useful two-year-old Crofter's Cline.

Gay Kelleway has always been among our strongest and most effective young girl riders and it is

another sad sign of the times that she is reported to be considering emigrating to New Zealand to further her career.

Let us hope that more young jockeys do not feel they have to follow her example. The success of Willie Ryan, with 56 winners and the plum No 2 job to Henry Cecil, should act as encouragement, although former top apprentice Paul Eddery has lost his retainer with Peter Walwyn to Brent Thomson.

Much though we like to see the big names in action, racing should be wary of going the way of cricket, which has suffered from the policy of encouraging foreign stars at the expense of home-grown talent.

One who will never fall into this trap is Henry Candy. He has another impressive young rider on his books in Chris Rutter, whose partnership with useful sprinter Polykratis emphatically showed he can ride on level terms with the best.

If only more trainers followed the example of Candy, whose loyalty in keeping faith with the much-troubled Billy Newnes shone like a beacon last term. □

Quiz of the Year

by JOHN RANDALL (Answers on page 267)

1. Whom did Jonjo O'Neill replace as Dawn Run's regular jockey?

2. Whom did Peter Scudamore replace as Burrough Hill Lad's regular jockey?

3. Which race at Sandown Park in February did Burrough Hill Lad win for the third consecutive year?

4. Which race at Sandown Park in February gave See You Then his only success of the year apart from the Champion Hurdle?

5. Which owner had a treble at Sandown Park on 8 March with Special Cargo, Insular and The Argonaut?

6. What was new in betting shops on 10 March?

7. Which Cheltenham Festival winner is a half-brother to 1983 Champion Stakes heroine Cormorant Wood?

8. Which 11-year-old, trained by Fulke Walwyn, won the Waterford Crystal Stayers' Hurdle for the second time?

9. Which seven-year-old, named after a character in the television series M*A*S*H, fell when second favourite for the Champion Hurdle?

10. Which ten-year-old, trained by David Elsworth, was carried out when third favourite for the Cheltenham Gold Cup?

11. Which three horses gave 5lb to Dawn Run in the Cheltenham Gold Cup and finished within five lengths of her?

12. Which trainer and jockey had their first Cheltenham Festival winner when Solar Cloud landed the Triumph Hurdle?

13. Which 40-1 shot, trained by the late John Thorne, beat Wayward Lad for the Whitbread Gold Label Cup at Liverpool?

14. Which colt, trained by Dermot Weld, was officially rated the champion juvenile hurdler after a runaway win at Liverpool?

15. Who became the first woman rider to win a race over the Grand National fences?

16. Which horse came from Czechoslovakia to run in the Grand National?

17. Which gelding, owned by Terry Ramsden, came fourth when favourite for the Grand National?

18. Name the trainer and jockey of Grand National winner West Tip.

19. Which subsequent Group One winner landed the European Free Handicap at Newmarket under top weight?

20. Which gelding came third in the Champion Hurdle and unseated Jonjo O'Neill in the Scottish Champion Hurdle on the latter's last ride in public?

21. Which Lambourn trainer won the first Pattern race of his career with Lemhill in the John Porter Stakes at Newbury?

22. Which Epsom trainer won the Great Metropolitan Handicap and City and Suburban Handicap at Epsom on 22 April?

23. Explain the significance of Geordie's Delight's win at Epsom on 23 April.

O **Q13?** Picture: PRESS ASSOCIATION

O **Q15?** Picture: ALAN JOHNSON

24. Which ill-fated rival did Dawn Run beat in a match at Punchestown on 23 April?

25. Who rode Plundering to victory in the Whitbread Gold Cup and led Peter Scudamore in the jump jockeys' table for most of the season?

26. Who became champion trainer of jumpers for the first time?

27. Which colt, trained by Clive Brittain, was runner-up in the Kentucky Derby?

28. Which grey gelding was runner-up in the Triumph Hurdle before beating Shardari for the Ormonde Stakes?

29. Which champion suffered his only defeat of the year when sixth in the Aston Park Stakes at Newbury in May?

30. Apart from Dancing Brave, which of Guy Harwood's colts lost his unbeaten record in the Derby?

○ Q28?   Picture: ALAN JOHNSON

○ Q21?   Picture: ALAN JOHNSON

31. Which colt was Vincent O'Brien's representative in the Derby but finished last?

32. Who trained both winner and runner-up in the Royal Hunt Cup?

33. Which Newmarket trainer won the first Pattern race of his career with Sizzling Melody in the Norfolk Stakes at Royal Ascot?

34. Which Royal Ascot winner did Taffy Thomas ride for David Thom?

35. Which jockey had his first win since 1983 on My Buddy at Catterick Bridge on 10 July?

36. Which Royal Ascot winner was pacemaker for Shahrastani and Shardari in the King George VI and Queen Elizabeth Diamond Stakes?

37. Which Melton Mowbray trainer won the first Pattern race of his career with Gemini Fire in the Molecomb Stakes at Goodwood?

38. Which stablemates were first and second in the Sussex Stakes?

39. On which gelding did Princess Anne score the first win of her riding career?

40. Which controversial trainer died on 16 August, his 74th birthday?

41. Which is the youngest racecourse in Great Britain, having celebrated 60 years of racing with the Diamond Jubilee Handicap on 25 August?

42. Which colt, trained by Jeremy Tree, was the only European-trained horse to be placed in the Arlington Million?

43. Explain the significance of Doronicum's win in the Racing Post Handicap Hurdle at Southwell on 3 September.

44. Which horse was disqualified for the second time in the Doncaster Cup?

45. Explain the significance of Veryan Bay's win at Lingfield Park on 16 September.

46. Which South African jockey won the Royal Lodge Stakes at Ascot on Bengal Fire?

47. Which record-priced yearling became the only son of Shergar to win a Classic?

40. Ajdal became the sixth Dewhurst Stakes winner sired by which great American-based stallion?

49. Which Hong Kong jockey rode Triptych to victory in the Champion Stakes?

50. Which jockey broke his right ankle at Sandown Park in May but recovered to win the Cesarewitch on Orange Hill?

51. Which two trainers were banned for five years by the Jockey Club in October?

52. Which seven-year-old was having his first race for six months when winning the St Simon Stakes at Newbury?

53. Name the only European-trained horse to win a Breeders' Cup race at Santa Anita, California on 1 November.

54. Which of Fred Winter's horses was prevented by a penalty from winning his third consecutive Mackeson Gold Cup at Cheltenham?

55. Who rode Dual Venture into third place in the November Handicap on his last ride in Great Britain before his retirement?

56. Which great jockey committed suicide 100 years ago on 8 November?

57. Sir Gordon Richards died on 10 November aged 82. How many times was he champion jockey?

58: Name the trainer and jockey of Hennessy Cognac Gold Cup winner Broadheath.

59. What was the new name of the race at Cheltenham in December originally known as the Massey-Ferguson Gold Cup?

60. Name the only race won as a three-year-old by Bakharoff, Europe's champion juvenile in 1985.

61. Which colt beat Slip Anchor on the latter's only outing as a four-year-old, and in which race?

62. Which four horses finished in front of Shahrastani in 1986?

63. Which four horses finished in front of Dancing Brave?

64. In which race did Dancing Brave make his seasonal debut?

65. How many races did Pat Eddery win on Dancing Brave?

66. Which West German champion won 12 consecutive races but then finished seventh to Dancing Brave in the Prix de l'Arc de Triomphe?

67. Which gelding, trained by Jeremy Tree, won seven consecutive races including the Sagaro Stakes and Jockey Club Cup?

68. Which three-year-old, trained by Martin Pipe, won his first seven races over hurdles, three of them at Cheltenham?

69. Who became champion sire of jumpers for the seventh consecutive time?

70. Name the only two horses to win six races on the Flat in Great Britain.

71. Which of Robert Armstrong's fillies was unbeaten in four races including the Waterford Candelabra Stakes and Hoover Fillies' Mile?

72. Which of Michael Stoute's fillies won in both Italy and Canada?

73. Which 16-year-old steeplechaser won twice in 1986?

74. Which two champion hurdlers were fatally injured while racing in 1986?

75. Which two riders were fatally injured while racing in 1986?

○ Q52?   Picture: JOHN CROFTS

Answers

1. Tony Mullins.
2. Phil Tuck.
3. The Gainsborough Handicap Chase.
4. The Oteley Hurdle.
5. The Queen Mother.
6. Television and light refreshments were permitted for the first time.
7. River Ceiriog, the Waterford Crystal Supreme Novices' Hurdle winner.
8. Crimson Embers.
9. Corporal Clinger.
10. Combs Ditch.
11. Wayward Lad, Forgive'N Forget and Run And Skip.
12. David Nicholson and Peter Scudamore.
13. Beau Ranger.
14. Dark Raven.
15. Caroline Beasley, who rode Eliogarty to win the Liverpool Foxhunters' Chase.
16. Essex, who was pulled up before the Chair.
17. Mr Snugfit.
18. Michael Oliver and Richard Dunwoody.
19. Green Desert, the July Cup winner.
20. Nohalmdun.
21. Michael Blanshard.
22. Reg Akehurst with Owen's Pride and Nebris.
23. It was Lester Piggott's first win as a trainer.
24. Buck House, who won the Queen Mother Champion Chase in March and died of colic in June.
25. Simon Sherwood.
26. Nick Henderson.
27. Bold Arrangement.

28. Brunico.
29. Longboat, the stayers' triple crown winner.
30. Allez Milord.
31. Wise Counsellor.
32. John Dunlop with Patriach and Siyah Kalem.
33. Lord John FitzGerald.
34. Touch of Grey in the Wokingham Stakes.
35. Billy Newnes, who had just served a 2½-year suspension.
36. Dihistan, the Hardwicke Stakes winner.
37. Paul Felgate.
38. Sonic Lady and Scottish Reel, both trained by Michael Stoute.
39. Guilland at Redcar on 5 August.
40. Ryan Price.
41. Chepstow.
42. Pennine Walk, who was third to Estrapade.
43. It enabled Phil Tuck to equal Johnny Gilbert's 1959 record of ten consecutive wins by a jump jockey.
44. Petrizzo.
45. She was the first winner trained by Michael Dickinson for Robert Sangster.
46. Michael Roberts.
47. Authaal, the Irish St Leger winner.
48. Northern Dancer.
49. Tony Cruz.
50. Richard Fox.
51. David Moorhead and Stephen 'Flockton Grey' Wiles.
52. Jupiter Island, the subsequent Japan Cup winner.
53. Last Tycoon in the Breeders' Cup Mile.

54. Half Free.
55. Tony Murray.
56. Fred Archer.
57. Twenty-six.
58. David Barons and Paul Nicholls.
59. The Glen International Gold Cup.
60. The Geoffrey Freer Stakes at Newbury in August.
61. Phardante in the Jockey Club Stakes at Newmarket in May.
62. Dancing Brave (twice), Shardari, Triptych (twice) and Bering.
63. Shahrastani in the Derby, and Bering.
64. The Craven Stakes at Newmarket in April.
65. Two—the King George and the Arc.
66. Acatenango.
67. Valuable Witness.
68. Melendez.
69. Deep Run, sire of Dawn Run, Run And Skip, Half Free and Aonoch.
70. Moon Madness, the St Leger winner, and Sarfraz, the Goodwood Stakes winner.
71. Invited Guest.
72. Ivor's Image, who won the Oaks d'Italia in May and the E P Taylor Stakes in October.
73. Kirkstyle.
74. For Auction (1982) at Fairyhouse in April, and Dawn Run (1984) at Auteuil in June.
75. Michael Blackmore on Silent Shadow at Market Rasen in May, and Jayne Thompson on Hot Betty at Catterick Bridge in November.

News Diary

by MARK COTON

January

8: Newbury announce sponsorship deals worth more than £750,000 for 14 days' Flat racing

20: John Oxley dies, aged 55.

21: Jockey Club amend Rule 153; cases of accidental interference to be judged on individual merits.

23: Somerset-based Stuart Pattemore quits as public trainer.

27: Lincoln trainer David Morrill declared bankrupt with debts of over £36,000

February

1: Burrough Hill Lad and See You Then win at Sandown Park.

13: Jockey Club announce that Billy Newnes will get jockey's licence back on 1 July.

24: Jockey Club announce 20 replacement fixtures for April and May, to compensate for 95 meetings lost to weather.

○ **TRIPLE TONIC: The Queen Mother and one of her three winners on 8 March, Special Cargo.**
Picture: DESMOND O'NEILL

27: Levy Board 1986 strategy review promises more than £10m for improving on-course spectator facilities.

March

6: Burrough Hill Lad, ante-post favourite for Tote Cheltenham Gold Cup, to miss race because of leg injury.

8: Queen Mother has 134-1 Sandown hat-trick with Special Cargo, Insular and The Argonaut, her first since 1962. Malton trainer Mick Lambert to quit; blames bad payers.

11: New legislation brings live TV coverage and refreshments in betting shops. See You Then (Steve Smith Eccles) lands second Waterford Crystal Champion Hurdle.

13: Dawn Run (Jonjo O'Neill) wins Tote Cheltenham Gold Cup. Meeting attracts record crowd of £41,732.

17: Sporting Life drops cover price from 40p to 25p.

19: Terry Ramsden buys Grand National favourite Mr Snugfit.

21: Terry Higgs, owner of TNS bookmakers, is jailed for 14 years, having stolen more than £3m to fund gambling.

23: Fire causes £250,000 damage to main stand at Nottingham.

April

5: West Tip (Richard Dunwoody) wins Grand National.

13: Peter Scudamore accepts offer to ride as first jockey to Fred Winter in 1986-87.

15: Racing Post launched. Sonic Lady wins Nell Gwyn Stakes.

17: Dancing Brave wins Craven Stakes.

22: Pat Eddery gets seven-day ban for careless riding on Land Of Ivory in Princess Elizabeth Stakes at Epsom and misses Guineas meeting.

○ **TERRY RAMSDEN: Big spender.**

○ **BRIGHT NEW DAWN: TV and refreshments in betting shops from 11 March.**

25: Monty Court, 57, takes over from Graham Taylor as editor of Sporting Life.

26: Shahrastani becomes ante-post favourite for the Derby after easy win in Guardian Classic Trial at Sandown.

28: Contractual problems mean Lester Piggott abandons plan to resume riding on Midway Lady in 1,000 Guineas. Tony Ives takes Piggott's proposed ride on Tate Gallery in 2,000. Richard Dunwoody to ride as first jockey to David Nicholson in 1986-7.

May

1: Midway Lady (Ray Cochrane) wins 1,000 Guineas.

2: Slip Anchor beaten by Phardante in Jockey Club Stakes.

3: Dancing Brave (Greville Starkey) wins 2,000 Guineas.

11: Amateur rider Michael Blackmore, 30, killed after hurdles fall from Silent Shadow at Market Rasen.

12: Robin Dickin quits riding to become trainer.

13: Dawn Run voted Racegoers Club NH Horse of Year.

14: Trainer John Hill banned for eight months for failing to pay correct percentage of prize money to staff.

18: Journalist and commentator Michael Seth-Smith, 57, dies. Tony Charlton retires from riding to concentrate on training; wins on last ride, Acercate at Uttoxeter.

19: Jockey Chris Pimlott to quit at end of jumps season; last ride on Starlight Rocky at Perth, 22 May.

20: Manton stable opened to Press after more than £14m spent on 230 acre site.

28: York racecourse reveal US bloodstock brokers Matchmaker as sponsor of old Benson & Hedges Gold Cup.

30: Jonjo O'Neill retires from riding to train in Cumbria.

31: Lester Piggott has first winner as trainer, Latch String at Nottingham. NH season ends; Nick Henderson champion trainer, Peter Scudamore jockey and Tim Thomson Jones amateur. Great Nephew put down at age of 25.

June

4: Shahrastani (Walter Swinburn) wins the Derby.

7: Midway Lady (Ray Cochrane) gains second Classic win, in the Oaks.

8: Bering wins French Derby.

9: Willie Carson rides 2,500th winner, on Flower Bowl at Leicester.

11: Petoski to stand at National Stud when retired.

12: Derby winner Slip Anchor retired to stand at owner Lord Howard de Walden's Plantation Stud. Eric Legrix sacked by Daniel Wildenstein.

26: Jockey Club turn down Edward Hide's bid to become Stewards' Secretary.

27: Dawn Run killed when falling in Grande Course de Haies d'Auteuil.

28: Shahrastani (Walter Swinburn) wins Budweiser Irish Derby.

July

1: Billy Newnes has first ride after 2½-year ban, on Chardonnay at Folkestone.

3: Trainer Barry Hills and jockey Brent Thomson split.

5: Dancing Brave wins Eclipse Stakes at Sandown.

○ BILLY NEWNES: Back in action   Picture: DAVID HASTINGS

7: Owner Jim Joel, 92, to disperse broodmare stud; failing eyesight and retirement of top groom reasons for decision.

9: Pebbles retired because of shoulder injury.

10: Billy Newnes rides double at Catterick Bridge, My Buddy and Great Exception, first winners since October 1983.

12: Colorspin (Pat Eddery) wins Irish Oaks.

20: Bridlington owner-trainer Clifford Watts, 81, dies.

21: Windsor racecourse purchase option for £5m gained by syndicate involving Toby and Ian Balding.

22: Pat Eddery named to replace Greville Starkey on Dancing Brave in King George at Ascot. David Wintle and Tony Carroll banned for three months over running of Terra Di Siena at Taunton on May 2 and 16.

23: Levy Board report income of £21.8m for 1985-6.

25: Tony Ives to ride as first jockey to Ian Balding in 1987.

26: Dancing Brave (Pat Eddery) wins King George VI and Queen Elizabeth Diamond Stakes.

29: Ron O'Leary quits riding because of weight problems.

30: Sonic Lady wins Sussex Stakes.

August

5: Princess Anne rides first winner, on 14th ride, Gulfland at Redcar. Tote take over sponsorship of Schweppes Gold Trophy at Newbury; Schweppes to back new race at course on Lincoln Day.

6: Pat Eddery accepts retainer for Khalid Abdullah in 1987; Cash Asmussen to take Eddery's job with Vincent O'Brien.

10: Minstrella beats Forest Flower and Polonia in Heinz 57 Phoenix Stakes.

11: Trainer Chris Bell quits after leading owner takes horses, including Rotherfield Greys, from yard. Trainer Ray Howe relinquishes licence.

14: Jonjo O'Neill announces he is suffering from cancer of lymph gland.

16: Ryan Price, 74, dies.

18: Midway Lady retired because of recurring leg injury.

19: Michael Stoute wins two Group One races at York, Matchmaker International Stakes (Shardari) and Yorkshire Oaks (Untold).

21: Last Tycoon wins William Hill Sprint Championship.

28: Lester Piggott fined £1,000 on firearms charge.

29: Tony Ives secures second retainer with Lester Piggott for 1987.

September

2: Bernard Penfold retires after six years as Chairman of Horseracing Advisory Council.

3: Phil Tuck equals Johnny Gilbert's record of ten straight NH wins, on Doronicum at Southwell, but is beaten on odds-on shot on next ride.

10: Michael Dickinson trains first winner, Veryan Boy at Lingfield Park.

11: Five runners withdrawn under starter's orders in a flag start for Portland Handicap. Petrizzo disqualified for second time in Doncaster Cup.

12: Channel 4 secure exclusive rights to cover Arc de Triomphe live.

13: Moon Madness (Pat Eddery) wins St Leger.

22: Mummy's Pet dies, aged 18.

○ RYAN PRICE: Drama might have been invented for him.
Picture: R H WRIGHT

Ryan Price

by GEORGE ENNOR

RYAN PRICE, who died on his 74th birthday, 16 August, was a man for whom drama might have been invented. His successes alone were enough to make him a trainer to remember, even if there had been no episodes of a less happy nature.

During his 45 years in racing he scaled the highest peaks and plumbed the lowest depths, from the training of Classic winners to the disgrace of being warned off.

His father bred show hacks at Hindhead in Surrey, and the young Price starred in local gymkhanas. Later he rode about 200 point-to-point winners, and in 1937 took up training at Hambleton in Yorkshire, where his nearest neighbour was Noel Murless.

His new career had hardly begun when World War II was declared. Price volunteered for the Commandos and distinguished himself by winning the Military Cross.

Soon after the war he was married, and he and his wife Dorothy moved to Lavant in Sussex. Price resumed training and shortly moved to the nearby Findon yard with which his name will always be associated.

It was not long before the French connection, which was to serve Price so well for so long, became evident. Many of his best early winners resulted from his friendship with jockey Charlie Elliott, then riding for Marcel Boussac. They included Claire Soleil, one of only two horses to win the Triumph Hurdle and Champion Hurdle, and Nuage Dore.

Claire Soleil won the Champion in 1955, and Price followed up with Fare Time (1959) and Eborneezer (1961). The Cheltenham Gold Cup eluded him until 1969, when the unorthodox preparation of What A Myth took him through the hunting field and hunter chases to the championship.

In between, Kilmore came out best in a battle of veterans for the 1962 Grand National. Later, Price won the Mackeson Gold Cup with Charlie Worcester, the Triumph Hurdle with Beaver II and Moonlight Bay, and the Whitbread Gold Cup with Done Up and Charlie Worcester.

But it was not all sweetness and light, especially from the moment the Schweppes Gold Trophy was launched. Price had his eyes on the season's richest handicap hurdle from the start, and won its first two runnings in 1963 and 1964 with Rosyth.

The horse's preparation for the second running did not convince the National Hunt Committee Stewards that all had been properly conducted, and Price was warned off. Four months later the ban was lifted, and to no-one's surprise Price was back in the Schweppes forefront in no time, winning in 1966 with Le Vermontois and 1967 with Hill House.

Even then the controversy was far from over. Hill House's 12-length success was greeted with a storm of booing, since his previous form hardly matched up to it, and once more Price went before the beak. After a series of lengthy inquiries, it was decided Hill House could have produced his own cortisol, and that could have affected his performance in the Schweppes.

Josh Gifford, who rode many of Price's best jumping winners, was sandwiched between Fred Winter and Paul Kelleway as Findon stable jockey, and when Gifford retired from race riding in 1970, he took over the Downs Yard, with Price building a small yard nearby called Soldiers Field.

Any plans to restrict his operation soon fell by the wayside, and by 1975 he had more than 100 horses.

He had already made his mark on the Flat in the 1960s, winning the Cesarewitch with Utrillo, Persian Lancer and Major Rose. In 1972 Ginevra's Oaks success gave him his first Classic victory, to be followed three years later by Bruni in the St Leger.

Having trained a career total of nearly 2,000 winners, Price retired at the end of the 1982 season, but his later years were marked with a deal of unhappiness.

His former assistant Con Horgan took over Soldiers Field but he and Price had what almost amounted to a public row in the first season, and they went their separate ways at the beginning of 1985. John Dunlop bought the yard as an overflow.

By now Price was far from well, and though he used to go racing fairly regularly during his early retirement, he was seen increasingly rarely.

Many an old Findon standard-bearer lived in honourable and pampered retirement at Soldiers Field. Price's affection for them was totally genuine, as was everything about him. For all the big winners he trained, he would perhaps have preferred simply to be remembered as a man who loved his horses. □

24: Stavros Niarchos to pull out of Robert Sangster bloodstock syndicate. Bruce Raymond disqualified for three months and fined £7,000 in Hong Kong betting case. Petoski valued at £2.3m.

29: Satellite Information Services sign heads of agreement with RCA to cover racing by satellite in betting shops; Ladbrokes, Hills, Corals and Mecca, have a 45% holding in company. Dick Hern out in public for the first time in nearly two years at Highflyer Sales.

October

1: Forest Flower survives Stewards' inquiry after beating Minstrella in Cheveley Park Stakes.

5: Dancing Brave (Pat Eddery breaks course record to wil Arc de Triomphe.

7: Trainer David Moorhead banned for five years for altering horses' passports.

14: Forest Flower disqualified from Cheveley Park and jockey Tony Ives suspended for 12 days for reckless riding,

O WELL DONE, DAD: David Tuck is well pleased with his father Phil's record-equalling success at Southwell.
Picture: ALAN JOHNSON

on appeal to Jockey Club Disciplinary Committee.

15: Ridley Lamb rides 500th winner, on Newlife Connection at Wetherby.

17: Ajdal wins Dewhurst Stakes.

18: Triptych wins Champion Stakes.

19: Shahrastani retired to stand at Three Chimney's Stud, Kentucky.

20: Writer Jeffrey Bernard fined £200 plus costs for illegal bookmaking.

21: Trainer Stephen Wiles warned off for five years in wake of Flockton Grey case; father Fred Wiles banned for three years. John Sanderson to quit as York Clerk of the Course. Ladbrokes to sponsor replacement for Irish Sweeps Hurdle, worth at least IR£50,000.

22: Tony Murray, 36, to quit riding.

23: Michael Albina to leave Newmarket to train for Mahmoud Foustok in US.

24: George Duffield fractures cheekbone in a football match and misses rest of season.

25: Reference Point wins William Hill Futurity.

28: Final Try sold for 100,000gns, record for prospective jumper.

O DICK HERN: Glad to be back. Picture: DESMOND O'NEILL

O JEFFREY BERNARD: Illegal betting. Picture: SPORT & GENERAL

Tattersalls Committee announce changes to Rule 4 governing deductions to bets in event of withdrawn horses.

30: Ladbrokes refuse to accept bets at Pari-Mutuel odds on Breeders' Cup races. Mecca follow next day.

November

1: Dancing Brave fourth to Manila in Breeders' Cup Turf; Sonic Lady and Green Desert also well beaten, but Last Tycoon wins Mile for France.

6: Two-year driving ban for Walter Swinburn after drinks case.

8: Jayne Thompson in coma after fall from Hot Betty at Catterick. Flat season ends; Michael Stoute champion trainer, Pat Eddery jockey.

10: Sir Gordon Richards, 82, dies.

11: Ken Richardson, key figure in Flockton Grey case, banned for 25 years.

13: New five-day entry system to become operational in winter 1988-9. Trainer Roger Fisher in court on nine charges including theft and deception.

14: Jayne Thompson, 22, dies of head injuries.

23: Jupiter Island wins Japan Cup.

24: Michael Dickinson sacked as private trainer to Robert Sangster.

25: Barry Hills to take over from Dickinson at Manton.

December

2: Jim Joel dispersal of 20 mares at Tattersalls makes 3.9 million guineas; Fairy Footsteps top at 720,000gns.

3: Ever Ready agree to back Derby until 1991.

8: Graham McCourt banned 28 days for "causing intentional interference". Princess Anne elected honorary member of Jockey Club; other new members include Peter O'Sullevan.

9: In Gimcrack Dinner speech Robert Sangster calls for European Breeders' Cup day.

10: Queen Elizabeth II Stakes (Ascot) to become Group One in 1987. Fillies' allowance in two-year-old Pattern races to go up from 3lb to 5lb.

12: Sir Gerald Glover, owner-breeder of Privy Councillor, dies, aged 78.

16: Dancing Brave top three-year-old and Reference Point top two-year-old in International Classification.

19: Lester Piggott charged with Income Tax fraud and given 72 hours to produce bank draft for £950,000 as bail. France to reduce Grand Prix de Paris distance from 15f to 10f.

20: Jenny Pitman saddles first, second and fourth in Coral Welsh Grand National.

22: Lester Piggott lodges bail 25 minutes before deadline.

23: High Court cuts Lester Piggott bail to £500,000.

26: Desert Orchid wins King George VI Rank Chase.

31: Sir Woodrow Wyatt made life peer in New Year Honours list.

◐ SAD DAY: Dick Hern and Joe Mercer at Sir Gordon Richards' funeral.
Picture: PRESS ASSOCIATION

O **CONGRATULATIONS: The Queen says well done to Gordon Richards after his Derby success on Pinza.** Picture: SPORT & GENERAL

Sir Gordon Richards

by GEORGE ENNOR

SIR GORDON RICHARDS, who died at the age of 82 on 10 November, was in many people's view the greatest jockey of the 20th Century. He was champion jockey 26 times; he rode a British record of 4,870 winners, of which 14 were in Classics, and set a British record for one season of 269 in 1947.

Though he had been in poor health for some time before he died, he had already survived one serious illness and a number of bad falls in a riding career which spanned more than 30 years.

It was tribute to his honour and integrity, as much to his riding skill, when in 1953 he became the only jockey ever to be knighted.

He was one of of eight surviving children of a Shropshire coalminer, and had his first ride in 1920. His first winner was on Gay

Lord in an apprentice race at Leicester the following season.

His first Classic victories were in 1930 when Rose of England won the Oaks and Singapore the St Leger. He lost the jockeys' title though, to Freddie Fox by one.

Richards topped the riding list for the next ten years, during which there were Classic wins on Chulmleigh in the 1937 St Leger and Pasch in the following year's 2,000 Guineas. In 1933 he beat Fred Archer's record of 246 winners, set in 1885, by riding 259 in the year. That season he also rode 12 winners in a row, starting with his last mount at Nottingham one day and then the next 11 over two days at Chepstow.

In 1943 he passed Fred Archer's career total of 2,748 but that should be put into perspective by pointing out, as Richards would have done,

that Archer was only 29 when he died and that Richards was by then ten years older.

In 1953 the Queen conferred a knighthood on him for his services to racing and in line with the best fairytale scripts, his finest moment followed immediately after.

It had seemed that Derby glory would elude him. He had been placed several times, and one year was was sent off 4-7 favourite on Tudor Minstrel without success. But it all came right in Coronation year on a colt called Pinza, who stormed home to beat the Queen's Aureole by four lengths.

That was Sir Gordon's final Derby ride. He was injured the following year, and though he came back for Ascot, a fall in the paddock at Sandown Park on Eclipse day resulted in his breaking his pelvis and dislocating four ribs.

He started training in 1955 at Beckhampton, and though he had several big-race successes, notably with Reform, Greengage and Dart Board, it would have been impossible for that part of his life to be as outstandingly successful as his days in the saddle. It may be that he did not enjoy training as much as he did riding.

By the end of 1969 he could not find suitable premises from which to train and did not renew his licence. Instead he acted as racing manager to Lady Beaverbrook and the Ballymacoll Stud team of Sir Michael Sobell and Lord Weinstock.

In the autumn of 1982 he suffered a major blow with the death of his wife Marjorie, mother of their three children Jack, Peter and Marjorie. He probably never got over it.

It would be hard to find a man who had a harsh word to say about Sir Gordon Richards, and Roger Mortimer summed up admirably when he wrote, "The sport of horse racing has never had a better friend than Sir Gordon Richards".

Unique is a dangerous word to use about anyone. In Sir Gordon's case, it might just be the right one.

Ascot Flat

Course Characteristics

Right-handed triangle, galloping and stiff, with few undulations. Just over 1m 6f round, with 2½f run-in. Straight mile and round mile. All races up to 7f on straight course

Draw: When stalls on stands side on straight course, low numbers slightly favoured; on round course, high numbers slightly favoured.

How to get there

Road: W of town on A329 Bracknell road. M4(Jctn6); M3(Jctn3). **Rail:** 500 yds, Ascot Stn (from London Waterloo). **Air:** 15m, London (Heathrow); 12m, White Waltham Airfield.

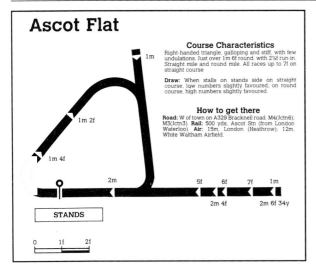

Ayr Jumps

How to get there

Road: E of city on A758 Mauchline road. **Rail:** ½m, Ayr Stn (from Glasgow). **Air:** 3m, Prestwick Airport; 40m, Glasgow Airport.

Course Characteristics

Left-handed, mainly flat. Circuit 1m 4f.

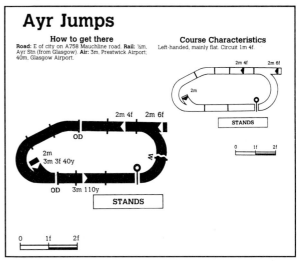

Ascot Jumps

Course Characteristics

Right-handed, galloping, with stiff fences. Circuit 1m 5f.

How to get there

Road: W of town on A329 Bracknell road. M4(Jctn6); M3(Jctn3). **Rail:** 500 yds, Ascot Stn (from London Waterloo). **Air:** 15m, London (Heathrow); 12m, White Waltham Airfield.

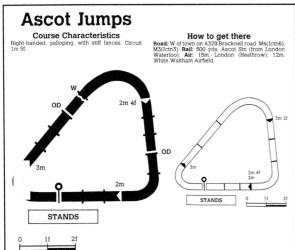

Bangor

How to get there

Road: 5m SE of Wrexham off B5069 Bangor-Oswestry road. **Rail:** 5m, Wrexham Stn. Bus to Bangor.

Course Characteristics

Left-handed, sharp and flat with a long run-in. Circuit 1m 4f.

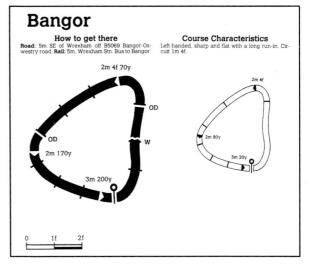

Ayr Flat

Course Characteristics

Left-handed oval, galloping with minor undulations. About 1m 4f round.

Draw: When stalls on stands side on straight course, high numbers favoured; on soft going, low numbers slightly favoured.

How to get there

Road: E of city on A758 Mauchline road. **Rail:** ½m, Ayr Stn (from Glasgow). **Air:** 3m, Prestwick Airport; 40m, Glasgow Airport.

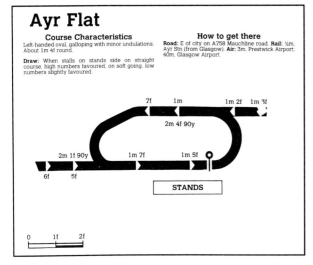

Bath

How to get there

Road: 2m NW of city at Lansdown (access A431 Bristol road). M4(Jctn18). **Rail:** 2m, Bath Stn (access London Paddington, or Bristol Temple Meads from N).

Course Characteristics

Left-handed oval, galloping, just over 1m 4f round. 4f run-in, bending to left, against collar throughout. Ground seldom testing.

Draw: Up to 1m, low numbers slightly favoured.

BEVERLEY

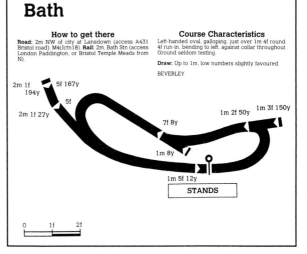

Beverley

How to get there

Road: 1m W of town off A1035 Market Weighton road. M62(Jctn38). **Rail:** 1m, Beverley Stn (Hull-Scarborough line).

Course Characteristics

Right-handed oval, generally galloping, with very stiff 5f course. 1m 3f round.

Draw: When stalls on far side, high numbers greatly favoured over 5f.

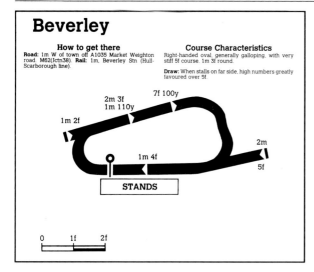

Brighton

Course Characteristics

Left-handed, U-shaped, markedly undulating and sharp. Suits handy types. 1m 4f in length.

Draw: Low numbers generally favoured.

How to get there

Road: E of town off A27 Lewes road. **Rail:** 1m, Brighton Stn (from London Victoria).

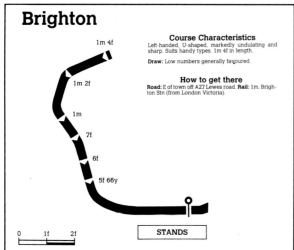

Carlisle Flat

How to get there

Road: 2m S of town on Durdar road. M6(Jctn42). **Rail:** 2m, Carlisle Stn (main west coast route).

Course Characteristics

Right-handed, pear-shaped, galloping and against collar over last 4f. Just over 1m 4f round.

Draw: High numbers slightly favoured.

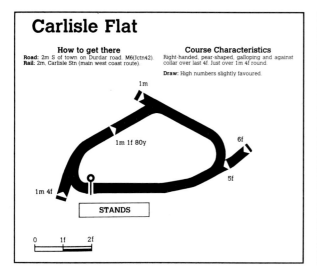

Carlisle Jumps

How to get there

Road: 2m S of town on Durdar road. M6(Jctn42). **Rail:** 2m, Carlisle Stn (main west coast route).

Course Characteristics

Right-handed, undulating, stiff and galloping. Circuit 1m 5f.

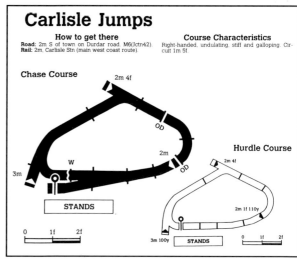

Cartmel

How to get there

Road: 1m W of town, 2m off B5277 Grange-Haverthwaite road. M6(Jctn36). **Rail:** 2½m, Cark and Cartmel Stn (Carnforth-Barrow line).

Course Characteristics

Left-handed, sharp and undulating, with stiff fences and a 4f run-in for chases. Circuit 1m.

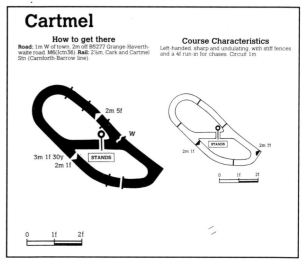

Catterick Bridge Flat

Course Characteristics

Left-handed oval, undulating and very sharp with handiness essential. About 1m 1f round.

Draw: When stalls on far side, low numbers slightly favoured over 5f.

How to get there

Road: 1m NW of town on A6136 (via A1). **Rail:** 14m, Darlington Stn (London King's Cross-Newcastle line). Bus to course.

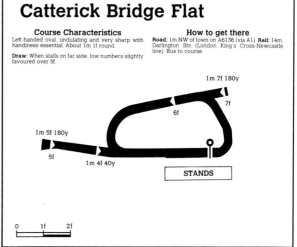

Catterick Bridge Jumps

How to get there
Road: 1m NW of town on A6136 (via A1). **Rail:** 14m, Darlington Stn (London King's Cross-Newcastle line). Bus to course.

Course Characteristics
Left-handed, sharp and undulating, suiting handy types. Circuit 1m 3f.

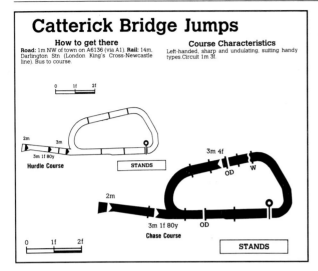

Chepstow Flat

How to get there
Road: 1m NW of town on A466 Monmouth road. M4(Jctn22). **Rail:** 1m, Chepstow Stn (from Newport).

Course Characteristics
Left-handed oval, undulating, 1m 7f round with 4½f run-in. Races up to 1m on straight course. Tends to have extremes of going.

Draw: Up to 1m on good or fast going, high numbers slightly favoured; on soft going, low numbers slightly favoured.

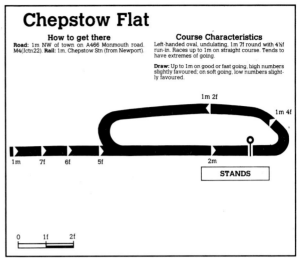

Cheltenham Old

How to get there
Road: 1½m N of town off A435 Evesham road. M5(Jctn10 or 11). **Rail:** 2m, Cheltenham Spa Stn (from London Paddington, Bristol or Birmingham). **Air:** 6m, Staverton Airport.

Course Characteristics
Left-handed, galloping, with stiff fences. Old Course circuit 1m 4f. New Course slightly longer.

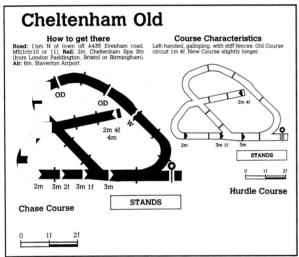

Chepstow Jumps

Course Characteristics
Left-handed and undulating. Going can be very testing. Circuit 1m 7f.

How to get there
Road: 1m NW of town on A466 Monmouth road. M4(Jctn22). **Rail:** 1m, Chepstow Stn (from Newport).

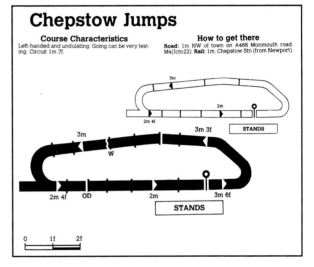

Cheltenham New

How to get there
Road: 1½m N of town off A435 Evesham road. M5(Jctn10 or 11). **Rail:** 2m, Cheltenham Spa Stn (from London Paddington, Bristol or Birmingham). **Air:** 6m, Staverton Airport.

Course Characteristics
Left-handed, galloping, with stiff fences. Old Course circuit 1m 4f. New Course slightly longer.

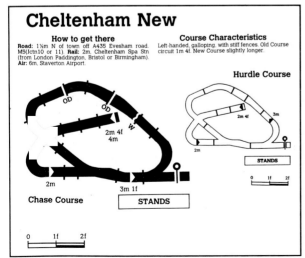

Chester

Course Characteristics
Left-handed, flat, just over 1m round with short run-in. Very sharp, not favouring long-striding horses.

Draw: Up to 7f 122yds, low numbers slightly favoured.

How to get there
Road: In SW of city on A548 Queensferry road. Junction of M56 with M53. **Rail:** 1m, Chester General (from London Euston). **Bus:** ¾m, Crosville Stn. **Air:** 2m, Hawarden Airport.

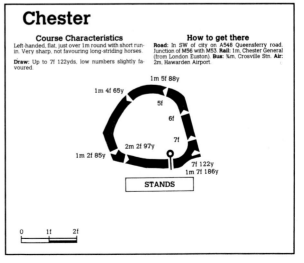

Devon & Exeter, Summer

How to get there
Road: At Haldon 5m SW of Exeter on A38 Plymouth road. **Rail:** Three stations in Exeter (St Davids on main London Paddington-Cornwall route). Bus to course.

Course Characteristics
Right-handed and undulating.Stiff test of stamina. Circuit 2m.

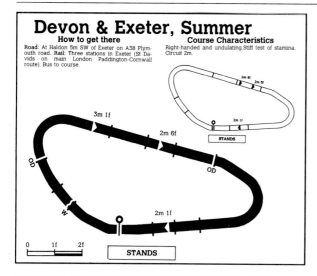

Doncaster Jumps

How to get there
Road: E of town off A638 Bawtry road. M18(Jctn3 or 4). **Rail:** 1½m, Doncaster Stn (London King's Cross-NE line). **Air:** Airport nearby.

Course Characteristics
Left-handed, pear-shaped, galloping. Almost 2m round with 4½f run-in. Round and straight miles. Mainly flat, providing fair test.

Draw: When stalls on stands side on straight course and going is soft, high numbers slightly favoured; on round course, low numbers slightly favoured.

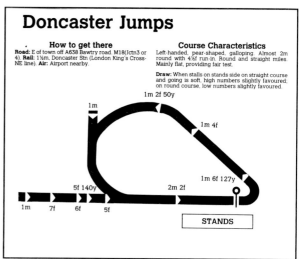

Devon & Exeter, Winter

How to get there
Road: At Haldon 5m SW of Exeter on A38 Plymouth road. **Rail:** Three stations in Exeter (St Davids on main London Paddington-Cornwall route). Bus to course.

Course Characteristics
Right-handed and undulating.Stiff test of stamina. Circuit 2m.

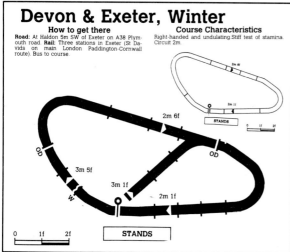

Edinburgh Flat

How to get there
Road: 5m E of city on A1 in Musselburgh. **Rail:** 5m, Edinburgh Stn. Bus to course.

Course Characteristics
Right-handed oval of 1m 2f with tight turns. 4f run-in. Going rarely testing.

Draw: When stalls on stands side on straight course, low numbers greatly favoured; on round course, high numbers favoured.

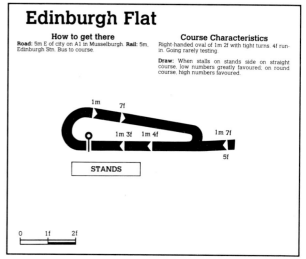

Doncaster Flat

Course Characteristics
Left-handed, galloping, generally flat. Heavy ground rare. Circuit 2m.

How to get there
Road: E of town off A638 Bawtry road. M18(Jctn3 or 4). **Rail:** 1½m, Doncaster Stn (London King's Cross-NE line). **Air:** Airport nearby.

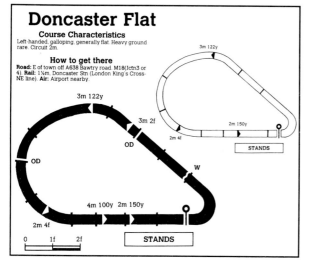

Edinburgh Jumps

How to get there
Road: 5m E of city on A1 in Musselburgh. **Rail:** 5m, Edinburgh Stn. Bus to course.

Course Characteristics
Level, right-handed oval of 1m 3f with tight turns.

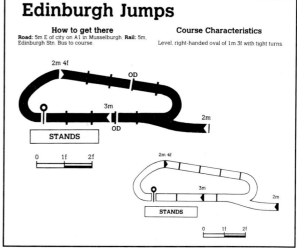

Epsom

How to get there

Road: 2m S of town on B290 Tadworth road. M25(Jctn8 or 9). **Rail:** ½m, Tattenham Corner Stn (from London Bridge, Charing Cross, Victoria or Waterloo, change at Purley). **Air:** 20m, London (Heathrow) and London (Gatwick).

Course Characteristics

Left-handed, U-shaped course of 1m 4f noted for steep undulations. 3½f run-in with pronounced camber, initially downhill, rising in final furlong. Races up to 8½f essentially sharp, particularly on 5f track, which is fastest in world.

Draw: Over 5f, high numbers favoured; 1m 110yds to 1m 2f, low numbers greatly favoured.

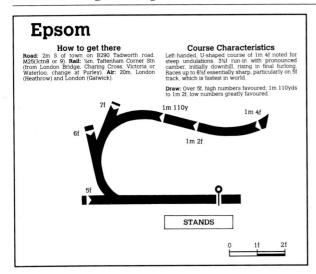

Folkestone Jumps

How to get there

Road: 6m W of town at Westenhanger, off A20 Ashford road. M20(Jctn11). **Rail:** Adjoining course, Westenhanger Stn (London Charing Cross-Ramsgate line).

Course Characteristics

Right-handed, undulating. Circuit 1m 2f.

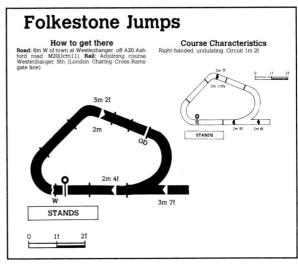

Fakenham

How to get there

Road: 1m S of town off B1146 East Dereham road. **Rail:** 26m, Norwich Stn (from London Liverpool Street). Bus to Fakenham.

Course Characteristics

Left-handed, sharp and undulating, suiting nippy types. Circuit 1m.

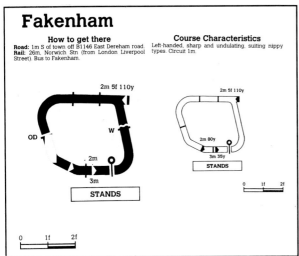

Fontwell Park

How to get there

Road: S of village at junction of A29 Bognor road with A27 Brighton-Chichester road. **Rail:** 2m, Barnham Stn (Brighton-Portsmouth line, access London Victoria).

Course Characteristics

Left-handed hurdle course. Figure-of-eight chase course does not suit long-striding gallopers. Ground can be very testing. Circuit 1m.

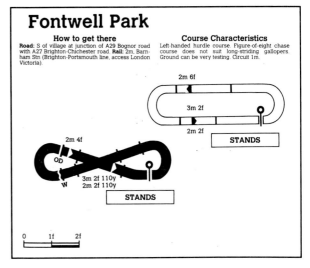

Folkestone Flat

How to get there

Road: 6m W of town at Westenhanger, off A20 Ashford road. M20(Jctn11). **Rail:** Adjoining course, Westenhanger Stn (London Charing Cross-Ramsgate line).

Course Characteristics

Right-handed, undulating oval of 1m 2f with 2f run-in.

Draw: On straight course on soft going, low numbers slightly favoured; on round course, high numbers favoured.

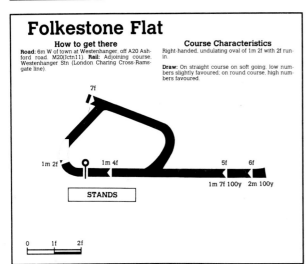

Goodwood

Course Characteristics

Right-handed with a loop for longer races. Long run-in, but primarily sharp, particularly on downhill sprint course.

Draw: When stalls on stands side, low numbers slightly favoured over 5 and 6f; 7f to 1m 4f, high numbers favoured.

How to get there

Road: 6m N of Chichester between A286 Midhurst road and A285 Petworth road. **Rail:** 6m, Chichester Stn (Brighton-Portsmouth line, access London Victoria). Bus to course. **Air:** 2m, Goodwood Airfield; 25m, Shoreham Airport.

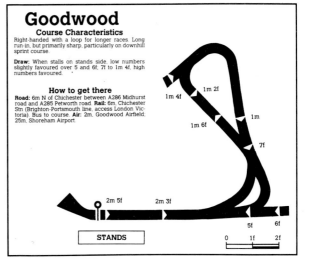

Hamilton Park

How to get there
Road: N of town off A74 close to Junction 5 of M74.
Rail: 1m, Hamilton West Stn (from Glasgow). **Air:** 20m, Glasgow Airport.

Course Characteristics
Right-handed, loop course with 5f run-in part of straight 6f. Undulating, with pronounced finishing climb. Can become very testing.

Draw: High numbers slightly favoured.

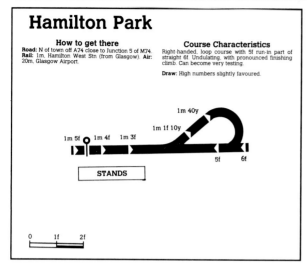

Hereford

How to get there
Road: 1m NW of city off A49 Leominster road. **Rail:** 1m, Hereford station (access Oxford, Birmingham, S.Wales).

Course Characteristics
Right-handed, sharpish and generally flat. Suits nippy types. Circuit 1m 4f.

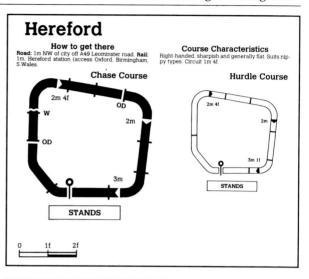

Haydock Park Flat

Course Characteristics
Left-handed oval, galloping, 1m 5f round, with 4½f run-in.

Draw: When stalls on stands side, high numbers slightly favoured over 5f.

How to get there
Road: On A49 Wigan road. M6(Jctn23). **Rail:** 2m, Newton-le-Willows Stn (Manchester-Liverpool line). Warrington Bank Quay or Wigan Stns better from London Euston. **Air:** 20m. Manchester International and Liverpool Speke Airports. Light aircraft on course.

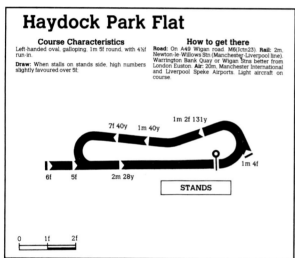

Hexham

How to get there
Road: 2m SW of town off B6305 Allendale road. **Rail:** 2m, Hexham Stn (Newcastle-Carlisle line).

Course Characteristics
Left-handed, severe and undulating, placing emphasis on stamina. Circuit 1m 4f.

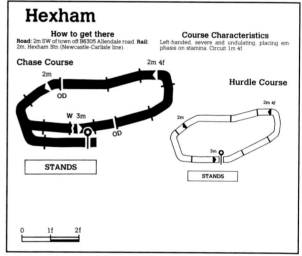

Haydock Park Jumps

How to get there
Road: On A49 Wigan road. M6(Jctn23). **Rail:** 2m, Newton-le-Willows Stn (Manchester-Liverpool line). Warrington Bank Quay or Wigan Stns better from London Euston. **Air:** 20m. Manchester International and Liverpool Speke Airports. Light aircraft on course.

Course Characteristics
Left-handed, flat and galloping. Drop fences and long run-in on chase course. Old hurdle course suits gallopers; New Course much sharper. Circuit 1m 5f.

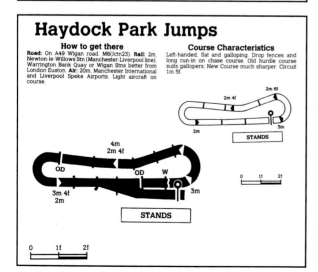

Huntingdon

How to get there
Road: 2m W of town off A604 Kettering road. **Rail:** 2m, Huntingdon Stn (London King's Cross-Peterborough line).

Course Characteristics
Right-handed and galloping. Circuit 1m 4f.

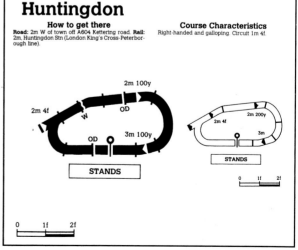

Kelso

How to get there
Road: 1m N of town off B6461 Berwick road. **Rail:** 23m, Berwick-on-Tweed Stn. Bus to Kelso.

Course Characteristics
Left-handed and undulating. Hurdles course of 1m 1f is sharp, more so than chase track of 1m 3f, which has 2f run-in.

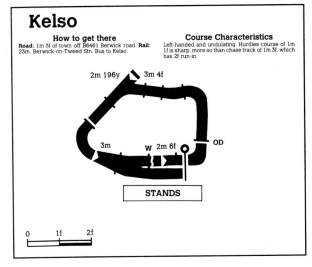

Leicester Flat

How to get there
Road: 2½m SE of city (signs to Oadby) off A6 Market Harborough Road. M1(Jctn21, with M69). **Rail:** 2½m, Leicester Stn (London St Pancras-Sheffield line).

Course Characteristics
Right-handed, undulating oval, about 1m 6f round with 5f run-in. Straight mile.

Draw: When stalls on far side, low numbers favoured up to 1m, especially on soft.

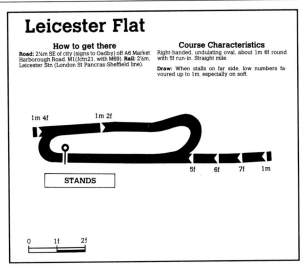

Kempton Park Flat

How to get there
Road: On A308 Kingston road, close to Junction 1 of M3. **Rail:** Adjoining course, Kempton Park Stn (from London Waterloo). **Air:** 6m, London (Heathrow).

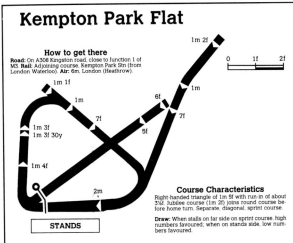

Course Characteristics
Right-handed triangle of 1m 5f with run-in of about 3½f. Jubilee course (1m 2f) joins round course before home turn. Separate, diagonal, sprint course.

Draw: When stalls on far side on sprint course, high numbers favoured; when on stands side, low numbers favoured.

Leicester Jumps

Course Characteristics
Right-handed and slightly undulating, placing emphasis on stamina. Circuit 1m 6f. Lingfield

How to get there
Road: 2½m SE of city (signs to Oadby) off A6 Market Harborough Road. M1(Jctn21, with M69). **Rail:** 2½m, Leicester Stn (London St Pancras-Sheffield line).

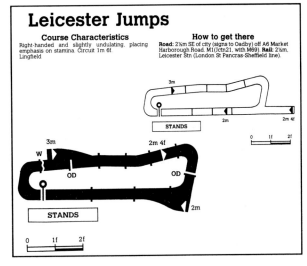

Kempton Park Jumps

How to get there
Road: On A308 Kingston road, close to Junction 1 of M3. **Rail:** Adjoining course, Kempton Park Stn (from London Waterloo). **Air:** 6m, London (Heathrow).

Course Characteristics
Right-handed, flat and fair. Circuit 1m 5f.

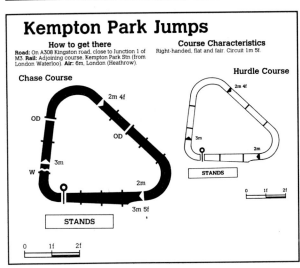

Lingfield Park Flat

Course Characteristics
Left-handed, undulating triangle of 1m 2f with 3½f run-in. Straight 7f 140yds.

Draw: When stalls on stands side on straight course, high numbers favoured; when on far side, low numbers favoured.

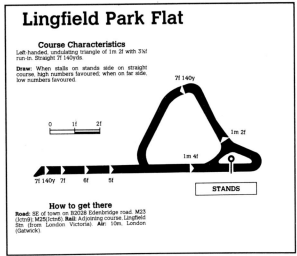

How to get there
Road: SE of town on B2028 Edenbridge road. M23 (Jctn9); M25(Jctn6). **Rail:** Adjoining course, Lingfield Stn (from London Victoria). **Air:** 10m, London (Gatwick).

Lingfield Park Jumps

Course Characteristics
Left-handed, undulating and sharp. Chase circuit 1m 5f, hurdles shorter.

How to get there
Road: SE of town on B2028 Edenbridge road. M23 (Jctn9); M25(Jctn6). **Rail:** Adjoining course, Lingfield Stn (from London Victoria). **Air:** 10m, London (Gatwick).

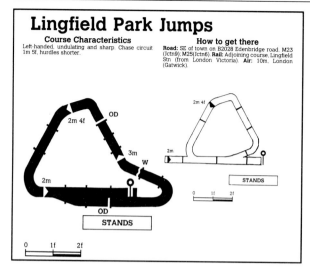

Ludlow

Course Characteristics
Right-handed. Chase course flat with sharp bends, circuit 1m 4f. Hurdles track, 150 yds longer, slightly undulating, with easier bends.

How to get there
Road: 2m NW of town off A49 Shrewsbury road. **Rail:** 2m, Ludlow Stn (Hereford-Shrewsbury line).

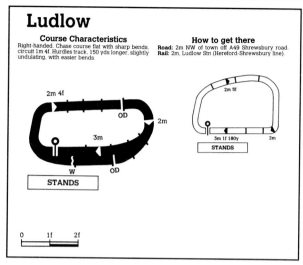

Liverpool Grand National

Course Characteristics
Two left-handed courses. Grand National circuit, 2m 2f, is flat and has big fences with drop on landing side. Long run-in. Mildmay Course of 1m 3f, flat with conventional fences, is sharper than hurdles course.

How to get there
Road: N of city, 1m S of junction of M57 and M58 with A59 Preston road. M6(Jctn21a). **Rail:** Adjoining course, Aintree Stn (London Euston-Liverpool Lime Street then local service). **Air:** 10m, Liverpool Speke Airport.

Market Rasen

How to get there
Road: 1m E of town on A631 Louth road. **Rail:** 1m, Market Rasen Stn (Lincoln-Grimsby line). **Air:** Light aircraft on course.

Course Characteristics
Right-handed oval, sharp and somewhat undulating. Circuit 1m 2f.

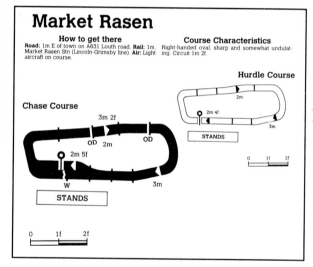

Liverpool Mildmay

How to get there
Road: N of town, 1m S of junction of M57 and M58 with A59 Preston road. M6(Jctn21a). **Rail:** Adjoining course, Aintree Stn (London Euston-Liverpool Lime Street then local service). **Air:** 10m, Liverpool Speke Airport.

Course Characteristics
Two left-handed courses. Grand National circuit, 2m 2f, is flat and has big fences with drop on landing side. Long run-in. Mildmay Course of 1m 3f, flat with conventional fences, is sharper than hurdles course.

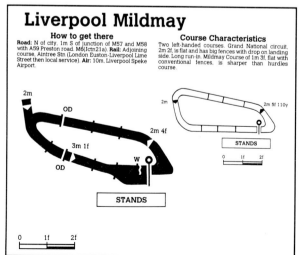

Newbury Flat

How to get there
Road: E of town off A34 Winchester road. M4(Jctn12) from E; M4(Jctn13) from W. **Rail:** Adjoining course, Newbury Racecourse Stn (from London Paddington). **Bus:** 1m, Newbury Bus Stn. **Air:** Light aircraft on course.

Course Characteristics
Left-handed, almost flat, roughly 1m 7f with 4½f run-in. Races on round mile and over 7f 60yds start on chute. Straight mile has minor undulations.

Draw: When stalls on stands side on straight course,high numbers slightly favoured, especially on soft going; up to 1m on round course, low numbers favoured.

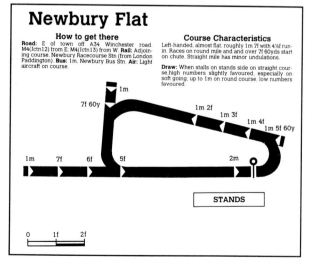

Newbury Jumps

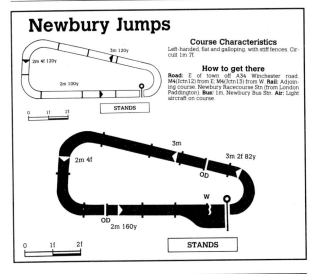

Course Characteristics
Left-handed, flat and galloping, with stiff fences. Circuit 1m 7f.

How to get there
Road: E of town off A34 Winchester road. M4(Jctn12) from E; M4(Jctn13) from W. **Rail:** Adjoining course, Newbury Racecourse Stn (from London Paddington). **Bus:** 1m, Newbury Bus Stn. **Air:** Light aircraft on course.

Newmarket July

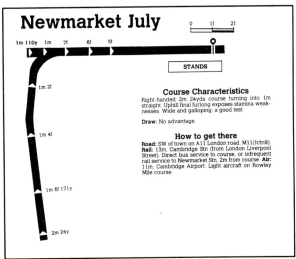

Course Characteristics
Right-handed 2m 24yds course turning into 1m straight. Uphill final furlong exposes stamina weaknesses. Wide and galloping; a good test.

Draw: No advantage.

How to get there
Road: SW of town on A11 London road. M11(Jctn9). **Rail:** 13m, Cambridge Stn (from London Liverpool Street). Direct bus service to course, or infrequent rail service to Newmarket Stn, 2m from course. **Air:** 11m, Cambridge Airport. Light aircraft on Rowley Mile course.

Newcastle Flat

How to get there
Road: 4m N of city off A6125. From S use Tyne Tunnel (A19/A1) then B1318 Killingworth road. **Rail:** 4m, Newcastle Stn (London King's Cross-Scotland line). Metro to Four Lane Ends then bus. **Air:** 6m, Newcastle Airport.

Course Characteristics
Left-handed oval of 1m 6f with easy bends. Uphill 4f run-in places emphasis on stamina. Straight 7f. Can become very testing.

Draw: Low numbers generally favoured, especially on soft.

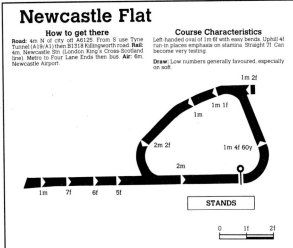

Newmarket Rowley Mile

Course Characteristics
Right-handed 2m 4f Cesarewitch Course turning into undulating 1m 2f straight. Uphill final furlong exposes stamina weaknesses. Wide and galloping; a good test.

Draw: Up to 1m, high numbers slightly favoured.

How to get there
Road: SW of town on A11 London road. M11(Jctn9). **Rail:** 13m, Cambridge Stn (from London Liverpool Street). Direct bus service to course, or infrequent rail service to Newmarket Stn, 2m from course. **Air:** 11m, Cambridge Airport. Light aircraft on Rowley Mile course.

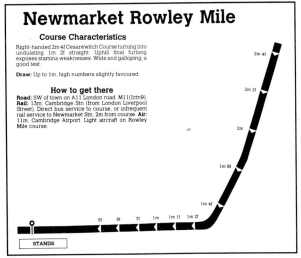

Newcastle Jumps

How to get there
Road: 4m N of city off A6125. From S use Tyne Tunnel (A19/A1) then B1318 Killingworth road. **Rail:** 4m, Newcastle Stn (London King's Cross-Scotland line). Metro to Four Lane Ends then bus. **Air:** 6m, Newcastle Airport.

Course Characteristics
Left-handed, with uphill finish. Going can be very testing. Circuit 1m 6f.

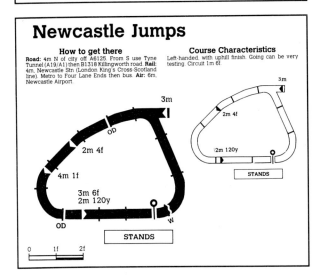

Newton Abbot

How to get there
Road: N of town on A380 Exeter road. **Rail:** ¾m, Newton Abbot Stn (on main line from London Paddington). **Air:** 20m, Exeter Airport.

Course Characteristics
Left-handed oval, sharp, with short run-in. Circuit 1m 2f.

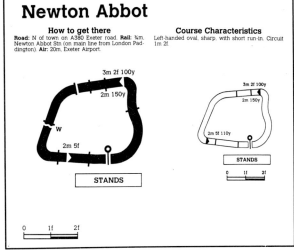

Nottingham Flat

How to get there
Road: 2m E of city off B686 Colwick road. M6(Jctn24 or 25). From E use A612 then Colwick road. **Rail:** 2m, Nottingham Stn (London St Pancras-Sheffield line).

Course Characteristics
Left-handed oval, galloping, flat with easy turns. About 1m 4f round with 4½f run-in.

Draw: When stalls on stands side on straight course, high numbers favoured, markedly so on soft going; up to 1m 2f, low numbers slightly favoured.

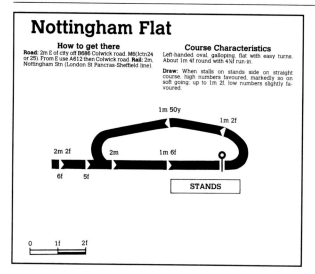

Plumpton

How to get there
Road: 2m N of village off B2116 Lewes-Keymer road. **Rail:** Adjoining course, Plumpton Stn (from London Victoria).

Course Characteristics
Left-handed, undulating, sharp. Circuit 1m 1f.

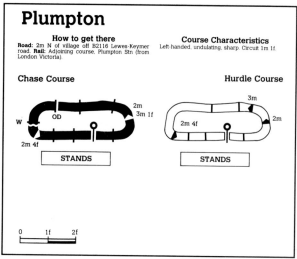

Nottingham Jumps

How to get there
Road: 2m E of city off B686 Colwick road. M6(Jctn24 or 25). From E use A612 then Colwick road. **Rail:** 2m, Nottingham Stn (London St Pancras-Sheffield line).

Course Characteristics
Left-handed, galloping, with easy turns and long finishing straight. Circuit 1m 4f.

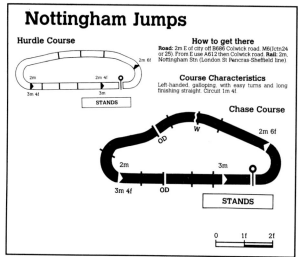

Pontefract

How to get there
Road: 1m N of town on A639 Castleford road. M62(Jctn32). **Rail:** 1½m, Pontefract Baghill Stn (Sheffield-York line).

Course Characteristics
Left-handed, undulating, 2m circuit, with straight of just over 2f. Last 6f essentially uphill.

Draw: Up to 1m2f, low numbers slightly favoured.

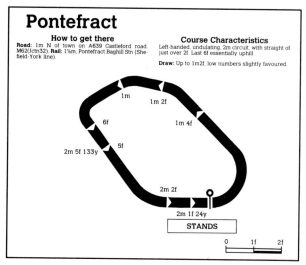

Perth

How to get there
Road: 4m N of town off A93 Blairgowrie road. M85(Jctn1). **Rail:** 4m, Perth Stn (from Dundee). Bus to course.

Course Characteristics
Right-handed and flat, with tight bends. Chase course has long run-in. Circuit 1m 2f.

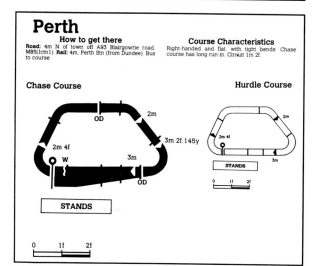

Redcar

How to get there
Road: In town, off A1085 Middlesbrough road. **Rail:** ½m, Redcar Stn (Darlington-Saltburn line). **Air:** 20m, Teesside Airport.

Course Characteristics
Left-handed oval, 1m 6f round, with tight, banked, turn into straight. Run-in 5f. Races up to 1m run on straight course.

Draw: Up to 1m, high numbers slightly favoured; on round course, low numbers slightly favoured.

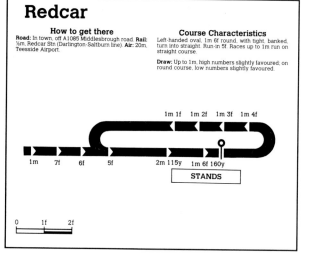

Ripon

Course Characteristics
Right-handed, 1m 5f oval with slight undulations and sharp bend before 5f run-in.

Draw: When stalls on stands side, low numbers slightly favoured; on round course, high numbers favoured.

How to get there
Road: 2m SE of town on B6265 Boroughbridge road. **Rail:** 11m, Harrogate Stn (Leeds-York line) and Thirsk Stn (York-Darlington line). Bus to Ripon.

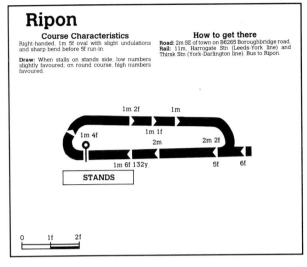

Salisbury

How to get there
Road: 3m SW of city off A3094 at Netherhampton. **Rail:** 3m, Salisbury Stn (London Waterloo-Exeter line). Bus to course.

Course Characteristics
Right-handed and galloping. Loop course for races of 1m 2f plus. 7f run-in (part of a nearly-straight mile) is mainly uphill and makes for a stiff test.

Draw: When stalls on stands side on straight course, low numbers markedly favoured up to 1m.

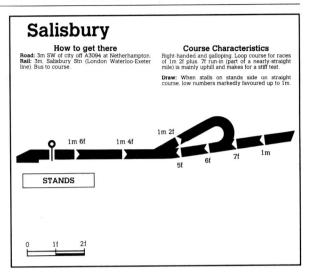

Sandown Park Flat

How to get there
Road: 4m SW of Kingston on A307 Esher road. M25(Jctn10). **Rail:** Adjoining course, Esher Stn (from London Waterloo). **Bus:** 4m, Kingston Bus Stn, direct to course. **Air:** 12m, London (Heathrow).

Course Characteristics
Right-handed oval of 1m 5f with 4f uphill run-in. Essentially galloping. Separate diagonal 5f also uphill.

Draw: When stalls on far side on sprint course, a high draw is vital, particularly on soft ground; when on stands side, low numbers favoured.

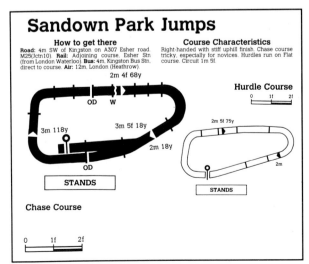

Sedgefield

Course Characteristics
Left-handed, undulating oval. Sharp bends. Chase course has easy fences and particularly long run-in. Circuit 1m 2f.

How to get there
Road: ¾m SW of town near junction of A689 Bishop Auckland road with A177 Durham road. **Rail:** 9m, Stockton-on-Tees Stn, or 12m, Durham Stn. Bus to Sedgefield.

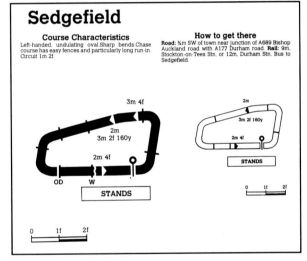

Sandown Park Jumps

How to get there
Road: 4m SW of Kingston on A307 Esher road. M25(Jctn10). **Rail:** Adjoining course, Esher Stn (from London Waterloo). **Bus:** 4m, Kingston Bus Stn, direct to course. **Air:** 12m, London (Heathrow).

Course Characteristics
Right-handed with stiff uphill finish. Chase course tricky, especially for novices. Hurdles run on Flat course. Circuit 1m 5f.

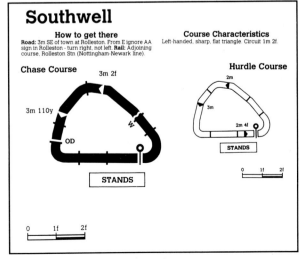

Southwell

How to get there
Road: 3m SE of town at Rolleston. From E ignore AA sign in Rolleston - turn right, not left. **Rail:** Adjoining course, Rolleston Stn (Nottingham-Newark line).

Course Characteristics
Left-handed, sharp, flat triangle. Circuit 1m 2f.

Stratford

How to get there
Road: 1m SW of town off A439 Evesham road. **Rail:** 1m, Stratford Stn (from Birmingham Moor Street or Leamington).

Course Characteristics
Left-handed, flat and sharp, with short finishing straight. Circuit 1m 2f.

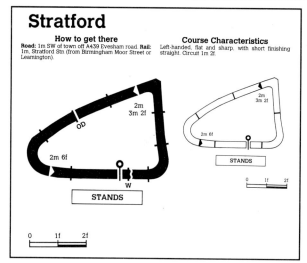

Towcester

Course Characteristics
Right-handed, with last mile uphill. Very testing. Circuit 1m 6f.

How to get there
Road: 1m SE of town on A5 Milton Keynes road. M1(Jctn16) from N; M1(Jctn15) from S.

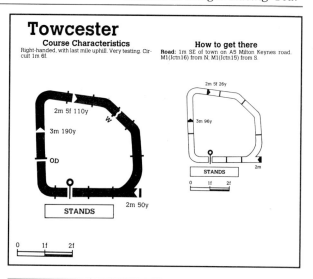

Taunton

How to get there
Road: 2m S of town on B3170 Honiton road. M5(Jctn25). **Rail:** 2½m, Taunton Stn (access London Paddington, Bristol Temple Meads, Exeter St David's).

Course Characteristics
Right-handed oval, on sharp side with short run-in. Circuit 1m 2f.

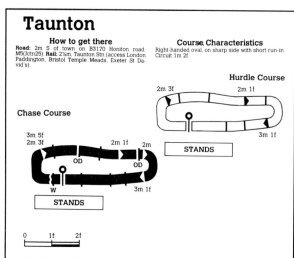

Uttoxeter

How to get there
Road: SE of town off B5017 Marchington road. **Rail:** Adjoining course, Uttoxeter Stn (Derby-Crewe line)

Course Characteristics
Left-handed with some undulations. Circuit 1m 3f.

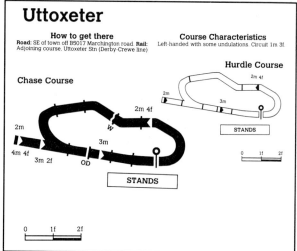

Thirsk

How to get there
Road: W of town on A61 Ripon road. **Rail:** 1m, Thirsk Stn (York-Newcastle line).

Course Characteristics
Left-handed oval of about 1m 2f with 4f run-in. Sharp and almost level.

Draw: When stalls on stands side on straight course, high numbers favoured on good or fast going; low numbers slightly favoured on soft.

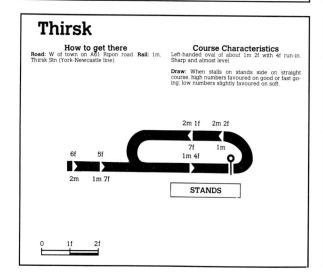

Warwick Flat

Course Characteristics
Left-handed, sharp, about 1m 6f. Dog-leg 5f course.

Draw: When stalls on far side and going not soft, high numbers slightly favoured over 5f.

How to get there
Road: W of town on A41 Birmingham road. **Rail:** 1m, Warwick Stn. Difficult from London.

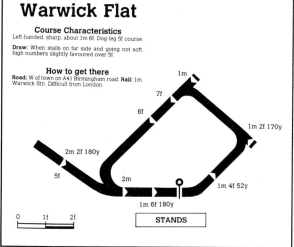

Warwick Jumps

How to get there
Road: W of town on A41 Birmingham road. **Rail:** 1m, Warwick Stn. Difficult from London.

Course Characteristics
Left-handed with tight turns and short run-in. Circuit 1m 5f.

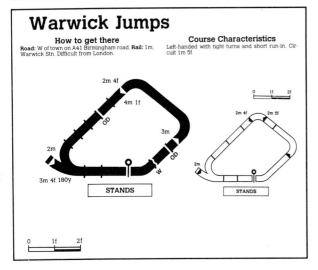

Windsor Flat

How to get there
Road: On A308 Maidenhead road N of town. M4(Jctn6). **Rail:** 2m, Windsor and Eton Riverside Stn (from London Waterloo) or Windsor and Eton Central Stn (from London Paddington). **Bus:** 1m, Greenline stop. **Riverbus:** Direct to course from near Riverside Stn (summer only).

Course Characteristics
Figure-of-eight course of 1m 4f, flat and, up to 1m 70yds, on sharp side.

Draw: In 1m 70yds races, high numbers slightly favoured.

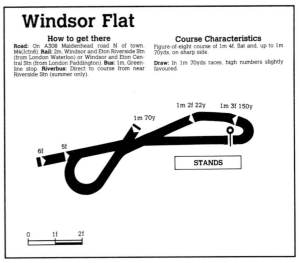

Wetherby

How to get there
Road: E of town, off B1224 York road. **Rail:** 12m, Leeds City Stn. Bus to Wetherby.

Course Characteristics
Left-handed oval, with easy bends. Circuit 1m 4f. Old hurdles course (used occasionally) much sharper.

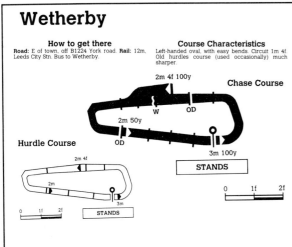

Windsor Jumps

Course Characteristics
Figure-of-eight shape, sharp and flat. Circuit 1m 4f.

How to get there
Road: On A308 Maidenhead road N of town. M4(Jctn6). **Rail:** 2m, Windsor and Eton Riverside Stn (from London Waterloo) or Windsor and Eton Central Stn (from London Paddington). **Bus:** 1m, Greenline stop. **Riverbus:** Direct to course from near Riverside Stn (summer only).

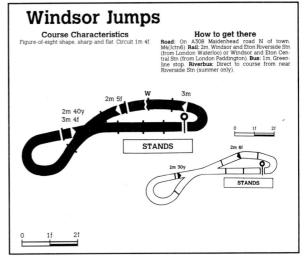

Wincanton

How to get there
Road: 1m N of town on B3081 Shepton Mallet road. **Rail:** 8m, Gillingham Stn (London Waterloo-Exeter line).

Course Characteristics
Right-handed, mainly flat. A fair test. Circuit 1m 3f.

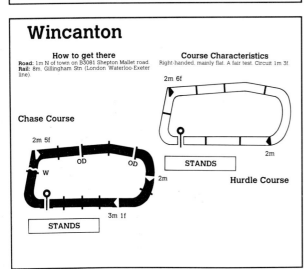

Wolverhampton Flat

How to get there
Road: 1m N of town off A449 Stafford road. M54(Jctn2) best from S. M6(Jctn12), A5, A449 best from N. **Rail:** 1m, Wolverhampton Stn (from London Euston).

Course Characteristics
Left-handed triangle, flat, about 1m 4f round with 5f run-in. 5f course easy.

Draw: When stalls on stands side on straight course, low numbers greatly favoured over 5f on soft going; up to 1m 1f, low numbers slightly favoured.

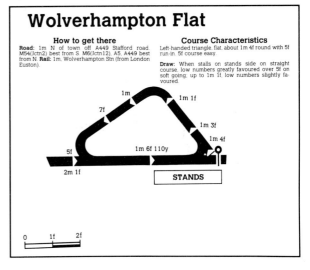

Wolverhampton Jumps

Course Characteristics
Left-handed triangle, essentially galloping. Circuit 1m 4f.

How to get there
Road: 1m N of town off A449 Stafford road. M54(Jctn2) best from S. M6(Jctn12), A5, A449 best from N. **Rail:** 1m, Wolverhampton Stn (from London Euston).

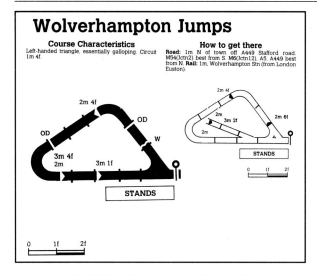

Yarmouth

How to get there
Road: N of town on A149 Caister road. **Rail:** 1m, Yarmouth Stn (from London Liverpool Street via Norwich).

Course Characteristics
Left-handed oval, flat and fair. About 1m 5f round with 5f run-in. Straight mile.

Draw: When stalls on stands side or in centre on straight course, high numbers slightly favoured up to 1m.

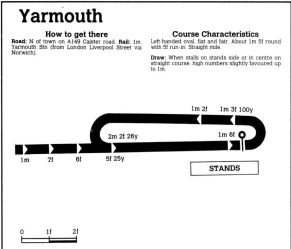

York

How to get there
Road: 1m S of city on A1036 Tadcaster road. **Rail:** 1m, York Stn (main line from London King's Cross). **Air:** 25m, Leeds/Bradford Airport.

Course Characteristics
Left-handed, U-shaped course, flat and fair. Ideal for powerful galloper. 2m with run-in of almost 5f. Races of 7f start on a spur. Can become very testing.

Draw: When stalls on stands side or in centre on straight course, low numbers favoured.

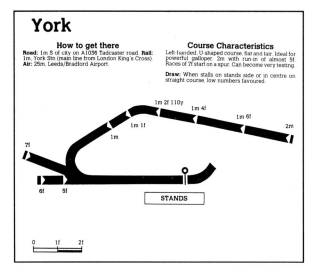